CLARE AND THE CIVIL WAR

CLARE AND THE CIVIL WAR

JOE POWER

Eastwood

First published by Eastwood Books, 2020
Dublin, Ireland

www.eastwoodbooks.com
www.wordwellbooks.com
@eastwoodbooks

First Edition

Eastwood Books is an imprint of The Wordwell Group

Eastwood Books
The Wordwell Group
Unit 9, 78 Furze Road
Sandyford
Dublin, Ireland

ISBN: 978-1-8380416-0-1 (paperback)
ISBN: 978-1-913934-04-0 (mobi)
ISBN: 978-1-913934-05-7 (epub)

British Library Cataloguing in Publication Data.
A catalogue record for this book is available from the British Library.

Typeset in Ireland by Wordwell Ltd
Copy-editor: Myles McCionnaith
Cover design and artwork: Ger Garland
Printed by: SprintPrint, Dublin

CONTENTS

PREFACE

This is my third book on County Clare during the revolutionary years c.1912–c.1924 and it begins where the second one ends – that is, with the truce on 11 July 1921. As in the others, this book has been a voyage of historical exploration and discovery for me. This study of the civil war is in many respects more difficult than that of the War of Independence. In the latter, it was simply a struggle between the Irish Republican Army (IRA) and the Crown forces, whereas the civil war pitted former comrades against each other in a bitter struggle over the terms of the controversial Anglo-Irish Treaty, which was signed on 6 December 1921.

After independence in 1922, an outline of the War of Independence was part of the history curriculum in primary and secondary schools, but the civil war was barely mentioned. Most Irish people may be broadly familiar with the outline of the civil war at national level: how former comrades in the struggle to establish an Irish republic during the War of Independence (1919–1921) were torn apart over the terms of the controversial Treaty, which was reluctantly accepted by a slight majority, 64 votes to 57, in Dáil Éireann on 6 January 1922. Most Irish people are also probably aware that the two main political parties in the Republic of Ireland today, Fine Gael and Fianna Fáil, were founded after the civil war, based on their support for, or opposition to, the Treaty. People may know about the civil war in general terms, especially about the controversial execution of prisoners, but very few people know much about the civil war at a local level. I have been enlightened and amazed at what I have discovered about the conflict in County Clare during my research.

While the press, the Catholic and Protestant hierarchies, the county councils, the farming and business leaders, and the majority of the public pragmatically accepted the unhappy Treaty as the best possible deal at the time, a significant body of republican zealots in Sinn Féin and among the IRA refused to accept the vote in the Dáil. Between January and June 1922, relations between the pro- and anti-Treaty factions deteriorated. The anti-Treaty republicans led by Éamon de Valera, President of the Irish Republic, rejected the Treaty and withdrew from the Dáil, and, on 14 April, a powerful body of IRA officers took over the Four Courts in Dublin. The anti-Treaty IRA then set up an army executive to defend the republic and to challenge the Provisional Government, which was formed once the Treaty was ratified in January 1922. The civil war began when government forces, under pressure from the British, shelled the Four Courts garrison on 28 June 1922; this bitter conflict lasted until the ceasefire declared by republican forces on 30 April 1924.

The hostility between the pro- and anti-Treaty forces at national level was reflected at local level, as a large number of Volunteers led by Frank Barrett, former commandant of the Mid-Clare Brigade and a member of the Army Executive, opposed the Treaty and tried to maintain the Irish republic through force of arms. On the other hand, Michael Brennan, former commandant of the East Clare Brigade and now commandant general of the 1st Western Division, took the pro-Treaty side. Just as it was at a national level, the press, the church hierarchies, the county and local councils, the farming and business leaders, and most of the general public in Clare supported the Treaty.

The civil war was contested as bitterly in Clare as in any other part of Ireland, and the legacy of that conflict lingered for many decades. The pattern of the war in Clare was similar to the military conflict at a national level; there was a brief conventional phase, when the government forces captured all the main cities and towns, and this was followed by a longer guerrilla war phase. The war ended on 30 April 1924, when the anti-Treaty forces called off their military struggle. By then, most of the leadership of the anti-Treaty forces were either dead or under arrest, and thousands of republican adherents were in jail.

This book is arranged into four chapters. Chapter One studies the mood of the county between the truce and the signing of the

Treaty, along with the political and military developments from this time. Chapter Two examines the continued impact of the War of Independence on many different groups in Clare long after the Treaty was signed. Chapter Three explores the civil war in the county from the beginning of the conflict up to the hunger strike of thousands of republicans long after the civil war was officially over. Chapter Four examines sectarianism in Clare during the revolutionary years, spanning both the War of Independence and the civil war eras.

The Treaty was passionately debated by men and women on both sides who held strong views on the political status of Ireland – whether it was to be an independent Irish republic or a Free State maintaining some associations with the Crown and the British Empire. The civil war was a fratricidal conflict between former colleagues, and the passions aroused by this conflict, which took place one hundred years ago, can still evoke strong feelings in supporters of those who fought on opposite sides. Emotional terms such as traitor or Free Stater were used to describe those who reluctantly supported the Treaty, while the opponents of the Treaty were described as Irregulars, wreckers, fanatics and murderous assassins. In this study, the terms 'government forces' and 'republicans' will be used to describe the protagonists in this conflict, except when citing quotations.

Unlike the War of Independence, the civil war was not regarded as a heroic struggle; instead it was viewed with horror by most Irish people. Maybe that is why there was a general amnesia about the civil war – the bitterness, passions and sorrows aroused by that unhappy conflict were perhaps too painful to be remembered. Growing up in Clarecastle during the 1950s, I heard many stories about the War of Independence, but I heard little about the civil war in the district, except that a local republican, Tommy Kinnane, lost an eye during the conflict and that republican forces, led by Marty Slattery and the Barretts from Darragh, launched an unsuccessful attack on the government garrison at the castle and barracks.

I am aware that there were people of sincere conviction on both sides of the struggle, and I have endeavoured to respect those sincerely held views. There were controversial issues and incidents during this tragic conflict, and I have striven to find out the facts and separate the truths from the myths and propaganda about what happened in Clare at this time. I have also tried to be objective. Some of my conclusions may be unpalatable to adherents of one side or the other, or indeed to both sides, even one hundred years later. Whether I have succeeded in the aspiration of being objective and impartial, you the reader can judge for yourself.

ACKNOWLEDGEMENTS

I wish to thank many people for their assistance in my research over the past four years. Without them, this work would not have been completed. My late father, Bernard Power, who was born in 1901, told me several stories about life in Clarecastle, which was a British garrison, during the 'troubles'. For example, he told how he and many young men around the village were rounded up by the Black and Tans in order to repair Latoon bridge, which had been blown up by the IRA several times in 1920 and 1921. He also told me about the burning of the Protestant church in the village in 1920 and about the attack on the army barracks by anti-Treaty forces in 1922. Bernard Power was secretary of the memorial committee and he gave the oration at the unveiling of a monument to a local anti-Treaty republican, Tommy Kinnane, on 22 July 1950 at Clarehill, Clarecastle.[1] My late mother, Margaret (Peggy) Power, née Ryan, of Kilcommon, Co. Tipperary told me the story of her 36-year-old aunt, Mrs Margaret Ryan, who was shot by an Auxiliary during the funeral of an RIC man in Callan, Co. Kilkenny on 21 December and who died on 23 December 1920.[2]

At primary school in Clarecastle, my teacher in second, third and fourth class was Mrs Maura Hanley, née Falvey, who had been officer commanding (OC) of the Ballyea Company, 2nd Battalion Mid-Clare Cumann na mBan during the War of Independence. She was a formidable woman whose favourite expression as she administered corporal punishment was, 'There will be wigs on the Green!' I remember being moved by George Morrison's film *Mise Éire*, with haunting music by Seán Ó Riada, which I saw first in 1960 at Ennis cinema when I was 9 years old. I was 15 years old on the fiftieth anniversary of the Easter Rising, and the documentaries and publicity on RTÉ One and in the newspapers were very impressive. President de Valera undertook a farewell tour of Co. Clare before his retirement in 1973, and I remember the time he passed through the old village of Clarecastle in which a guard of honour was provided by some surviving members of the 2nd Battalion Mid-Clare Brigade, including Bernie Barrett, Jim O'Reilly, John Bradley, Mick Carmody and Joe Reidy, all of whom opposed the Treaty.

Growing up in Clarecastle during the 1950s, I heard of some of the exploits of old republicans from the parish, such as the Barretts of Bearnageeha, Tommy Kinnane of Clarecastle and Marty Slattery from Darragh, who had been involved in the War of Independence and all of whom had taken the anti-Treaty side. I was also fortunate to have had an interview around 30 July 1977 with an old republican named Jim O'Reilly of Ardsollus, Quin, who gave me first-hand information about his role in the formation of a Sinn Féin club in Clarecastle in 1917 – of drilling the local Volunteers in 1917 and the wrecking of the Sinn Féin club house by Scottish soldiers of the Black Watch Regiment in 1918. Jim also told me about the Manusmore cattle drive of February 1918; he was central to the operation and was imprisoned for several months, but he was later released without charge. The killing of John Ryan by the RIC during the cattle drive precipitated the introduction of military rule in the county at that time. Jim O'Reilly was prominent in the formation of the Volunteers at Clarecastle, and the county police inspector, Mr Gelston, stated in October 1917, 'James O'Reilly appeared to be their leader [...] sooner or later he will have to be arrested. He is a very disturbing element in Clarecastle.'[3]

I owe an enormous debt to the many historians, both at local and national level, who have written about and published works on the War of Independence. Most of my early research was done at local level, especially at the Local Studies Centre, Ennis, Clare and Clare County Library, and I am very grateful to the staff of both for their support and assistance over many years. I am also thankful to three Ennis local historians, Declan Barron, Ollie Byrnes and Sean Spellissy, who gave me valuable information. I am indebted to the staff of many other libraries and institutions for their assistance over the years: the Irish National Archives, Dublin; the Military Archives at Cathal Brugha Barracks, Dublin; the Archive Collection, UCD, Dublin; the National Library, Dublin; the Royal Irish Academy,

Dublin; Trinity College, Dublin; NUI Galway; the Glucksman Library, University of Limerick; the Killaloe Diocesan Archives, Westbourne, Ennis; and the Limerick Diocesan Archives. I am also indebted to Dr Paul O'Brien, Mary Immaculate College, Limerick for giving me access to the Joe Barrett papers. I am also grateful to Mrs Grania Weir, née O'Brien, Whitegate, Clare for allowing me to access some of her family papers from Dromoland Castle. I am grateful to Ronan Colgan and Una McConville at Wordwell for supporting my project and to Myles McCionnaith for his forensic editorial work. Finally, I wish to thank my wife Fionnuala and my daughters Maria, Rachel and Bronwyn for their love and support.

This book is dedicated to all who suffered during the Irish Civil War.

1
FROM TRUCE TO CIVIL WAR

After months of tortuous negotiations, Ireland's plenipotentiaries, led by Arthur Griffith and Michael Collins, reluctantly signed a treaty with the British government under Prime Minister David Lloyd George on the night of 5–6 December 1921. The most controversial terms of the Treaty were that Ireland was to remain as a dominion in the British Commonwealth, that members of the Irish legislature were to swear an oath of allegiance to the British monarch, and that a boundary commission was to decide the border between Northern Ireland and the Irish Free State (which came into being exactly one year after the Treaty was first signed). This Treaty gave the Irish Free State far more independence than what was envisaged under the Home Rule bill of 1912, but it was a far cry from the independent Irish republic proclaimed in the Easter Rising of 1916 and declared by the Dáil at the Mansion House, Dublin in January 1919. The controversial terms of the Treaty divided the Sinn Féin party and the IRA into two bitterly opposed groups, the pro- and anti-Treaty sides, with de Valera, who had been elected President of the Irish Republic by the first Dáil in January 1919, being passionately opposed to its terms. Nationalist Irish society was also divided over the controversy. After passionate debates in the Dáil in December 1921 and January 1922, the Treaty was ratified by a majority of 64 votes to 57. Though the Treaty was accepted by most of Irish society, there was a significant body of republicans who rejected its terms, and this, tragically, led to the outbreak of the civil war on 28 June 1922.

Debating the Treaty
Between the signing of the Treaty on 6 December 1921 and its ratification on 14 January 1922 its terms were the main topic of conversation. The Treaty was hotly debated all over the country: in

the media, in churches, in urban and county councils, among nationalists and unionists, in farmers' organisations and chambers of commerce, and in probably near every household in the country.

The local newspapers were strongly in favour of the Treaty. The *Saturday Record* editorial was in favour of the Treaty and hoped that it would be accepted by the Dáil:

> At last, a Treaty, the outcome of the London conference seems to have the approval of both countries, with little dissent in both countries [...] We trust sincerely that neither will be disappointed [...] The Irish delegates seem to have splendidly acquitted themselves and the terms are of a sufficiently wide and comprehensive character to disarm all fair criticism. Ireland becomes a Free State [...] On Irishmen themselves will now depend how she will for the future have the peace and prosperity for which we have been so long praying [...] It is a time of great and golden promise and it will be the prayer of all classes and creeds in the country that we shall soon see our long-suffering island at last a haven of security and happiness.

An editorial in the *Clare Champion* also welcomed the Treaty:

> Clare with all its history from the days of the great Brian Boru to the election of Éamon de Valera will stand as one man behind the fateful decision of Ireland's plenipotentiaries [...] We welcome the terms of the settlement and we believe we may, on behalf of the people of Clare, send a message of congratulations to those, who sitting in conference, surmounted so many difficulties, and came to a settlement acceptable to all.

Two weeks after this statement, while the political storm over the Treaty was raging all over Ireland, the *Clare Champion* again urged acceptance of its terms:

> It has now been made abundantly clear that the terms which the Irish representatives brought back from London were the very best they could get and that the alternative to acceptance was, and is chaos [...] The Treaty does not give all that was asked for [...] The outstanding fact is that the people of Ireland are prepared to accept the Treaty and hope that Dáil Éireann will ratify it.[4]

'Clare County Council declares for Peace – An emphatic majority'. This was the heading in the *Saturday Record* when it published details of the council's meeting and vote at the courthouse in Ennis on 22

December 1921. Michael Brennan, chairman of Clare County Council and also commandant of the East Clare Brigade, called a meeting of the county council on 22 December to discuss the Treaty. At that meeting, Joseph O'Connor proposed, and Sean O'Keefe seconded, a long-winded resolution from the council in favour of the Treaty:

> That we the members of Clare County Council view with the greatest apprehension the differences prevailing in Dáil Éireann. The representatives of the nation, irrespective of party, have appealed to the sovereign people as the final authority in this matter of ratifying or rejecting the Treaty between Ireland and England, and we feel, therefore, that it is our duty to bring before our representatives what we know to be the wishes of the people of Clare. The people of Clare consider that the Treaty is the substance of independence, that it will lead inevitably, and within a short time, to the complete fulfilment of our national aspirations, and therefore, we believe that the Treaty should be ratified. We do not attempt to minimise the grave objections to the Treaty. But we see no rational alternative to its acceptance. The rejection of this Treaty is certain to involve us in a war of annihilation [...] It is our deepest conviction that national unity can only be preserved only by accepting the Treaty [...] we would request President de Valera to use his immense influence and political capacity for the maintenance of national unity.

After a long discussion, the council carried the motion by 17 votes to 5. Copies of the resolution were sent to the four TDs from Clare: President de Valera, Brian O'Higgins, Sean Liddy and Patrick Brennan. The vote was hailed in another editorial in the *Saturday Record*, which claimed that most of the people of Clare were in favour of the Treaty, 'The County Council acted on the general desire of the people of Clare, who are practically unanimous in the feeling and wish for peace. What effect can non-ratification of the Treaty have? Only to plunge the country back again into the horrors of the last 12 months.'[5]

The special correspondent of the London *Times*, who spent Christmas in Ennis and the surrounding districts, wrote:

> I found the people not a little proud of the action of the county authority in courageously seeking to support the men who have seemed to offer peace to Ireland. But the Clare man will tell you that it is fitting that his county should show the way to the rest

of Ireland [...] Clare has done so in the past. The significance of the majority in the Clare County Council, lies in the fact that, as in the Dáil, it is the fighters who demanded peace.[6]

In his Christmas Day sermon in Ennis cathedral, Dr Fogarty, Bishop of Killaloe and a staunch advocate of Sinn Féin since at least 1917, spoke passionately in favour of the Treaty:

> Make no mistake about it, the rejection of the Treaty must lead inevitably to war of such a destructive character as will lay Ireland out dead in a very short time, if indeed the country wants war, be it observed, not for any advance of the Treaty powers, but for the pleasure of writing 'external Association', over the door [...] but I will take no responsibility for such a policy, which I consider would be national madness. But the country does not want war, nor does it want the rejection of this Treaty. The country has made its mind up definitely that this supreme question must be settled by reason and common sense and not by 'heroics'. The discussions in the Dáil have, however, revealed a disquieting fact, I mean the callous disregard openly avowed by some deputies for the national will and the wishes of their constituents on this awful question. In my opinion the position is wholly indefensible and morally wrong. It is a negation of representative government. No man or group of men has a right to lead the country into a ruinous war against the considered judgement of the nation.

On 8 December, two days after the Treaty was signed, Bishop Fogarty, in a letter to Erskine Childers (who was bitterly opposed to the Treaty), described the Treaty as 'marvellous' and congratulated all those involved. On the same day that de Valera publicly denounced the Treaty, Bishop Fogarty publicly approved of it in letters to the *Freeman's Journal* and the *Irish Independent*, in which he 'expressed confidence that the Irish Free State will soon have the cordial allegiance of every Irishman'. Shortly after the publication of Bishop Fogarty's letter in the *Independent*, Edward MacLysaght, a prominent businessman from Raheen, sent a letter to Bishop Fogarty supporting his view:

> This lamentable and really serious crisis which has arisen causes me to send you this note post haste. I observe by the paper which has just arrived that you have no doubts on the advisability of acceptance of the Treaty. I want to let you know that as a fairly

prominent constituent of Mr de Valera, who has always hitherto supported him, but I regard it as our duty to adhere to a Treaty signed by our plenipotentiaries [...] I entirely agree with your pronouncement given in today's Independent and know well that the great majority of Irishmen agree with it. Does not de Valera realise this?

In fact, by September 1921 Bishop Fogarty had reached the conclusion that the time had come for the Irish side to reach an accommodation with Britain. He wrote a letter to Collins criticising de Valera's intransigence in dealing with proposals made by Lloyd George, 'Apart from partition, which may be resolved in whole or in part, the people feel that there is in the proposals something very substantial to negotiate and work upon [...] The alternative was a war of devastation without the good will of the people behind it.'[7]

The *Saturday Record* published other reports on what it called 'the crisis', including when Catholic priests organised public meetings in several parishes to get a consensus on the matter, 'A public meeting was held after Mass on Christmas Day at Clonlara to discuss the Treaty. Rev James Kennedy, PP [parish priest], took the chair and a motion to accept the treaty was proposed by Mr O'Shea, and seconded by Mr Lenihan. The motion was unanimously accepted by a show of hands.' Another public meeting was held in the parish of Dysart, 'Following a meeting at Dysart, chaired by Rev Fr Breen PP, a motion was passed by a large majority, in favour of accepting the Treaty, two people dissenting and one person declining to vote, in favour of accepting the Treaty.'

Significantly, T.V. Honan, the chairman of Ennis Urban Council, who was also president of the East Clare Executive of Sinn Féin, was interviewed on the political controversy and he stated that he was in favour of the Treaty at Christmastime:

Under the present circumstances, personally, I see no practical alternative, but to accept the terms of the Treaty as signed. Then, let the Irish Government and the Irish people settle down to work its provisions to the very marrow. This course, I am certain, will eventually prove the shortest and surest to our complete independence.[8]

The vote by Clare County Council on 22 December caused some controversy. Sean O'Keefe, who had seconded the motion, claimed that he had been misinformed by the chairman of the council, Michael Brennan, who had told him that the Irish Republican Brotherhood (IRB) had instructed its members to vote in favour of the Treaty. O'Keefe wrote a letter to President de Valera explaining his action in seconding the motion, 'I seconded the resolution recommending ratification of the Treaty today as a soldier obeying an order of the divisional commandant [Michael Brennan]. He informed me that orders were issued by the IRB and GHQ [General Headquarters] to do so. It is contrary to my principles. I am a republican.' Upon hearing of this allegation, the IRA chief of staff, General Richard Mulcahy, immediately repudiated such an order from GHQ and ordered Commandant Michael Brennan to make a report on the matter.

At another meeting of Clare County Council on 3 January 1922, Michael Brennan asserted that there was some misunderstanding on the issue and allowed another vote on the subject. He stated that at the previous meeting of the council on 22 December he had correctly informed Sean O'Keefe that the IRB had allowed a free vote on the Treaty. He said that he was not an officer of the IRB and had no authority to order O'Keefe, a fellow member of the IRB, to support the Treaty. Brennan added that four or five other IRB members on the council, who were also army officers, had voted against the Treaty. He emphasised that he did not, as commandant of the 1st Western Division, order O'Keefe to second the motion. Brennan also stated that he greatly resented the role of Frank Barrett, commandant of the Mid-Clare Brigade, who was not a councillor, in interfering in the matter; he alleged that Frank Barrett had telegraphed President de Valera, informing him that the resolution of Clare County Council 'was carried by intimidation and canvassing'.

Clare County Council re-confirmed its vote to ratify the Treaty at the meeting on 3 January 1922 by 18 votes to 9. On the second vote, Sean O'Keefe voted against the Treaty. The chairman of Clare County Council, Michael Brennan, stated that he had a letter from Sean Liddy, TD stating that if he were present at the council meeting, he would vote for the resolution. John D. Moloney also said that he had a letter from Councillor Michael Hehir from Tiermaclane, who was then in Cork Prison, stating that he too would be in favour of the resolution.[9]

At local councils, the urban and district councillors were also voicing their opinions on the Treaty, as reported in the *Saturday Record*:

> At a special meeting of Kilrush Urban Council on Friday night, Mr Bart Culligan in the chair, a motion in favour of the Treaty was unanimously passed. The members hoped that the Dáil would ratify the Treaty. The Kilrush Board of Guardians also passed a resolution in favour of the Treaty ratification.

At that meeting, the chairman stated that this motion reflected 'the emphatic wish of all their constituents as more than 95% of the people of West Clare are in favour of the Treaty. Of course,' he added, 'there are some extremists who want nothing but an Irish Republic.' Meetings of the Kildysart Union and Rural District Council unanimously approved of the Clare County Council vote in favour of the Treaty and called on the four TDs in the county to support the Treaty. A meeting of Scariff Guardians and District Council adopted the following resolution, 'That we the members of the Scariff Board of Guardians, embracing the amalgamated unions of Tulla and Scariff, endorse the action of Clare County Council in calling on our representatives in Dáil Éireann to vote for ratification of the treaty.' Twenty-two members voted in favour, while only one member voted against the motion.[10]

Besides elected urban and county councillors, the members of Sinn Féin clubs and county executives also hotly debated the controversial Treaty over the Christmas holiday season, and most of the delegates seemed to be in favour of supporting the Treaty. At a meeting of the Miltown Malbay Sinn Féin Club, presided over by Rev. Fr O'Molloy, CC (Catholic curate), a motion in favour of ratifying the Treaty was passed by a show of hands in the club. On Sunday, 1 January, a meeting of the East Clare Executive of Sinn Féin was held in the town hall in Ennis to discuss the Treaty. The meeting was chaired by T.V. Honan, chairman of the Ennis Urban Council. A motion was proposed by the chairman and seconded by Fr Hamilton of St Flannan's College in Ennis, 'That we are of the opinion that under the circumstances the Treaty as signed is the best road towards our goal of independence.' After a long debate, with passionate arguments on both sides, the motion was passed by 17 votes to 0, with nine members abstaining. Canon O'Kennedy sent a letter of apology for non-attendance (he was imprisoned in Spike Island at the time) and stated, 'I cannot see any way out of the present crux but ratification. I hope the delegates will consider the matter dispassionately.'

At a meeting of the West Clare Executive of Sinn Féin at Kilrush on Wednesday, 4 January, a motion was proposed by Rev. A.J. Moloney and seconded by M. Haugh:

> That we the members of the West Clare Executive of Sinn Féin accept the terms of the Treaty as a foundation on which the prosperity, happiness, and future independence of our country may be built and we call upon our deputies to give effect to the will of their constituents.

The proposal was passed by 17 votes to 4.[11]

The farmers of Clare also met to express their opinion on the merits of the Treaty. At a meeting of the West Clare Farmers Union, which was held in Kilrush on Saturday, 31 December, a motion urging the Clare TDs to ratify the Treaty was unanimously passed. Also, at a branch meeting of that union on 31 December, the Carrigaholt Farmers Union was unanimous in supporting a motion calling on President de Valera and the other Clare TDs to accept the Treaty. On the same Saturday as the Kilrush meeting, Colonel George O'Callaghan Westropp chaired a meeting of the East Clare Farmers Union at the courthouse in Ennis. There was a large attendance, and the secretary, C. Quinn, read letters from branches of the Farmers Union in Ennistymon, Kilshanny, Tulla and Killimer, who were all in favour of the Treaty ratification. The Feakle branch of the Farmers Union also called for ratification of the Treaty. At the Ennis meeting, a motion calling for 'ratification of the Treaty in deference to the wishes of the great majority of the Clare people' was passed by a large majority of the farmers present.[12]

The businesspeople of Ennis and Clarecastle also held a meeting to express their opinion on the Treaty. A large number of Ennis traders and merchants were in attendance, and they voted overwhelmingly in favour of accepting the Treaty, stating that this was the wish of most Ennis people. The following motion was proposed by Denis Roughan and seconded by Matthew Kenny:

That we believe that the Treaty offers a basis for freedom, by giving us control of our vital national resources; by opposing the Treaty we are in direct opposition to the men who worked hard for the freedom of Ireland. We strongly urge our public representatives for Clare to vote for the Treaty and in doing so, we believe that we are expressing the practically unanimous wishes of the people of the town of Ennis.

The motion was passed unanimously, and copies of the resolution were sent to the four Clare TDs.[13]

Some Catholic archbishops also gave their opinion on the Treaty, urging the people and politicians to accept it. The Archbishop of Cashel said, 'The voice of the people must prevail [...] the people of Ireland, by a clear majority are in favour of the Treaty.' The Archbishop of Armagh and Primate of Ireland, Cardinal Logue, also called for peace and acceptance of the Treaty, 'It would be a terrible calamity for Ireland if the Treaty were rejected because of mere verbal quibbles [...] the Treaty held forth the only hope for the peace, prosperity and welfare of Ireland.'

Finally, the editor of the *Clare Champion*, having considered all the opinions of diverse people and interests in the county, again welcomed the Treaty and was confident that it would be passed in the Dáil:

Our people hope earnestly that the vote will be for peace and for Ireland [...] Whatever happens, and we have every confidence that it will be ratified, we trust no bitterness will be left behind [...] Let us hope that we are on the eve of great events, and at last the dawn of freedom is going to light up the hills of Ireland.[14]

A secret military report compiled by the intelligence officer of the 18th Infantry Brigade at Limerick, which fell into the hands of the IRA, gives another insight into opinions among different classes of Clare people on the truce and peace talks:

The merchants, farmers and shopkeeper classes are all for peace. They considered the terms offered to be generous and are quite willing to accept them. However, should negotiations fail, they are such rabbits that they would assist the IRA as hitherto [...] The labouring class, including rank and file of the IRA are not keen on fighting, but if ordered out, they have not sufficient character to refuse [...] The loyalists view with horror the present terms and have decided in the event of their being accepted to clear out of the county. They realise that they will only live on the sufferance of the IRA.

Significantly, the secret report also gives us an interesting insight into the thinking of Frank Barrett at this crucial time:

> Among IRA personnel, Frank Barrett, commandant Mid-Clare Brigade was seen on the 16th of August. He seemed very depressed and would not say much about his views on the Truce. The impression gained from him was that he expected negotiations to fail and did not want to resume operations. He is not in good odour at GHQ, who think he is too slack.

However, another contemporary source suggests that Frank Barrett was committed to the republic. The intelligence officer of the Mid-Clare Brigade wrote, 'Frank Barrett never discusses the present situation only at council meetings. He has always encouraged the idea of another fight. From my own knowledge, he will not be satisfied with anything less than a Republic.' Ironically, the county inspector, William Attridge, reported in October 1921 that 'Michael Brennan is stated to have said at Corofin that they [the IRA members] would accept nothing less than a republic.'[15]

Funding the IRA

Long before the Treaty was signed, and while the republicans were still united, the IRA organised collections around the county to support the men of the flying columns (a highly trained and active unit of between twenty and thirty IRA men, who were full-time soldiers and carried out most of the attacks against the Crown forces) during the truce period. In a letter to Diarmuid O'Hegarty, the adjutant general, in September 1921, Frank Barrett argued that a levy on every householder was necessary:

> as people with the most means, who should pay £20 to this levy, would only give on average five shillings, if we left the collection to themselves. The people in the towns did absolutely nil in the war and it is only right that they be asked to do their bit.

In September, the Royal Irish Constabulary (RIC) reported that the IRA were collecting money through intimidation. County Inspector Attridge reported as follows:

> A number of dances, sports and race meetings have been held

and the profits handed over to the IRA. In the case of the dance at Ennis, the local shopkeepers were compelled to supply the refreshments free and all the money made by the sale of tickets was profit for the IRA.

During October 1921 the RIC were informed that many shopkeepers, especially loyalists, were being intimidated and forced to subscribe to the republican cause:

> The IRA were collecting money throughout the county through collections and dances. They were collecting money by threats to loyalists in amounts varying from £5 to £25 and the people are afraid to complain. Collections are being vigorously continued. In Ennis many loyalist shopkeepers have subscribed, one to my knowledge gave £25.

A suggested levy by the IRA was based on a valuation of two shillings in the pound of rateable valuation. Thus, a ratepayer, with a property valuation of £1 would pay a levy of two shillings to the IRA (there were twenty shillings in £1). The collection of the levy in mid-Clare was controversial, as indicated by the intelligence officer of the brigade:

> Speaking for Mid Clare, the only area in Clare in which we know of a levy being made, some opponents stirred up a sort of opposition and spread some false rumours. The opposition came from the people who are always trying to interfere in the affairs of the Mid-Clare Brigade. The levy is still being collected. The IRA has suffered no loss of prestige as a result of the levy. The people are willing to support the Dáil in any action we take.

In November 1921, Michael Brennan, commandant general of the 1st Western Division, sent a circular regarding collections for the IRA. In this he stated levies could not be imposed and that no force or threats be used to compel people to subscribe to the IRA funds. Brennan stated that the British were aware that the IRA were short of funds, and he cited an RIC report from the 5th Divisional Bulletin, no 24, dated 26 August 1921, in which allegations were made that the funds were being misappropriated:

> There is reason to believe that Rebel funds are running low. Collections are being made all over the country ostensibly for the IRA. Some cases have come to light, however, in which money collected was spent on buying beer in the nearest public house.

> Some rebels are resorting to robbery of inoffensive inhabitants,
> mostly shopkeepers to make good their present shortage of funds,
> no doubt IRA pay has ceased for the time.

The English were not lying about IRA stealing collection money and spending it on beer in the nearest public house, because a court of inquiry sat at Feenagh House on 8 November 1921 at 4 p.m. to investigate and decide what had happened to the £50 rate money that was missing from a collection in Newmarket.

Because of these allegations of misappropriation of the collection money, Brennan issued new directives: each battalion and company was to have its own funds; fetes in aid of battalion funds must have permission of the brigade commandant; and a brigade staff officer had to superintend and check the receipts of fund-raising activities in aid of each battalion.[16]

Keeping their powder dry

Following the truce, the IRA leadership became concerned about the discipline and training of the IRA Volunteers. If the talks were to break down and a renewal of war became necessary, they wanted the Volunteer army to be prepared for war. Training camps were established in various places around the county between September and November 1921. Joe Barrett, adjutant of the 1st Western Division, sent out notices regarding training sessions for engineers at Lissycasey, Mountshannon and Whitegate in mid-September. Another training session was organised for Duggan's Hotel, Scariff on 4 November. The notice on this occasion stated, 'The men selected should be of the toughest dare devil type [...] as they will be trained in hand to hand fighting, which will require utmost determination [...] all ranks will carry revolvers or automatics.'

The RIC were still monitoring the activities of the IRA during the truce, and County Inspector Attridge's reports indicate that many training sessions were organised by the IRA between July and December 1921. The police reported IRA training sessions at venues such as Crusheen, Kilfenora, Kilmihil, Scariff and Quin in July. In August Attridge noted:

> The county has been during the past month an IRA armed camp.
> Large bodies in uniform have been seen drilling and manoeuvring

in Crusheen, Kilfenora, Kilmihil, Scariff and Quin. A great many young men have been conscripted [...] The IRA rule the whole life of the county, social, political and commercial.

A month later, County Inspector Attridge noted, 'Apart from attacks on the Crown forces and the courts, the truce is being broken in every way by the IRA, with drilling, intimidation and enforcing under threats subscriptions to IRA funds.' Meetings were reported at Ballynacally, Broadford, Carrigaholt, Cooraclare, Ennistymon, Fanore, Kilfenora, Kilmihil, Miltown Malbay and Rineanna in September. Training sessions were reported at Kilshanny, Corofin, Ogonnelloe and Spancilhill in October, and the IRA were reported 'to be taking full advantage of the lull to recruit, equip and train every able-bodied young man in the county, while officer training camps were reported at Kilmihil, Ruan and Quin.' The county inspector also noted that the IRA were seeking to get in touch with 'traitors' amongst the RIC, Black and Tans, Auxiliaries, British army and Royal Marines for the purpose of acquiring arms and ammunition. On 28 October the police recorded that a Lewis machine gun, a revolver and ammunition were stolen from G Company, Auxiliary Division at Corofin.

During IRA training sessions, the Volunteers were billeted among the local community, with or without their consent. The RIC noted that the men were billeted during the autumn at places such as Carerhue, Clenagh, Kilfenora, Kilkee, Rineanna, Spancilhill and Quin. According to the RIC, the loyalists in Kilkee were given a hard time by the IRA during September. The RIC families remaining in Kilkee after the officers and men were removed to Kilrush were treated harshly:

> being pushed and jeered as they walked the streets [...] The only levees reported during the month were from Kilkee, where a general collection was made from house to house. Eighty Volunteers arrived in Kilkee on 29th and were billeted on people who had been friendly to the police [...] a hundred more were expected to be accommodated in Moore Hall.

County Inspector Attridge reported that Michael Brennan had expressed regret to the district inspector (DI) at Kilrush for the treatment of constables' wives in Kilkee following the evacuation.

Following criticism of the West Clare Brigade during the latter stages of the war, GHQ sent an officer, Michael Ryan, to reorganise the 5th Battalion, West Clare Brigade over a period of three weeks in July and August 1921. On arrival Ryan found that the battalion was badly led and badly trained, demoralised and riven by land disputes:

> When I arrived, the commandant had resigned, the vice-commandant was considering resignation, while the adjutant and quarter master had a serious quarrel. The officers were rather slow and un-enterprising, they were too cautious and lacked initiative, the men did not respect them [...] there were infrequent parades, the officers were ignorant of drilling, there were no intelligence officers in any company and none of the companies ever saw a grenade [...] A company in Carrigaholt ought to have been the best, but it was divided by land disputes [...] B company at Kilbaha was also frustrated by land disputes [...] In C company, Kilkee and Kilferagh, the captain of Kilferagh had resigned and the company at Kilkee had ceased to function; D company, Doonaha, was the best in the battalion, with an excellent captain; the men of E company, Moveen, were untrained but eager to learn; the men of F company, Cross, were not remarkable; while G company, Blackweir, was satisfactory.[17]

The Dáil vote on the Treaty

Judging from the opinions expressed privately and publicly by many groups and noted individuals in Clare, it seems that a significant majority of the population were in favour of the Treaty. In July, the county inspector of the RIC, Mr Attridge, reported that 'the people generally are anxious for peace', while in October he wrote that 'about 90% of the people would be opposed to a renewal of hostilities, but of them 90% are a mere herd that can be driven anywhere or obliged to do anything at the point of a rifle or revolver.' The four Clare TDs in the Dáil were aware of the views of people in the county, and that every vote on the matter was critical. The Dáil voted on a motion to support the Treaty on Thursday, 7 January 1922, and it was carried by 64 votes to 57. The Clare TDs were evenly divided in terms of the vote; two of the TDs, Patrick Brennan and Sean Liddy, voted to accept the Treaty, while Éamon de Valera and Brian O'Higgins voted to reject it.

During the Treaty debate in the Dáil, Brian O'Higgins stated that he was going to vote against it on principle and principle alone, 'It may be said that my constituents were in favour of it, but though they be masters of my position in the Dáil, they were not captains of my soul.' Éamon de Valera voted against the Treaty 'to stand by the Republic'. Patrick Brennan stated that 'the army in Clare have not said a word about the Treaty, they look upon themselves as soldiers. The civil population are out for the Treaty.' It is interesting that the two soldiers, Sean Liddy, former commandant of the West Clare Brigade, and Patrick Brennan, former commandant of the Clare Brigade between 1917 and 1919 (before it was divided into three separate brigades), both voted to accept the Treaty, while the politicians Éamon de Valera and Brian O'Higgins voted against it. De Valera was commandant at Boland's Mill in Dublin during the Easter Rising but had not played any significant military role in the War of Independence; O'Higgins, a poet and Gaelic Leaguer, was in the GPO during the rising but had not taken part in the War of Independence.[18]

In the bitter aftermath of the vote, de Valera and his followers walked out of the Dáil, having refused to accept its democratic decision; they chose 'to stand by the Republic'. Arthur Griffith became president of Dáil Éireann while de Valera and his supporters boycotted the Provisional Government. Over the next few months, the relations between the two camps, the pro- and anti-Treatyites, deteriorated. Despite many efforts made by churchmen and politicians to reunite the sundered republicans, the country sadly drifted towards civil war in the summer of 1922.

Good news?

The vote in favour of the Treaty was welcomed in many quarters. The *Saturday Record* reported:

> The Peace Treaty was welcomed in Kilrush as the steam whistles and sirens of Messrs Glynn's Mills loudly proclaimed the good news, and it was joyously and quietly received by the public generally. At last Mass, Fr Molony asked the people to be united in working the peace treaty [...] In a similar spirit the news was received throughout West Clare.[19]

The editor of the *Clare Champion* was upset by the bitterness of the debate in the Dáil and the dramatic scenes following acceptance of the Treaty in which de Valera and his followers withdrew from the building, 'The insinuations against Mr de Valera were deeply regretted, the vulgarities, a painful topic [...] we hope that there would be no sordid splits.' Nevertheless, the paper welcomed the result, 'We have had no more history-making week than the present one [...] The Provisional Government has become a reality and Irishmen for the first time since the Act of Union are governing themselves and the evil history of Dublin Castle has come to an end.'[20]

The Dáil vote was also welcomed by the unionists and Protestants of Clare. At a meeting of Clare unionists held at Harmony Row Schoolhouse, Ennis on Tuesday, 17 January, the following resolution was proposed by Richard John Stacpoole, DL (deputy lieutenant), seconded by W.J. McNamara and passed unanimously:

> That we the unionists of County Clare assembled at Ennis this 17 January 1922, recognise that a new form of government accepted by a majority of the Irish people has now been legally established and we therefore deem it to be both the duty and the interest of all loyal subjects and good citizens, as it will be our own most sincere wish, to do everything possible to strengthen the hands of the new administration and to assist them in the discharge of the arduous duties which they have undertaken.
>
> We are gratified by the assurances given that their administration will be impartial, and we believe that this policy steadfastly adhered to, will prove to be the best means calculated to produce general peace and contentment, and ultimately to bring the whole of Ireland under one form of government again, as we feel that the best interests of the whole country must suffer so long as its people remain divided, and therefore in many respects, disunited.[21]

To counteract the accusations of being anti-republican, Patrick Brennan wrote a letter to the *Clare Champion* to assert the republican principles of those who supported the Treaty, 'The term Republican is equally the property of Free Staters and anti-Free Staters [...] our aim is the complete independence of Ireland with a republican form of government [...] We differ from the anti-Treaty group only in method [...] we accept the Treaty as a means of securing absolute independence for Ireland.'[22]

Meanwhile, members of Sinn Féin were meeting at clubs around the county to select candidates for a forthcoming Ard Fheis (national convention). At a meeting of the Liscannor Sinn Féin Club on 29 January to elect delegates, Fr J. Meehan, as presiding chairman, decided to hold a vote on the Treaty in the parish. The vote gives some idea of public opinion in a rural parish at the time. The meeting voted in favour of the Treaty by 235 votes to 124 – a majority of 111 (about 65 per cent) in support of the Treaty. Rev. Fr Meehan and T. Gardiner were elected to support the Treaty at the Sinn Féin convention.[23]

In Ballyea, the curate Fr Cahill called a meeting of the Killone Sinn Féin Club for 29 January. The purpose of the gathering was to reorganise the branch, elect officers, ascertain the opinions of the parishioners regarding the Treaty and select two delegates to represent the views of the majority of parishioners at the Ard Fheis on 7 February. Ironically, this club was the bailiwick of the Barrett family of Bearnageeha, who had taken a strong anti-Treaty position at this time. Incidentally, the previous president of the club was Fr Marcus McGrath, who was a strong Sinn Féin supporter and a founding member of this club and the Sinn Féin club at Clarecastle in 1917. Fr McGrath had been transferred to Roscrea at the beginning of December 1921.[24]

Bishop Fogarty and the Catholic clergy of the diocese of Killaloe were endeavouring to influence the selection of pro-Treaty candidates for the forthcoming Sinn Féin Ard Fheis in Dublin. It is significant that most of the clergy who had been prominent supporters of Sinn Féin from 1917 up to the Treaty took the pro-Treaty side. This was evident at the meetings of the East Clare and West Clare executives of Sinn Féin on 1 January and 4 January. At the East Clare Executive meeting, Fr Crowe (Barefield), Fr Breen (Ruan) and Fr Hamilton (St Flannan's College) were all in favour of the Treaty. Canon O'Kennedy, of St Flannan's College, who was then in Spike Island prison, also stated his support. In the West Clare Executive, Fr Molony, Kilrush, also spoke in favour. Other clergy who tried to influence the votes at Sinn Féin clubs around the county included Fr Kennedy, Clonlara; Fr O'Molloy, Miltown Malbay; Fr Meehan, Liscannor; and Fr Cahill, Killone.

The meetings of the East Clare and West Clare executives to select delegates for the Ard Fheis took place on Sunday, 29 January. Delegates from Killaloe, Crusheen, Inch, Newmarket-on-Fergus, Noughavill, Kilnamona, Quin, Ennis, Doora, Corofin, Tradaree, Ballycorick, Ballyea, Ruan, Connolly, Barefield, Kilmaley and Dysart attended the East Clare meeting in Ennis, and Henry J. Hunt was presiding. Michael Hehir proposed, and Mr Malone seconded, a motion that the delegates appointed to the national convention should support the Treaty, and the motion was passed. However, in Kilrush the delegates at the West Clare Executive meeting voted by 27 to 6 in favour of supporting de Valera and the anti-Treaty side. At the Ard Fheis, de Valera was re-elected President of Sinn Féin by a large majority, and many attempts were made to restore unity within the republican community.[25]

Settling old scores
After the Dáil vote to accept the Treaty and the establishment of the Provisional Government, the British forces began to withdraw from Ireland. In January and February 1922, soldiers, sailors, the RIC, the Black and Tans and the Auxiliaries departed from their barracks, and the local units of the IRA took over. But some barracks were occupied by pro-Treaty IRA men, while others were taken over by anti-Treaty IRA. The Union Jacks were taken down in the Ennistymon, Kilrush and Tulla workhouses, the Ennis Ordnance Survey building, the Quilty coastguard building and the police barracks in Clarecastle, Corofin, Broadford, Ennistymon, Feakle, Kildysart, Kilkee, Killaloe, Kilrush, Lisdoonvarna, Tulla, Miltown Malbay and Tirmaclane. The Home Barracks (the main British army garrison) in Ennis was evacuated on 21 February, and finally, Ennis RIC barracks, the largest in the county, was evacuated on Wednesday, 25 February. It was then occupied by the anti-Treaty IRA, with the tricolour flying proudly overhead. The Ennis Ordnance Survey building, the former Erasmus Smith College, became the new divisional headquarters of the 1st Western Division in Clare.[26]

Some old scores were settled before the withdrawal was completed. Bombs were thrown by Auxiliaries or Black and Tans on the evening of their departure from Ennistymon on 1 February. A bomb was thrown from the barrack window, and four people were injured in the blast, including school children. Two people, a schoolboy and a labourer, were compensated later, as the injuries were inflicted by Crown forces. Perhaps as a reprisal, two Black and Tans, constables William Guerley and Francis Kershaw, were shot dead at Lisdoonvarna after coming out of Green's pub at 8.30 p.m. on Friday, 3 February; about twenty shots were fired at them.

Also, an ex-RIC policeman named Sergeant Gunn, 52 years old, was shot dead on Saturday, 22 April. He had been stationed in Ennis for most of his career. A Presbyterian, he was shot dead by a party of IRA men at around 11.30 p.m. in the Market area outside his fiancée Miss Morrissey's home. It was felt at the time that Sergeant Gunn was shot because he planned to stay on in Ennis and he knew many people, including IRA members, who had spied for the British in the area during the 'troubles'. Fr Pat Gaynor stated in his memoir that Paddy 'Conn' McMahon had shot Sergeant Gunn for passing some remark about him. Historian Sean Spellissy told me that the IRA party included Aimee Barron, Bernie Barrett, Paddy 'Conn' McMahon and Jack Spellissy, who pursued Sergeant Gunn from Lyons' Bar on High Street and shot him in Market Lane. Spellissy informed me that 'more than likely, his father, Jack Spellissy, shot Sergeant Gunn'.

Sergeant David Findlay of the Royal Scots Regiment was badly beaten by the IRA after leaving the Queen's Hotel in Ennis; he died of his injuries on 13 January 1922. Findlay was allegedly associated with the torturing of prisoners such as the Doonbeg republicans – Willie Shanahan and Michael McNamara – who were murdered in December 1920. Another ex-RIC policeman, Sergeant J. Cotter, 37 years old and a Clare native, was shot dead in Cabra, Dublin on Friday, 13 March 1922 by three men who were shadowing him. He was survived by a widow and three children.[27]

Army Executive

The departure of the British presented many difficulties, both nationally and locally, as the IRA was divided over the Treaty. Pro- and anti-Treaty officers and IRA men took over the vacated barracks in different areas, and the military situation was confusing and volatile. It seems that most of the IRA officers at GHQ supported the Treaty, while most of the IRA officers outside of Dublin were against the Treaty. Seven anti-Treaty commandants called for an army convention in March. The Provisional Government allowed it at first, but as the situation in the country became more strained, permission was revoked. Despite this, the convention went ahead and an army executive council was formed on 26 March. Frank Barrett was one of sixteen members elected to the Army Executive on 9 April 1922. The Army Executive rejected the Treaty and pledged to defend the independence of the Irish Republic. The sixteen members of the Army Executive were: Liam Lynch, Liam Mellows, Rory O'Connor, Joe McKelvey, Florence O'Donoghue, Sean Moylan, Sean O'Hegarty, Liam Deasy, Seamus Robinson, Ernie O'Malley, Peadar O'Donnell, Joe O'Connor, Frank Barrett, Tom Maguire, P.J. Ruttledge and Tom Hales. The crisis worsened when officers of the Army Executive Council took over the Four Courts as their headquarters on 13 April.[28]

Anarchy
During the interregnum between the departure of the British forces and the takeover by government forces and republicans – a time that included the formation of a new Irish army and a new police force – law and order deteriorated in the county. Bitterness and tensions between the pro- and anti-Treaty camps increased and sometimes flared up into violence. Besides these political rows, some agitators began to take advantage of the political and security vacuum and renewed the old land campaign in the county – cattle drives became common in the months after the Treaty was ratified, especially in north Clare. In one agrarian-related dispute, a 91-year-old man named James McGuane, from Coolmeen, was taken out of his bed and shot; he subsequently died of his wounds.[29]

A proclamation 'banning cattle drives for three months owing to increased frequency and danger of very serious trouble arising from it' was issued on 29 April; it was issued by the military authority in Clare, and signed by General Michael Brennan and other officers of the 1st Western Division – Michael Hehir, John Joe Neylon and

William Haugh.[30] Despite this proclamation, land agitation continued and resulted in a harrowing tragedy two months later in Carron. A 45-year-old woman, Margaret Kilmartin, living in Meggah, Carron, was shot dead by six masked and armed men who raided the house at about 12.30 a.m. on Saturday, 17 June. Her husband Stephen was a herdsman on some lands in the Carron district. The men, armed with shotguns and revolvers, came to the house after midnight and demanded that Stephen Kilmartin come out. He refused, and after a struggle with the raiders, who broke in, several shots were fired in the house. Mrs Kilmartin received the fatal bullet intended for her husband, and nine young children were left without a mother.[31]

Law and order deteriorated in April, and the government authorities in the county ordered a curfew in Ennis and Ennistymon. General Michael Brennan issued the proclamation, 'Because of the danger of further bloodshed, there will be a curfew in Ennis in view of happenings in Ennistymon and Ennis last night, I hereby order that all persons be indoors by 7 pm this Thursday evening until 5 am Friday. Armed Volunteers will patrol the streets.'[32]

Canvassing in Clare

Éamon de Valera returned to Clare on a propaganda mission in late February. He sought to canvass support for the republican cause in the forthcoming election. De Valera arrived at the train station in Ennis and was welcomed by a guard of honour provided by the Mid-Clare Brigade, a sub-division of the 1st Western Division under the command of Frank Barrett. There was a monster meeting in Ennis; it was chaired by T.V. Honan, who had reversed his earlier pro-Treaty stance and now allied himself with the anti-Treaty side. The speakers included Éamon de Valera, Liam Mellows and Brian O'Higgins.

Liam Mellows TD, a leading republican socialist, was the commandant of the 1916 Rising in Galway. After the rebels dispersed, Mellows and two other officers, Alf Monaghan and Frank Hynes, went 'on the run'. They found refuge in the hills of north Clare at a place called Knockjames in the parish of Tulla, where they remained in hiding for about five months, until September 1916.

They were assisted by the local IRA under Sean McNamara of Crusheen. Mellows subsequently escaped to America.

At the monster meeting in Ennis, all three speakers called on the people of Clare to renew their allegiance to the Republic of Ireland, which was established in the Easter Rising and ratified by the Dáil in 1919, and to reject the Treaty. The editor of the *Clare Champion* praised de Valera for the moderation of his speech in Ennis; however, a few weeks later, de Valera denounced the Treaty in sanguinary language. Speaking at Thurles on 17 March, he said:

> The Volunteers would have to complete it over the dead bodies of their own countrymen. They would have to wade through blood, through the blood of the soldiers of the Irish Government, and through perhaps the blood of some of the members of the Government in order to get Irish freedom.[33]

Bishop Fogarty did not welcome de Valera to Ennis on this occasion. On his previous visit to Clare, between 30 November and 1 December 1921, a few days before the Treaty was signed, de Valera had stayed overnight at Westbourne, the bishop's residence. The friendship between Bishop Fogarty and Éamon de Valera was sundered when de Valera rejected the Treaty. That breach was never healed, even though Dr Fogarty was Bishop of Killaloe until 1955. Nevertheless, there were some Franciscan clergy at Ennis railway station to welcome de Valera, including Fr Leopold, Order of Friars Minor (OFM), and Fr Aloysius, OFM.

Bishop Fogarty had communicated with Michael Collins, the chairman of the Provisional Government, shortly after the Dáil's vote on the Treaty. Michael Collins replied on 13 January 1922; the letter describes what Bishop Fogarty referred to as the 'heart-breaking' division over the Treaty and gives some insights into Michael Collins's thoughts on the issue:

> My Lord Bishop, it was a great pity that President de Valera did not think better of my proposal as I think it did indicate a means to keep us together, or at least to avoid any acute division. It is my firm belief that if the proposal had been listened to, we all could have accepted the Treaty with any reservations we wished. It is, however, now too late from that point of view as we are going wider and wider apart. The whole thing is, as your lordship says, heart-breaking, and one can only hope it will come right in

the end. It is certain, however, that the Treaty was unavoidable and if there had not been such violent opposition the necessity for advocating it would have been much less and in this way the possibility is that very much more could have been made of the Treaty in its application than can now be made, but we shall do our best in any case.

As regards Dáil money, there is no change to be made for the present. The Trustees continue, and the Funds and Departments are administered as before.

I am, your lordships most obedient servant.[34]

Around this time there was an impressive demonstration at Cloonagh, Ennistymon on the second anniversary of the death of Volunteer Martin Devitt, the first IRA man to be killed in Clare during the War of Independence. More than 500 Volunteers attended the ceremony in his memory. At the memorial, a letter from Commandant Frank Barrett was read:

> Commandant Martin Devitt gave his life for the Republic, and all of us in the Brigade, his comrades, stand unflinchingly for the same sacred object. We mean to be true to our gallant dead and at his graveside we renew our allegiance and pledge our lives to the Irish Republic.[35]

A week after de Valera's monster meeting in Ennis, the Provisional Government held an election meeting in Ennis, which was attended by President Arthur Griffith, General Sean McEoin (GOC Western Command) and thousands of supporters. Canon William O'Kennedy, who was released from Spike Island prison after the Dáil voted to accept the Treaty, was the first speaker. Before the meeting, Bishop Fogarty sent a letter of support to Michael Brennan, who chaired the meeting; in this letter, Dr Fogarty stated:

> The people of Clare, soldiers and civilians, have fought as much as any other part of Ireland, if not more so. They are able to recognise freedom when they meet it in the concrete and by whatever name it is called. They are now free to live their lives their own way without interference from any foreign power; and they have no notion of 'going another round of the course' for the difference between the Treaty and Document Number 2 [de Valera's alternative proposal] merely to secure the applause of

the galleries. I wish success to your meeting, which is held not so much to instruct the people who have already made up their minds and who will give Mr Griffith a cordial welcome, but to assert the nation's right to liberty against armed despotism of a few. If I were at the meeting, my one appeal would be to let us look after our common sufferings, settle our differences like brother Irishmen not by violence but in a peaceful and constitutional way, with my blessings for peace and unity, yours sincerely, M Fogarty.[36]

Ecclesiastical Advice

In his Lenten pastoral, a pastoral letter to the parishioners of the Diocese of Killaloe, usually issued at the beginning of Lent, Bishop Fogarty warned the people in the diocese about the dangers of civil conflict over the terms of the Treaty and appealed for unity:

> We give thanksgiving for the liberation of our country; the terror is gone and with it the foreign power that held our country in destructive grip for 700 years. Even though we have not achieved all we would wish, Ireland is now the sovereign mistress of her own destiny, the rusty chains of bondage are scrapped for ever unless indeed by our own folly we put them on again.

> Unfortunately, there is a cloud hanging over us. Those who held so firmly together are now divided, and to the general dismay, divided on points, which in their original form did not seem to differ very substantially. It would appear to be a question of one form of association with the British empire as against another. Their ardent aspirations deserve respect, but an attempt to realise them will mean another sanguinary conflict. They have done their part nobly and heroically. Unless I am in error, the bulk of people are sick and tired of war. It is cruel and crude patriotism to plunge them into fratricidal strife, with the prospect of another 'terror' worse than they have gone through, ending perhaps in the loss of the freedom they purchased at so high a ransom.

> Already the evil effects of disunion are visible with demoralisation of the unscrupulous terror. The dissentions and consequent weakening of the Provisional Government have opened a gate for the malefactors, robbers and murderers now preying on society to such an alarming extent. It will need the combined efforts on all sides to avoid chaos. I appeal to the young men to take up religious practices again, they fought bravely, let them now live nobly.

Dr Berry, the Church of Ireland Bishop of Killaloe and Kilfenora, appealed for Irish unity while addressing the annual diocesan synod (an assembly of the diocesan clergy and lay representatives), stating that

> we have been living through dark days, days of mourning, days of trouble, but now there has come a day of a new hope [...] We hope that the dawn of a new and brighter day for Ireland is very near – a day of peace and prosperity, a day of unity and brotherhood [...] an Ireland now divided, but an Ireland yet to become one under the controlling influence of the Holy Spirit of unity, peace and concord.[37]

Funding the anti-Treaty forces

The anti-Treaty forces needed funds for electoral and other purposes, and they tried to organise a national church gate collection on Sunday, 24 April for Cumann na Poblachta, an Irish republican political party founded on 15 March by de Valera, 'to support those who stand for the unity and independence of Ireland and the maintenance of the republic'. However, Bishop Fogarty banned the collection at the church gates in Ennis.[38]

Desperate for money, the Army Executive sought funding for propaganda, the maintenance of an anti-Treaty republican army and the purchase of weapons. Ennis Post Office was raided on 1 April 1922 by a party of men in IRA officer uniforms, who stole £82. This raid seems to have been a local initiative in Clare. A month later, however, soldiers acting on behalf of the Army Executive carried out several major bank raids around the country, including Ennis. Dorothy McArdle, an Irish writer, republican and historian, wrote, 'The Republican army without funds felt justified in taking money from banks and post offices to arm and provision the republicans, the executive took full responsibility for the raids on 1 May 1922. On that day more than £50,000 was taken.'[39]

On Monday, 1 May at about 11 a.m., a party of armed and masked men, acting on the orders of Commandant Frank Barrett, raided the Bank of Ireland in Ennis. The raiders informed the staff that they were acting under orders from the Army Executive, and they left a document to this effect. A total of almost £36,000 was taken from the bank, of which £17,000 were cancelled notes. The raiders departed in a motor car; they were armed with Mauser rifles.[40]

In November 1924, responding to an anonymous letter to the local press that enquired into the proceeds from the raid on the Bank of Ireland, Frank Barrett publicly admitted that he was the officer responsible for the operation. Garrett Barry and Frank Butler also stated that they were involved as officers. They stated then that the amount stolen was £18,600, and they said that they acted entirely in accordance with orders from military superiors. They claimed that the money was surrendered to the brigade commandant and vice-commandants for the payment of bills contracted by the anti-Treaty IRA in the divisional area.

The 1st Western Division had been formally established on 11 November 1921 with Commandant Michael Brennan as OC and Frank Barrett as Vice-OC. The new divisional area compromised the three former Clare Brigade areas – West, Mid- and East Clare – along with two Galway brigades, South-east and South-west. However, after the split over the Treaty, the Army Executive set up a rival 1st Western Division with Frank Barrett in command.[41]

Fr Pat Gaynor, CC, in his memoir, stated that the men involved in the bank robbery were Frank Butler, Peter O'Loughlin and Paddy McCormac, and that they were acting on the orders of Frank Barrett. Fr Gaynor and others alleged that the money from the bank robbery was not used solely for the republican cause, and that most of it ended up in private hands after the civil war was over. Gaynor stated that the stolen money was buried in a pot in McMahon's garden, Ballynacally, except for a small amount that was sent to Dublin and perhaps a sum that was spent locally on uniforms and supplies. Gaynor added that Frank Barrett did not use the money for himself. Finally, Gaynor alleged that upon his release from prison after the civil war ended, Paddy 'Conn' McMahon demanded the pot of stolen money from Frank Barrett at the point of a gun and used the money for his own purposes.[42]

Confusion and tension in Clare

There was tension in many areas around the country and the county as rival groups of IRA men occupied the barracks vacated by the British forces. However, a truce negotiated between the two factions was unanimously ratified by the Dáil and the Sinn Féin Ard Fheis.

In early April 1922 the republicans took over the former police barracks in Miltown Malbay from government forces. The takeover of Miltown Malbay barracks on Monday, 10 April caused 'intense excitement' in the town. A party of six armed republicans led by Captain Michael Barrett arrived in two cars and entered the barracks, which was occupied by twenty-four government troops. They demanded possession of the barracks, and it was handed over to them without any resistance being offered. Four of the government soldiers then decided to join the republicans. The departing forces had to find temporary accommodation in the town. It was reported that the government troops only held four rifles and some revolvers. The republicans also took over Quilty coastguard station, as well as the former police barracks in Ennistymon, Kilkee and Kilrush.[43]

On the national stage, momentous events were taking place as the rival parties – the Provisional Government, led by Griffith, and Cumann na Poblachta, led by de Valera – struggled to assert their military authority and win the support of the people in a forthcoming election. This was the case in Limerick, where there was almost a military clash between the anti-Treaty and pro-Treaty IRA groups in March. The Provisional Government did not want the city falling under the control of the anti-Treaty forces led by General Ernie O'Malley of the 2nd Southern Division. General Michael Brennan was ordered to secure the city with troops from the 1st Western Division, and the rival forces came very close to military engagement at this time.[44]

General Michael Brennan was ordered by the Provisional Government to withdraw his troops from several garrisons in north Clare, as his actions in ordering government troops to take over several evacuated barracks in north Clare were deemed to be in breach of the truce between the Army Executive and the Provisional Government. The following correspondence from Brennan, under the *Clare Champion* heading 'Evacuation of posts by Regular Troops', illustrates the tension between the rival groups:

> Owing to the state of lawlessness in certain districts in Clare and in consequence of hundreds of appeals from people, I found it necessary to establish several new posts, amongst them being, Miltown Malbay, Ballyvaughan and Lisdoonvarna. Shortly

afterwards, the Minister for Defence was contacted by representatives of the Four Courts that this action was in breach of the truce. I was instructed by the Chief of Staff to forward a report. I had an interview with Commandant Frank Barrett. I pointed out to him that I was actuated solely to give protection to the law-abiding population. He agreed that in accordance with the spirit of the truce, it would be better to remove any cause of friction between the two forces, and if I evacuated these posts, he would guarantee protection to the people.

I sent the following letter to Commandant Barrett on 7 June: 'Further to our conversation on Saturday last re evacuation of new posts, I am willing to recommend to the chief of staff that he sanctions this course of action if you agree to accept responsibility for maintaining law and order in these districts and affording people and property all necessary protection.'

Commandant Frank Barrett in his written reply stated: 'I am prepared to accept responsibility for the maintenance of law and order in these districts referred to following the evacuation by you of your troops in the stations concerned.'

Following this reply, the evacuation was proceeded with, and Balyvaughan, Lisdoonvarna and Miltown Malbay have already been evacuated. My object in making these details public is to dispose of charges being made against regular troops of having 'deserted' the people. There is no question of desertion, as it must be quite clear that we only left these districts on being satisfied that the people would get every protection they required.[45]

A negation of democracy

Even though the various parties had already selected their candidates for the forthcoming election to be held in June, on 20 May Éamon de Valera and Michael Collins agreed to an election pact that allowed each branch of the Sinn Féin party to return the same proportion of candidates already elected to the Dáil – after the split following the Treaty, there were 64 pro-Treaty Sinn Féin TDs and 57 anti-Treaty Sinn Féin TDs. In many constituencies, the electorate were not being allowed to freely express their opinion or vote for non-Sinn Féin candidates. In Clare at least three other candidates had been nominated to contest the election: Patrick Hogan, for the Labour Party; Conor Hogan, representing the Farmers Party; and

Edward MacLysaght, an independent. However, whether through intimidation, subtle pressure or other means, all of these candidates withdrew their names just before the nomination period. The result was that four candidates – Éamon de Valera and Brian O'Higgins, representing the anti-Treaty party, and Patrick Brennan and Sean Liddy, representing the pro-Treaty party – were elected without a ballot in what the *Clare Champion* editor called 'a negation of democracy'.

Some months earlier, on 26 April, the Catholic hierarchy had met at Maynooth and issued the following statement, urging a pro-Treaty vote, 'We think that the best and wisest course for Ireland is to accept the Treaty and make the most of the freedom it undoubtedly brings to us, freedom for the first time in 700 years.'

Despite the electoral pact between Collins and de Valera, it was not accepted by other parties and individuals in Ireland, and by the electorate in many other constituencies. The results of the election showed that only 36 anti-Treaty Sinn Féin TDs were elected out of a total of 128 TDs; of the 92 remaining seats, 58 went to pro-Treaty Sinn Féin candidates. The rest were divided among the Labour Party, the Farmers' Party and independents. Clearly, most people in the country voted for pro-Treaty candidates.[46]

The anti-Treaty republicans did not accept the electoral verdict of the Irish people. Historian Tom Garvin contrasted the attitudes of both sides towards democracy:

> The Free State side argued in favour of the will of the people. The anti-Treaty side argued that the will of the people was tainted, because the Irish had a slave mentality [...] the 'true' republicans looked with contempt on the slave mentality of most of the Irish people, who voted pro-Treaty.

Éamon de Valera stated that the majority had no right to do wrong.[47]

Some members of the anti-Treaty IRA also attacked the press. In Dublin, they smashed the printing presses of the *Freeman's Journal*, which had been critical of their actions. Perhaps taking inspiration from this attack on the press, some republicans in Clare also attacked the freedom of the press. On 8 April a group of armed and masked men held up the newsagents at Kilrush after the West Clare railway had delivered the newspapers; they seized bundles of the *Freeman's Journal* and burnt them with paraffin oil. Another gang of armed and masked men seized and burnt parcels of the *Freeman's Journal* at Ennis railway station on 30 April.[48]

Death and terror

The tension between the two rival forces in Clare resulted in a tragedy at Broadford. An armed party of anti-Treaty republicans attacked the barracks at Broadford, which was held by government forces, and captured the barracks on Saturday evening, 8 April. The next morning a party of government soldiers arrived and recaptured the barracks. During this operation, William O'Brien, one of the republicans, was shot and died from his injuries. He was the first Clare victim of this period, and the civil war had not yet officially begun.[49]

Some weeks later, some trigger-happy soldiers fired a few shots at each other. A shot was fired and a bomb exploded at Ennis County Club, the headquarters of the pro-Treaty forces in the county, on Saturday, 22 April 1922. A week later, four shots were fired at a sentry guarding the government headquarters in Ennis; shots were returned, but there were no reports of injury. A 'land war' ambush took place at Corofin on the night of Thursday, 1 June. While patrolling 'driven' farms (farms from which the cattle and other stock had been driven by people seeking to break up the ranches and large estates) outside the town, a sergeant and four soldiers were ambushed; they returned fire, and there were no reports of casualties.[50]

An ominous and very disturbing sectarian development occurred on Friday, 2 June, when threatening notices were posted in Kilrush warning Protestants to clear out of the town within twelve hours or take the consequences. Several Protestants received these written notices, which were posted on their doors. Notices were also posted up in the Market Square. The recipients were very disturbed by the sectarian threats, and they reported the matter to the local military authorities. The West Clare Brigade commandant, Simon McInerney, who was anti-Treaty, took prompt action and issued a proclamation denouncing the threats and asking the citizens of

Kilrush to help in tracing the culprits. He stated that the military authorities would protect the Protestants of Kilrush. The Very Rev. Dean McInerney, PP, of Kilrush, strongly denounced the letters at Mass on Sunday. Also, Fr Culligan, a local Catholic priest, presiding over the district court at Kilrush, strongly denounced the threats to the Protestant people of Kilrush.

Incidentally, according to County Inspector Attridge's report of August–September 1921, John J. Liddy, a member of the Dáil and commandant of the West Clare Brigade, was charged at a Sinn Féin court with embezzlement of £1,600 in rate money owed to Clare County Council. Another police report noted that he was accused of misappropriating over £26,000 belonging to Clare County Council. No source or evidence was given by County Inspector Attridge for these damaging allegations. However, three days later, Attridge stated that Liddy was suspended from his role as brigade commandant. The police report noted that Liddy, accompanied by Thomas Marrinan, visited the former RIC barracks at Kilkee. County Inspector Attridge noted, 'Simon McInerney of Kilferagh had replaced John J. Liddy in command of the West Clare Brigade. McInerney, had been in the Dublin district for the past two years, but returned after the Truce.'[51]

Besides robbing the Bank of Ireland in Ennis, the republicans in Clare were also gearing up for war by stealing motor cars, which would increase their mobility. Between April and May 1922, a total of sixteen motor cars were stolen by armed men from prominent people in the county. Landlords were prime targets; these included the Inchiquins of Dromoland, the Stacpooles of Eden Vale, Colonel Tottenham of Mount Callan, Edward O'Brien of Roslevan and Major Blood of Ballykilty. Two cars were stolen from Lord Inchiquin. Cars were also stolen from prominent businesspeople in Ennis, Kilrush and other towns, and from a Church of Ireland minister in Ennis.[52]

About ten days after the result of the June election was announced, the stand-off between the government and the republicans in the Four Courts finally came to a head. The Provisional Government issued an ultimatum to the anti-Treaty forces to vacate the building by 3.40 a.m. on 28 June 1922. The republicans inside the Four Courts refused to surrender, and shortly after the deadline, the government forces shelled the Four Courts and the civil war began.

Summary
The controversial Treaty of 6 December 1921, which provided for the establishment of the Irish Free State within a year, had bitterly divided the county. It was rejected by de Valera and a significant number of republicans as a betrayal of the Irish Republic declared by the rebels of the Easter Rising and ratified by the Dáil in January 1919. Between the signing of the Treaty by the plenipotentiaries on 6 December and the Dáil's vote to have it ratified on 7 January 1922, the issue was passionately debated all over the country.

In Clare, the Treaty was supported by most people. Clare County Council voted twice on the issue, and a significant majority voted to accept the Treaty on each occasion; the first vote was 17 votes to 5, the second was 18 votes to 9. Likewise, urban councils in Ennis and Kilrush voted in favour of the Treaty, as did rural district councils and the boards of guardians in Kildysart, Scariff and Kilrush. The farming and business leaders of Clare, at meetings in Ennis and Kilrush, also overwhelmingly supported the Treaty. The two most influential local newspapers published in Ennis and circulated widely in the county, the *Clare Champion* and the *Saturday Record*, also urged the politicians to ratify the Treaty in the Dáil vote. Both county executives of Sinn Féin, in east and west Clare, supported the Treaty by large majorities of 17 votes to 9 and 17 votes to 4. Besides the public bodies, plebiscites in various parishes around the county indicated that a significant majority of the public were in favour of the Treaty.

Bishop Fogarty, Bishop O'Dea (the Bishop of Galway), the Irish hierarchy and most of the Catholic clergy urged the people and politicians to accept the Treaty as the best possible deal on offer. Bishop Fogarty was active in seeking a bishop's conference at this critical time. The bishops met on 26 April 1921 and issued a statement afterwards, 'We think that the best and wisest course for Ireland is to accept the Treaty and make the most of the freedom it undoubtedly brings to us, freedom for the first time in 700 years.'

Historian Patrick Murray asserts that the Catholic hierarchy accepted the moderate view on the Treaty, which was the view of most of the people. The bishops denounced the extreme republicans' claim that the army, or part of it, can, without any authority from the nation, declare itself independent of all civil authority; such a claim to 'military despotism' would amount to 'an immoral usurpation and confiscation of the people's rights [...] There was only one legitimate authority, the Dáil.'

Early in April 1922, Bishop Fogarty, in a letter to Monsignor Hagan at the Vatican, stated that de Valera's public behaviour had made conciliation impossible:

> You have only to read todays Independent, to see that de Valera has now identified himself with the army junta and has given his benediction to their schemes of suppressing elections by force [...] de Valera wanted no peace but his own, and having lost public sympathy and support was relying on intimidation as his last resource.[53]

Murray states that Bishop Fogarty appears to have imposed his moderate republican views on the great majority of his clergy, as 'very few Killaloe priests openly declared themselves republicans in a diocese with a considerable republican electorate.' Murray lists only four members of the clergy in the diocese of Killaloe who publicly opposed the Treaty: Fr M.J. Galvin, Ennis; Fr John O'Dea, CC of Killaloe; Fr Daniel O'Dea, CC of Sixmilebridge; and Fr Daniel O'Flynn, CC of Ballynacally and Clondegad. Fr O'Flynn had presided at a republican convention in Ennis that selected Éamon de Valera and Brian O'Higgins as candidates for the general election in June. Besides these four priests, Murray lists three clergymen belonging to Clare parishes in the diocese of Galway, Kilmacduagh and Kilfenora who also opposed the Treaty: Fr James Considine, administrator of Carron and Kilnaboy; Fr Marcus Conway, PP of Lisdoonvarna; and Fr John O'Kelly, administrator of Liscannor.[54] Fr Patrick Gaynor recalled that all but three or four Killaloe diocesan priests followed the bishop and were anti-republican.[55]

Despite overwhelming support from politicians, the media, farmers, businessmen, churchmen, and it would seem, the majority of the people of Clare (and, indeed, of Ireland), a significant body of republicans in the county, led by Commandant Frank Barrett, rejected the Treaty and stated that they would not accept the democratic will of the Irish people as expressed in the Dáil vote on the Treaty and in the June election. Two of the Clare TDs voted against the Treaty; de Valera 'stood by the republic' and Brian O'Higgins voted against it 'on principle', declaring that 'the constituents of West Clare were not the captains of my soul.'

Following the Dáil vote on 7 January, relations between the pro- and anti-Treaty camps deteriorated rapidly. The determination of the anti-Treaty republicans to overthrow the Treaty led them to form an army executive council and defiantly seize the Four Courts. They engaged in bank robberies, attacked the press and sought to undermine the authority and legitimacy of the Dáil and the democratically elected government through military means. Anti-Treaty republicans in Clare were involved in all these activities; there were also sectarian alarms in west Clare. Despite many pleas for unity and peace from the Catholic and Protestant hierarchies, the press and other bodies (which were ignored), there was a lot of nasty propaganda, and tension and bitterness between former comrades in armed garrisons in many areas around the country until the civil war finally erupted on 28 June 1922.

2
THE IRISH DISTRESS COMMITTEE

The Irish Distress Committee was established by the British government in 1923 to assess the claims of those in Ireland who had suffered mainly because of the activities of the republicans during the War of Independence. The compensation claims came from many categories of people: ex-RIC men and their families; ex-soldiers; people boycotted for associating with, or assisting, the police or Crown forces; unionists or loyalists whose properties had been destroyed, or whose lands had been seized by republicans and land agitators; and others who had fallen foul of the IRA for various reasons and were intimidated and traumatised by them. The records of this committee give some further insights into how the War of Independence was conducted and reveal some of the physical, economic, social and psychological suffering experienced by many people throughout Clare during this time – and for a considerable time after the war was over, during the truce and civil war periods.

There were a total of 354 claims sent to the committee from people associated with forty different towns, villages and parishes in the county. However, more than 65 per cent of all claims in the files came from the north-western part of the county, specifically from a cluster of four parishes: Ennistymon, Lahinch, Liscannor and Doolin. Significantly, more than 41 per cent of all the claims came from people in the Ennistymon area alone; 14.6 per cent came from Lahinch; 6.2 per cent were from Liscannor; and 3.1 per cent from Doolin. When we aggregate the claims from the top twelve parishes, the inordinate number of claims from the Ennistymon area stands in stark contrast to the rest of the county. The figures are as follows: Ennistymon, 146; Lahinch, 52; Ennis, 23; Liscannor, 22; Doolin, 11; Kilrush, 8; Kilkee, 6; Miltown Malbay, 6; Kilfenora, 6; Feakle, 6; Killaloe, 5; Lisdoonvarna, 4; Kilshanny, 4. These statistics are unusual and raise the question as to why such a high percentage of claims came from this relatively small portion of the county. Was it that people in this region were more persecuted or suffered more distress during the War of Independence than people in the rest of the county? Perhaps files for other parts of the county are missing. Or was it because people from this area were more litigious than people in other parts of the county in seeking compensation?

Ex-RIC

Thirty-six of the 354 claims for compensation, just over 10 per cent, were related to RIC men who had returned to Clare or tried to settle there after the end of the War of Independence and the disbandment of the RIC. Though the war was over, they were not forgotten or forgiven. In every case, they were intimidated, boycotted and given warning notices to leave the county or else face the consequences. However, only ten of the thirty-six RIC claims were granted some compensation. All of them would have been aware of the fate of Sergeant Gunn, who had returned to Ennis after the demobilisation of the police force and was shot dead. He left the force on 20 April 1922 and was shot dead on his return to Ennis three days later. He had served about twenty-five years in Ennis. The death of Sergeant Gunn was a salutary lesson to all ex-RIC men from Clare, and elsewhere, that they would be risking their lives by settling in the county. In almost every one of the thirty-six claims, the ex-RIC men had been given very short notices – in many cases as little as twelve hours – to leave the county. Some who had tried to return to their homes in Clare were visited by armed and masked men and given short notices to get out. Some who had retired, even before the War of Independence, and tried to set up a business were boycotted. Others claimed that they found it difficult to get employment in Ireland. Clearly, the ex-RIC men were *persona non grata* in Clare after the war was over, and they knew it.

The testimony of Patrick Connor from Cassernagh, Knock is typical:

> I was disbanded from the RIC on 20 April 1922. I returned home next day to my wife and family at Cassernagh, Knock, where we had a well-stocked freehold farm of 8 acres. About three weeks later I received a notice signed by the Commander in Chief West Clare Brigade IRA [Simon McInerney]: 'As you fought with and

assisted the enemy in shooting down the Irish people and depriving them of their freedom, you are hereby ordered to leave this area within 24 hours.' I ignored the notice but the next day my home was raided at 2 a.m. by armed men, who ordered me to leave the area. I at once left for England [...] I was held up at Limerick Junction and all my belongings taken [...] I arrived in England on 1 May '22 [...] my wife and four children joined me in October.[56]

William Burns was an intelligence officer; he and his wife Nora were living in Ennis. Nora Burns testified as follows:

my house was raided on the night of 23 April 1922 by ten or more armed men to murder my husband. I assisted him to escape through the back-room window. I heard shots as he ran [...] they searched my house, I, being in my night-dress, and my children screaming and believed my husband was murdered outside [...] my husband was a crime special intelligence officer and guide to the Crown forces up to the disbandment.

William Burns corroborated her claims on the attack:

I narrowly escaped shooting on the night of 23 April 1922, my house was raided by armed men determined to murder me, having murdered my colleague, Sergeant Gunn on the previous night. I escaped by jumping out the window in my shirt and trousers [...] I was fired at as I ran. I was a crime special intelligence constable and acted as guide to the Crown forces in all parts of County Clare up to the time of disbandment.

Nora Burns was awarded £100 by the Irish Grants Committee, a separate British government agency set up in 1924 to compensate the victims of IRA violence.[57]

There is a third testimony from Daniel Brougham of Newmarket-on-Fergus:

I was disbanded on 5 April 1922 [...] I left Dublin on 25 April and came home to live with my wife and family at Newmarket on Fergus. On 27 April I received a letter containing a typed notice signed 'Adjutant IRA Clare', ordering me to leave the area within 24 hours as my presence was a menace, otherwise I would be shot. I left home on 29 April taking my wife and family to London.[58]

The wives and families of ex-RIC men were also harshly treated. Agnes Clarke, a national teacher, 42 years old, was the wife of a sergeant in the RIC. She was a primary teacher in Ruan National School while he was based in Ennistymon. Her testimony illustrates the power of the IRA in local communities:

> Early in July 1921 a party of four members of the IRA visited the school, I was absent due to illness; they came to my home and ordered me not to teach again as I was the wife of an RIC man, they said that I was not fit to teach Irish children. They gave me ten days to leave the locality.

> They locked the school and took away the key. I did not leave the place, but things were made so difficult for me and it was impossible for me to get milk and vegetables; and previously, servants, whom I had engaged to mind my children, had been intimidated and forced to leave; so that I was forced to go to Ennistymon where my husband was then stationed and get rooms there leaving my own home locked. While I was there the parish priest of Ruan tried to persuade me to resign; I would not do so, though he said I might as well as the IRA would keep the school closed and would not allow me to teach there. [Note, at that time Fr Breen was the parish priest of Ruan; he was a member of the East Clare Executive of Sinn Féin.]

> Shortly after this I was told by the owner of the hotel I was staying in that the IRA had ordered me to leave and that I was better off leaving the country altogether. In desperation, I wired my husband who was in Mullingar awaiting demobilisation, we all then came to Liverpool [...] when I left Ireland the IRA opened my school again.

The National Educational Board and Bishop Fogarty provided references for Agnes Clarke, indicating that she was a teacher of good character. Sergeant Laurence Clarke, her husband, stated, 'After demobilisation, I and Sgt. Gunn were ordered to leave Ireland as soon as we could. Sgt. Gunn went back to Clare and was immediately shot.'[59]

The widows of ex-RIC men did not find much sympathy in Ireland either. Ellen Stanley was the widow of Constable William Stanley, who was killed at Feakle on 7 October 1920. She lived in the barracks for some time afterwards, but she had to move out during the civil war, as it was too dangerous. She tried to get a house in Ennis, Limerick and even Dublin, but because she was the widow of a murdered policeman, she could not find anywhere to live. She was forced to go to England. Ellen Stanley was awarded a sum of £250.[60]

Even RIC men who had retired before the War of Independence were victimised. Michael Hourihan, 69 years old, retired from the RIC on 31 July 1918 after forty-one years of service with a pension of £104 a year. He settled in Clarecastle, where he rented a small house with a garden for 6 shillings a week. To augment his pension, he used to sell vegetables, making on average between 2 shillings and 3 shillings per day. He was also a part-time agent for the Pearl Insurance Company; this earned him between £1 and £2 a week. However, after the truce he was boycotted owing to his previous service in the RIC. Two of his sons had also been members of the RIC until the force was disbanded in 1922. Hourihan claimed that he could not sell his vegetables and that his clients in the Pearl Insurance Company were warned to have nothing to do with him. In some instances, their policies were seized and destroyed. It became dangerous for him to go out; his home was raided by armed men and he was ordered to leave the country. His wife was terrified, and a bicycle was stolen. They went to England. The family had to leave in a hurry, and they had to sell their furniture at a considerable loss. He claimed that the threats to his life were due to his service in the RIC. He was awarded £150 by the Irish Grants Committee. He also received a sum of £20 from the Southern Irish Loyalist Relief Association.[61]

Ex-Sergeant Anthony Tunny, 39 years old and a native of Bohola, Co. Mayo, could not go back to Mayo after the RIC were disbanded, and he settled for a while in Clarecastle with his wife and child. They were threatened on several occasions, and his wife, who was expecting her second child, became 'a nervous wreck'. They decided to leave Clarecastle after several armed men visited their house and left word that he was to 'clear out at once'. He and his family left. Sergeant Tunny stated that after serving with the RIC for fifteen years he was 'a marked man' and had to leave the country with his wife and children. Sergeant Tunny was granted a sum of £405 by the Irish Grants Committee.[62]

Former soldiers

Ex-soldiers were also subject to intimidation during the War of Independence and the truce period. A total of twenty-four ex-servicemen applied for compensation; most of these men had served in the army, while only one had served in the navy. Those who were still serving up to the truce were naturally treated as enemies. Most of these ex-soldiers had difficulty in finding employment after demobilisation. In some instances where they set up enterprises, they were boycotted, especially if they dealt with the police or the army. Some who were approached to join the IRA and refused to do so were treated badly and were ostracised as spies; in many instances, they were threatened and assaulted, found it hard to get work and, in some cases, were forced to leave home. However, only five of the twenty-four ex-servicemen were granted some compensation.

Mrs Denis Callinan illustrated how her husband, an ex-soldier, was treated:

> He farmed 156 acres at Cahercullen, Cree, Co Clare. In 1917 he responded to the call to join the 'colours', he left his sister in charge of his farm and served as a gunner till he was demobilised in 1919. On one occasion, while home on leave from France, his tunic was taken and burnt and an effort was made to prevent him re-joining his regiment. From the time he joined the army he was subject to much persecution [...] the oak beams were stripped from the roofs of the out-offices and the lands were constantly grazed by trespassing cattle [...] his turf was also taken and he was boycotted, being unable to sell surplus turf [...] In 1921 he bought a mowing machine [...] the meadow was maliciously spiked with iron damaging the machine, the meadow could not be cut and he had to buy hay, the same thing happened in 1922.

The Callinans were members of the Church of Ireland. They received £10 in relief from the Southern Irish Loyalists Relief Association and a suit of clothes from the Irish Red Cross Society. She was awarded £75 by the Irish Grants Committee.[63]

Patrick Baker, an ex-soldier of Lower Quay, Liscannor, told another tale of persecution. He was demobilised on 27 June 1919 and returned to Liscannor, and from that date onward he said that he 'was a marked man'. In May 1920 he was asked to join the IRA but he refused, and he was then branded as an English loyalist and a spy. At the end of 1920, when the Royal Marines came to Liscannor, nobody was allowed assist them in any way. At the risk of his own life, he volunteered to cart their foodstuffs from Ennistymon until they were evacuated from Liscannor. At the end of December 1921, he was taken out of his house along with his son (another ex-soldier), accused of being a spy for the British government and told that he was sentenced to leave the country or be executed. He was threatened several times and in July 1922, he was severely beaten and became a nervous wreck. Baker earned his living as a carter, and he was so severely boycotted that he had to sell his horse and car. He was awarded £75 by the Irish Grants Committee.[64]

The cases of other ex-army men are similar. For example, Patrick Woods of Doolin was demobilised in 1919; he was hampered in every way by the IRA and accused of being a spy.[65] Anther ex-soldier named Simon O'Flaherty, from Lough, Doolin, was demobilised in 1920. When he refused to join the IRA, he was 'boycotted and harassed'.[66] John O'Donnell of Kilshanny was demobilised early in 1919, but when he returned home he received threatening letters and he had to leave.[67] Michael O'Connor of Ardnacolla, Ennistymon was demobilised from the army in 1917. He was approached by the IRA to join as an instructor. He refused to do so and was threatened in many ways.[68] Patrick O'Brien of Church Hill, Ennistymon was demobilised in 1919. He was attacked in the streets of Ennistymon and both of his legs were broken.[69] Steven Reynolds of Carhooduff, Kilshanny, an ex-serviceman who refused to join the IRA, 'was beaten unmercifully and ordered to go back to England'. He also alleged that the IRA stole £700 from him.[70]

Collaborators

The largest number of claimants for compensation came from those people who supported, assisted or worked for the RIC or the military. In fact, a total of seventy-six people put in claims for loss of business or intimidation. The list of those who were boycotted, intimidated, threatened or assaulted for assisting the police or army covered a broad spectrum of society; it included newsagents, grocers, builders, butchers, farmers, fuel merchants, laundresses, washer-women, stonecutters, bootmakers, cooks, cleaners, publicans, fishermen, hoteliers, restaurant owners, chimney sweeps, fish-mongers, hackney drivers, carpenters, undertakers, bakers, milk sellers, carters and tailors. Others affected included a doctor, a photographer, a town clerk, a dentist and even a Catholic priest. A couple of cases will suffice to illustrate this category of claimants.

Peter Blake was a blacksmith who lived in a pub beside the Bridge at Ennistymon; he also ran a coach-building business while his wife managed his pub. He repaired vehicles for the military and RIC, and officers visited his public house. He was threatened and boycotted, and he claimed his health was ruined.[71] Michael Garrahy was another blacksmith who served the Crown forces in Ennistymon. The IRA punished him by cutting his bellows to pieces.[72]

Charlotte Brennan, from Ennistymon, was the widow of an RIC sergeant who had died in 1911. She stated that she was unpopular with the 'rebels', because she opened a tearoom that was frequented by the military. In her application to the Irish Distress Committee for assistance, she described how in 1921 she received a threatening letter to clear out of Ireland within forty-eight hours – herself and the 'Peeler's children':

> Owing to threats and raids, I and my children often had to fly into the fields at night and sleep in ditches, with only light cover, being cold and hungry. On 22 August 1922, when the military were withdrawn and the police demobilised, I and the children had to flee the country with only our clothing [...] my son, Francis Anthony Brennan was fired at on three occasions and on 1 February 1922 a bomb was thrown at him, which wounded him in the legs and arms permanently impairing him.

Charlotte Brennan and her family went to Australia and she was awarded £1,200 in compensation.[73]

Other people were threatened because they publicly denounced IRA actions. For instance, William Cahir, who farmed 144 acres at Knockroe, Kilfenora, submitted a claim as he said that his house was raided all through the troubles. After the killing of two policemen at Illaunbaun in July 1919, some parishioners, including William Cahir, held a meeting at the local school the following Sunday. They passed a resolution condemning the outrage, which was sent to the county inspector of the RIC. Following this action, Cahir was threatened; he had to leave his house and move to Corofin until

March 1924, as he feared for his life. On 23 November 1922, his house was raided by five or six armed men and he had to flee from the house at 10 p.m. He was granted a total of £150.[74]

Henry Vincent MacNamara's associates

A total of fifty-three claimants were associated in some way with Henry Vincent MacNamara, JP (justice of the peace), DL, of Ennistymon House, a prominent landlord and unionist in Clare. At least twenty-five of them had been employees or dependant on H.V. MacNamara, while the rest were his tenants. He was threatened on many occasions by the IRA, and he eventually left the country in February 1920. His departure had a significant impact on employment in the area. Given that he was the dominant landlord in the Ennistymon district, and that a considerable number of claims came from that district, it is not surprising that many of those who applied for compensation were either his tenants or his employees, or both. There had been a massive campaign against him and other large landowners in north Clare, and his tenants as well as his employees were also harassed to boycott 'Henry Vee', as he was popularly known in the district. The following examples show how some of his tenants and employees were affected by the campaign against him.

Katie Considine of Kilconnell, Liscannor, a farmer's widow with a young family, was appointed as a tower keeper and shore ranger by H.V. MacNamara:

> I became very unpopular for doing my duty for him and was several times threatened and would get no one to work my lands after my husband's death [...] I suffered a loss of cattle for want of proper care and consequently owing to many threats my three children had to leave this country for the USA, as they could get no work.[75]

George Blood of Fantire, Kilshanny was another victim of the campaign against H.V. MacNamara. He claimed that he had been boycotted since 1920 and could not sell his banks of turf; 7 acres of his land were flooded when the IRA dug a road trench and put the material into a trench on his property. He was forced to leave MacNamara's employment in 1920, losing a salary of £16 per annum; he had paid MacNamara £6 to rent 1 acre of tillage ground in 1920 but was prevented from tilling it after receiving threats. He claimed that the cause of this persecution was that 'the rebels were hostile to my continuing to work for Mr MacNamara and I was blamed for giving information to the Crown forces.' Blood was awarded £200.[76]

Women were punished by the IRA in other ways beyond boycotting for assisting the RIC or British army. The following claims illustrate this. Nora Logan of Main Street, Lahinch was, in her own words, 'friendly with the RIC'. She had her hair cut several times in 1919 and 1921.[77] Katie McNamara of Bogberry, Ennistymon was a mother of eleven children who worked as a laundress and cook for the military in Ennistymon; she opened a tea room, which was frequented by the army and RIC. She was ordered to stop by the IRA and refused to do so. She then claims that she was kidnapped and held prisoner in 'wild mountainous country, where she was shamefully ill-treated. Because of this treatment, she miscarried and spent six weeks in hospital.' Her husband was an ex-employee of H.V. MacNamara.[78] Susan O'Loughlin of Chapel Road, Ennistymon was warned that she was going to be tarred for working in the RIC barracks. She stated that had to leave the country until 1926.[79]

Non-collaborators

Pressure was put on people to join the IRA or support them during the struggle. Those who refused to do so were punished. A common accusation against people who refused to support the IRA was for them to be called 'loyalists'. Patrick McNamara of Lahinch asserted that he was forced to leave home several times for refusing to join the IRA.[80] George Hynes, from Lahinch, was boycotted for refusing to give the IRA permission to approach his two sons in an effort to enlist them.[81] William Neylon, also from Lahinch, refused to fund the IRA, and his farm was damaged.[82] Margaret Marrinan of Ballyduff, Inagh refused to shelter a number of IRA men in April 1921. Three nights later, shots were fired into the house, 'which affected her husband's nerves'.[83] Stephen Neville of Glann, Ennistymon 'refused to join the IRA and was called an enemy of the people [...] he was beaten severely and treated like a dog.'[84] Patrick Fitzgerald of Fisher Street, Doolin refused to join or support the IRA. He and his family were boycotted and intimidated.[85] Michael Mulqueeny of Moymore, Ennistymon refused to subscribe to the IRA. Mulqueeny stated that because of this refusal his brother suffered 'Republican Court Justice' and paid a heavy fine to the IRA.[86] Edmund Cahill of Kildeema South, Miltown Malbay had four sons that were beaten up because they would not join the IRA.[87]

Justices of the peace

Another significant group of people who made claims for compensation were justices of the peace, and at least eleven of them made representations to the Irish Distress Committee seeking some recompense for their losses. Among these justices were: Joseph Browne, Knockerra, Killimer; Bartholemew Culligan, Kilrush; Dr Peter O'Dwyer, Ennistymon; William James Corbett, Wilbrook, Corofin; William Charles Doherty, Kilkee; Michael Gaynor, New Quay; W. Hogan, Main Street, Ennistymon; Joseph McInerney, Ennistymon; Marcus Patterson, Clifden, Corofin; William Jonas Studdert, Kilballyowen, Carrigaholt; and James Wakely, Mountshannon. The IRA put justices under enormous pressure to resign their positions as part of the campaign to undermine the British justice system and replace it with the Sinn Féin courts. The justices were intimidated, boycotted and suffered injuries to themselves and their properties.

The statement of Joseph Browne of Knockerra in his application to the Irish Distress Committee shows how intensely the justices were pressured to resign:

> I am a farmer farming 31 acres at my home farm, Knockerra and 23 acres of Coolmuinga. I held the position of Justice of the Peace for a number of years until the evacuation of the British military from Ireland. I sat alone, the country was then in a most disturbed state, especially the district where I live. I was on several occasions attacked and badly beaten for not giving up the position. My cattle were taken off my lands and disposed of, without giving me any money for them, this occurred on several dates, including August 1921 and April 1923. On the 1st September 1921, I had to leave my home and had to remain away for one month. During this time, my lands were allowed to run

into a state of disrepair and my cattle deteriorated during my absence. On the 7th January 1922, I was again beaten. In the month of November 1921, I was fired at and again in December the same year. As a Justice of the Peace a dead set was made against me [he was publicly ostracised] and I was cruelly treated in consequence of my loyalty to the Crown.

Joseph Browne was not given any compensation.[88]

Batt Culligan, from Cappa, Kilrush, wrote that he was threatened on many occasions and ordered to resign as a justice, but that he had refused to do so.[89] Dr Peter O'Dwyer, from the Cottage, Ennistymon, was a medical officer for the RIC and the military and was also a local dispensary doctor. He was a justice, and when he refused to resign the office, he was removed from his position as a dispensary doctor. He was unable to practice locally due to boycotting. He was awarded a sum of £350 by the Irish Grants Committee.[90]

William Charles Doherty, a justice of the peace from 3 Doherty Terrace, Kilkee, was also awarded a sum of £350. In his application for relief he claimed that he was boycotted when he refused to resign from the Peace Commission. Ironically, in 1914 Doherty, in a letter to the *Saturday Record*, stated that he had been elected to Kilkee Town Commissioners for six years, that he had topped the poll in one election and that he had been elected chairman of Kilkee Town Commissioners for four years – he was the only Protestant member of that body. He claimed that he had never known a Protestant to be injured in person, property, position or repute because of his religion (asserting that the people of west Clare were not sectarian towards the local Protestant minority).[91]

William T. Hogan was a justice and the owner of a hardware and grocery shop in Main Street, Ennistymon. Two of his daughters asserted in their claims to the Irish Distress Committee that their father's business was boycotted, that customers were discouraged, threatened and intimidated, and that their father died in penury.[92] Joseph McInerney, a justice of the peace and a shopkeeper who lived over his shop at Parliament Street, Ennistymon, claimed that he was also boycotted, and his son was shot and wounded, 'allegedly' for refusing to join the IRA.[93] William James Corbett, another justice of the peace, of Willbrook House, Corofin, was awarded compensation of £1,000 for damages. He stated that his house was burnt the day before the truce, and that he was 'persecuted' from then until January 1923. He stated that he 'was a well-known supporter of the Imperial Government'.[94]

Finally, James Wakely of Mountshannon, another justice, was awarded £2,560 in compensation for his sufferings. He could be classified as a 'strong farmer', with about 350 acres around Mountshannon. He claimed that he was targeted, boycotted and attacked because he was a magistrate and a well-known loyalist. James Wakely was a member of the Church of Ireland.[95]

Other Protestants affected by the boycotting of the British judicial system in Clare included solicitors and petty sessions clerks. F.F. Cullinan of Bindon Street, Ennis, a Crown solicitor (who acted for the state in prosecuting criminals), was awarded a sum of £1,500 because of loss of business due to intimidation and boycotting.[96] Francis C. Pilkington, an Ennis solicitor, was given £200 'for the loss of his business due to the activity of the Republican Courts'.[97]

Thomas Jonas Blackall of Killard, Doonbeg, a Protestant and a petty sessions clerk in the Kilrush area, was subjected to intimidation and property losses in attempts to force him to resign from his position in the local courts. On 11–12 July 1921, a large force of people took some sheep from Blackall's 122-acre farm at Tromera Castle. His cattle were driven off his lands and other cattle were put on his farm. He had to sell his cattle at a loss. Before this 'damage' was done to him, he was kidnapped and taken away by armed men. The armed men threatened him in an effort to make him resign his office; they claimed that if he didn't, he would be made do so. He was awarded £400. He was also granted an annual pension of £114 4s 4d by the Irish government for his services as a petty sessions clerk up to 31 December 1922.[98]

Marcus Keane, of Beechpark, Ennis and Doondahlin House, near Carrigaholt, was a member of the Church of Ireland. He believed that

> the outrages against him were committed to drive us out of the place. I have always been a loyalist and my sympathies opposed to separation from England. I belong to a class the people want to get rid of and that the house [Doondahlin] was burned so that I would not be able to work the lands, about 100 acres, so that they might then be divided.[99]

Informers

Patrick Sexton, from Upper Turnpike Road, Ennis, worked as an attendant at Ennis Mental Hospital. On 11 March 1922, he was shot by republicans and suffered wounds to his leg on his way to work. A week before this attack, the windows of his house were broken and he received threatening letters to clear out. He fled to England with his wife and child. In his application for compensation, Sexton admitted that he was an informer, 'I assisted His Majesty's forces and the Royal Irish Constabulary in many ways, viz., by giving information which came to my knowledge as to the movements and intentions of the Republicans.' Sexton, who was lucky to have escaped with his life, was awarded compensation of £350.[100]

One other application to the Irish Distress Committee is of interest, because it came from a Catholic priest, Fr James Russell, CC, of Ballina and Killaloe. He was appointed as curate of Ballina in July 1920, around the same time that the Auxiliary police came to the parish. He was friendly with the Auxiliaries, and because of this he claimed that he was boycotted. He was intimidated and many of his plans, including collections and dances, were hampered – this lasted for eighteen months. He and his housekeeper were suspected of being collaborators; given this, his clerical status may have saved him from a worse fate than boycotting. Fr Russell sought compensation of £200 for himself and £60 for his housekeeper, but no money was awarded to either of them.[101]

Compensation

Overall, the Irish Grants Committee paid a total of £77,440 to 81 out of 354 claimants from County Clare. However, of this sum, a total of £55,775 (72 per cent) was paid to eighteen members of the Protestant community as compensation for their losses – they suffered their houses being burnt down, their cattle being driven from their lands, and their lands being seized. Those compensated were: Lord Inchiquin, Dromoland, £1,000; the Hon. Edward O'Brien, Roslevan, £400; Dora Brew, Ballyerra, Kilrush, £700; Francis William Gore Hickman, Kilmore House, Knock (who also claimed for the destruction of his wife's property at Hazelwood), £16,575; Elizabeth MacNamara, (the widow of H.V. MacNamara),

Ennistymon, £7,750; Commander Reginald Gore, Ballinahinch and Derrygore, £14,775; William Corbett, Willbrook, Corofin, £1,000; James Wakely, Mountshannon, £2,560; Robert Goold Ellis, Sea View, Miltown Malbay, £1,800; Marcus Wyndham Patterson, Corofin, £75; William Jonas Studdert, Kilballyowen, Carrigaholt, £390; James D. Going, Gortnagonella, Claremount, £750; Marcus Keane, Doondahlen House, Carrigaholt, £750; Dr F.C. Sampson, Moynoe House, Scariff, £5,300; Loftus A. Studdert, Glenwood, Sixmilebridge, £1,500; John Alfred Studdert, Cragmoher, Corofin, £150; and Helena Skerett, Finnevara, £300.[102]

All of those named above were Protestants who had suffered losses during the War of Independence, the truce period and the civil war. Land agitation against landlords and graziers was rife in Clare before and during the First World War, and while Sinn Féin tried to suppress the cattle drives in February 1918, many of the landlords were victimised during the War of Independence and civil war by land-hungry people who wanted to see the estates and larger farms divided. It was also the case that many of the large landowners in Clare were Protestant and unionist. This confirmed the small Protestant community in their belief that there was a sectarian struggle being fomented against them – that some republicans sought to drive them out of the county and seize their lands and homes.

Andy Bielenberg argues that the records of the Irish Distress Committee and the Irish Grants Committee should be regarded with caution, as the objective of many of its claimants was to maximise their compensation – hence, there may have been exaggeration of claims. Nevertheless, he concludes that 'the evidence reveals serious difficulties faced by Protestant loyalist households. Their claims document many of the more extreme instances where such households were subjected to revolutionary violence, intimidation, arson and forced departure in the post-Truce period.'[103] This opinion is supported by Tom Garvin in his study of the period, 'The cost of the war was disproportionately borne by the Protestant community in country areas, who were sometimes murdered, commonly physically threatened, often hounded out of Ireland by the republicans, or by local agrarian opportunists; the bills were put on the ratepayers.'[104]

The War of Independence was conducted in many ways – through boycotting, intimidation, propaganda and violence. Many people who were boycotted or persecuted by the IRA during the War of Independence also suffered at the hands of the IRA during the truce and civil war. The atrocities committed against the nationalist community in Clare by the Crown forces, especially the Black and Tans and Auxiliaries, have been well documented in folklore, history and song. However, there were also victims on the unionist side, both Catholic and Protestant. They suffered at the hands of the republicans, and their distresses were largely ignored by most of the community because they were deemed to have associated with, or collaborated with, the Crown forces. These compensation claims give us further insights into the conduct of the War of Independence and the civil war. In an era of reconciliation, around one hundred years after these traumatic events, perhaps it is timely that the story of those who suffered in this way should be told, and that their anguish should also be recorded for a balanced historical analysis of the War of Independence and the civil war in Clare.

Bishop Michael Fogarty (Killaloe Diocesan Archives).

Taoiseach Éamon de Valera and Bishop Fogarty in 1954 (courtesy of *Molua*).

General Frank Barrett (*Clare Champion*)

Below: Note that President Arthur Griffith is to the left of Mr PJ Hogan, TD, while Kevin O'Higgins, TD, Minister for Justice, is to the right of the speaker. This photo was taken at a Cumann na nGaedhael election rally at Ennis in April 1922 (courtesy of Clare County Library).

The late Mr. P. J. Hogan, T.D., addressing a meeting in O'Connell Square, Ennis, on Sunday, April 30th, 1922.

SACRED TO THE MEMORY OF
VOLUNTEER PATRICK MAHONY.
AGED 25 YRS EXECUTED AT THE HOME
BARRACKS ENNIS 26TH APRIL 1923.
VOLUNTEER CHRISTOPHER QUINN.
AGED 21 YRS AND VOLUNTEER.
WILLIAM O SHAUGHNESSY.
AGED 18 YRS EXECUTED AT THE SAME
PLACE ON THE 2ND MAY 1923.
THE ABOVE WERE EXECUTED BY
FREE STATE FORCES BECAUSE OF
THEIR LOYALTY TO THE REPUBLIC.
OF IRELAND.
R.I P.

THIS MONUMENT WAS ERECTED BY
THEIR ENNIS EXILED COMRADES OF
NEW YORK CITY U.S.A
1ST NOV. 1928.

Memorial to Patrick Mahony, Christopher Quinn and William O'Shaughnessy at Drumcliffe (photograph by the author).

Below: Memorial to Conn McMahon, Patrick Hennessy and Joseph Considine at Clooney (photograph by the author).

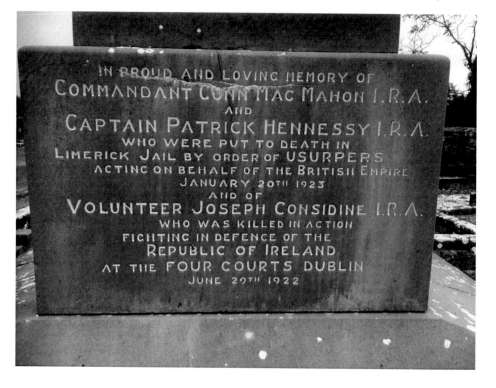

IN PROUD AND LOVING MEMORY OF
COMMANDANT CONN MAC MAHON I.R.A.
AND
CAPTAIN PATRICK HENNESSY I.R.A.
WHO WERE PUT TO DEATH IN
LIMERICK JAIL BY ORDER OF USURPERS
ACTING ON BEHALF OF THE BRITISH EMPIRE
JANUARY 20TH 1923
AND OF
VOLUNTEER JOSEPH CONSIDINE I.R.A.
WHO WAS KILLED IN ACTION
FIGHTING IN DEFENCE OF THE
REPUBLIC OF IRELAND
AT THE FOUR COURTS DUBLIN
JUNE 29TH 1922

General Michael Collins in 1922
(*Irish Independent*).

General Richard Mulcahy
(photograph from Wikimedia
Commons).

General Liam Lynch
(photograph from
Wikimedia Commons).

Éamon de Valera T.D.
(photograph from
Wikimedia Commons).

General Frank Aiken (photograph from Wikimedia Commons).

William T Cosgrave President of the Free State (photograph from Wikimedia Commons).

Katie and Peg Barrett from Bearnageha, dressed up in IRA uniforms. Sisters of General Frank Barrett, they were prominent members of Cumann na mBan, and they opposed the Treaty. Peg Barrett was injured by gunshots during the arrest of de Valera at an election meeting at Ennis on 15 August 1923 (courtesy of the Barrett family).

Civilians take cover as government troops arrest de Valera at Ennis on 15 August 1923. (Still From a newsreel by British Pathé News.)

Putting up election posters in August 1923 at Ennis in August 1923 (photograph from Wikimedia Commons).

'Up De Valera' outside the Town Hall, (old Ground Hotel), Ennis in August 1923 (photograph from Wikimedia Commons).

Old 'shawlies' and others studying the election posters for the 1923 General Election. (From Carlton Younger's *Ireland's Civil War*.)

EXECUTIONS =
WAS THIS THE WILL OF THE PEOPLE OF CLARE

CORNELIUS McMAHON.
Executed at Limerick Jan. 20th, 1923

PATRICK HENNESSY.
Executed at Limerick Jan. 20th, 1923.

PATRICK MAHONY.
Executed at Ennis April 26th, 1923.

CHRISTOPHER QUINN.
Executed at Ennis May 2nd, 1923.

WILLIAM SHAUGHNESSY.
Executed at Ennis May 2nd,

ELECTORS OF CLARE, do you approve of the
Execution of these boys ?

If you support the men who Executed them
you do ! !

SHOW YOUR DISAPPROVAL and

Vote for DE VALERA

Published by Sinn Fein Election Committee.

Sinn Fein Election poster at Ennis in 1923. Courtesy of The 19th.

Éamon de Valera at Ennis on 15 August 1923. Still from from British Pathé News newsreel, released in 2014.

An impassioned de Valera speaking just before his arrest at Ennis on 15 August 1923. T.V. Honan, Chairman of Ennis UDC, is on his right (British Pathé News).

Commandant Michael Brennan (National Library of Ireland).

3
'GIVE THEM A DEASANT WALLOPING'

When the anti-Treaty republicans occupying the Four Courts in Dublin refused to comply with an ultimatum to vacate the building by 3.40 a.m. on 28 June 1922, the Provisional Government's military forces shelled the building. A hastily drafted handwritten proclamation was issued by the anti-Treaty Army Executive on the date of the attack. This marked the beginning of the civil war:

> Fellow citizens of the Irish Republic, the fateful hour has come. At the dictation of our hereditary enemy our rightful cause is being treacherously assailed by recreant Irishmen. The crash of arms and the boom of artillery reverberate in this supreme test of the nation's destiny. Gallant soldiers of the Irish Republic stand vigorously firm in its defence and worthily uphold their noblest traditions. The sacred spirits of the illustrious dead are with us in this great struggle. 'Death before Dishonour' being an unchanging principle of our national faith, we therefore appeal to all citizens to rally to the defence of the Republic.

Among the sixteen officers who signed this document was Commandant General Frank Barrett of Bearnageeha, Darragh, representing the 1st Western Brigade. Four months later, on 28 October 1922, thirteen members of the Army Executive chose Éamon de Valera as president and called on him to form a government, 'In the name of the Army we proclaim Éamon de Valera to be President of the Republic of Ireland.'[105]

Though Frank Barrett was one of those who signed the proclamation on 28 June, he had, according to Liam Deasy, opposed a resumption of the war against England at an Army Executive meeting on 9 April, and he had supported a motion on army unity. Deasy, another member of the Army Executive, also stated that Frank Barrett attended a meeting of all available officers on 28 June at the Clarence Hotel in Dublin. The meeting included Liam Lynch,

Cathal Brugha and de Valera. After a brief discussion, those attending unanimously agreed to resist the attack on the Four Courts.

One of the officers involved in the shelling of the Four Courts was Ignatius O'Neill, from Miltown Malbay, whose aim with the cannons was not so good. Apparently, some of the shells fired from the cannon under his command landed on the Royal Hospital Kilmainham, and then the British army headquarters. Major General Emmet Dalton recalled the incident, which greatly annoyed General Macready and his staff (Macready had been GOC of the British army in Ireland from 1919 up to the departure of the British forces in 1922):

> I found Ignatius O'Neill, a great character from County Clare, with his gun canted up as he tried to hit a sniper in the dome of the Four Courts. He was using an 18 pounder like a rifle and the shells were going right through the dome and landing on the Royal Hospital. Macready, when he heard the story was not amused.[106]

Tragically, this war was to last for more than ten months, with hundreds of casualties up to the date of the anti-Treaty forces' ceasefire order on 30 April 1923. With superior weapons and a substantial army of over 50,000 troops, as well as a naval force and some aeroplanes, the National Army proved too strong for the anti-Treaty republicans. The civil war deeply divided Irish society and left a legacy of bitterness in Irish political life for generations. Charles Townshend, a historian, states, 'Fighting civil wars usually produces a sense of shame rather than of pride for victors as well as losers. For many, the response was a deep silence.' Anne Dolan agrees with Townshend about the silence the civil war has been met with, 'The memory of the Irish Civil War has been assumed, distorted, misunderstood. It has been manipulated, underestimated, but most of all, ignored.'[107] Writing in 1971, F.S.L. Lyons stated, 'The civil war was an episode which has burned so deep into the heart and mind of Ireland that it is not yet possible for the historian to approach it with the detailed knowledge or the objectivity which it deserves.'[108] Seán Lemass, the former taoiseach and an anti-Treaty republican, was asked, in 1969, about the civil war by journalist

Michael Mills. He replied, 'Terrible things were done by both sides and both sides knew it [...] I'd prefer not to talk about it.'[109] C.S. Andrews, another republican, stated:

> The real damage to the nation was the intense bitterness and hatred created by the split. The nation suffered a psychological wound which was largely unhealed until the second world war. Even then the psyches of many of the participants in the Civil War were never healed, it was a burden many carried all their lives.[110]

The Provisional Government (later the Free State government) enjoyed the powerful backing of the Irish Catholic hierarchy, along with that of the major national and local newspapers. Clare County Council, the urban councils in Ennis and Kilrush, and business and farming organisations also supported the Treaty. Dr Fogarty, the Bishop of Killaloe, was an ardent supporter of the government, and he was also a trenchant critic of the anti-Treaty republicans. The local press, both the *Clare Champion* and the *Saturday Record*, were strong advocates of the Treaty and were appalled by the outbreak of civil war. Moreover, the majority of the public in Clare seemed to have been in favour of the Treaty.

The witness statements from those who participated in the War of Independence were precluded from commenting on the civil war, as the wounds from that tragic conflict were too deep and raw in the 1940s and 1950s. The new police force, the Garda Síochána, were not yet established at the outbreak of the civil war, so they were not there to make official reports on the military situation in the county. The government forces did keep some records of the fighting, but naturally these documents supported the pro-Treaty side. Some prominent anti-Treaty republicans, such as C.S. Andrews, Tom Barry, Dan Breen and Ernie O'Malley, have given their side of the story from a republican perspective. The local Clare newspapers recorded the events taking place in the county, and they provide a valuable contemporary record of the conflict. However, one must remember that the local and national press were heavily censored, and they did not support the republican military actions. Early in the civil war, the republicans issued a proclamation directing all units to prevent the circulation of the *Irish Independent*, the *Freeman's*

Journal and the *Irish Times*, as 'they are channels of enemy propaganda.'[111]

Sarsfield Maguire, editor of the *Clare Champion*, captured the mood of the county at the start of the civil war when writing in the immediate aftermath of its outbreak:

> Every Irishman who has the welfare of his native land at heart will stand aghast at the awful happenings in Dublin and other parts of the country. The dreaded spectre of civil war has raised its head [...] in the long drawn out tragedy of our country there has hardly been a darker period.[112]

Maguire's opinion probably also reflected the majority opinion in the country. Tom Garvin states:

> The Civil War was deeply unpopular with the majority of the population, and was, in a sense an anomalous event. It involved only the elites and their immediate followers, the new political class. The split did not truly involve the general population. As shall be argued, the conquest of Leinster, Munster and Connaught by the Free State army in 1922–23 resembled a liberation rather than a conquest [...] West Clare gave a particularly enthusiastic welcome to the Free State forces [...] The Catholic bishops roundly denounced the intransigence of the anti-Treatyites and the press was almost unanimously pro-Treaty [...] Whereas de Valera had the allegiance of the guerrilla army, the Free State had the immediate allegiance of the vast bulk of the civilian and local population. The overwhelming majority of local authorities, county and borough, formally approved of the Treaty.

On the other hand, Garvin noted that republican military leaders such as Liam Lynch and Ernie O'Malley looked contemptuously on 'the slave mentality of the Irish people'.[113]

Townshend agrees with Garvin, stating that 'the republican view of public opinion was and remained generally dismissive'; he cites de Valera, who stated, after the general elections of 1922 and 1923, that 'the people had no right to do wrong.'[114] Seán Lemass maintained that the Irish public were intellectually anti-Treaty but had voted in favour of it in 1922 for the sake of peace, 'The IRA in the Civil War made the tremendous mistake, the fundamental mistake of forgetting the importance of public opinion [...] they began to adopt an attitude of hostility or indifference to public opinion.' General Liam Lynch, chief of staff of the anti-Treaty forces, had stated in August 1922, 'The people are simply a flock of sheep to be driven in any way you choose.'[115]

The course of the civil war in Clare was, to a large extent, dictated by military events outside of the county, especially in the struggle for control of the strategic city of Limerick. Nevertheless, there were significant military developments in the county in the early stages of the conflict, before Limerick's capture by government forces. Ironically, while the West Clare Brigade was the least active of the three brigades during the War of Independence in Clare (except in the early stages), most of the republicans' actions during the civil war in Clare seem to have been concentrated in the west Clare region. One newspaper report from January 1923 stated, 'Kilmihil is said to be the hot bed of the Irregular movement in Clare.'[116]

Fr Pat Gaynor, who was transferred to Tipperary in early 1922 and was the parish priest of Kilmihil during the 1930s, had great respect for the leaders on both sides of the conflict, but he was of the opinion that the rebel leaders lacked common sense:

> In general, the officers on either side, who had fought against the British, were men of high character and principle; they had soldierly instincts and conducted the warfare honourably. Those rebel leaders whom I knew never lost their place in my esteem [...] I appreciate the rebels' high motives, I understand their bewilderment and exasperation; but I can only deplore their lack of common sense.

Fr Gaynor had a low opinion of 'Trucileers', or Truce Patriots:

> I never ask for information about the Civil War, I have no interest in the details of that faction fight. Doubtless, many men who had been meek and mild during the Black and Tan regime emerged as heroes and patriots, deeming it fairly safe and patriotic to indulge in gasconade [boasting] when the British forces had withdrawn to Ulster. The free part of Ireland had become a happy-hunting ground for political adventurers and for strutting little war lords, for cattle thieves and robbers and most contemptible of all, Truce Patriots. I never lost my liking for the genuine men of the Sinn Féin war, whether they were for or against the Treaty. They, at least, had the right to their ideas, one way or another. Nearly all the real fighting men wanted peace,

even if they were opposed to the Treaty, but they were tricked into Civil War by a few skilful intriguers, who seem to have desired a social revolution.[117]

Given the fact that Éamon de Valera, a TD for Clare, was chosen as president of the Irish Republic by the Army Executive, and that General Frank Barrett was one of the sixteen members of the executive, it might be expected that Clare would play a prominent part in the civil war, but according to Michael Hopkinson, a historian, it didn't. However, Hopkinson states that Clare's pro-Treaty forces, led by General Michael Brennan, 'played an important role in the fighting in Limerick and Kerry'.[118] Also, Bishop Fogarty, who had been a prominent supporter of Sinn Féin and de Valera since the East Clare by-election in 1917 (which de Valera won), and who was one of the three trustees of the Sinn Féin funds, became one of the most vocal ecclesiastical opponents of the republican attack on the democratically elected government. Bishop Fogarty's trenchant condemnations of the republicans must have had a significant influence on public opinion in the diocese of Killaloe, and indeed in other parts of Ireland, during these turbulent years; his words probably dissuaded many Clare republicans from taking up arms against the government.

In Clare, like so many other areas around the country, former comrades in the three military brigades took different sides in the conflict. The rivalry between the brigade commandants during the War of Independence – especially between the Barretts of the Mid-Clare Brigade and the Brennans of the East Clare Brigade – continued into the truce and civil war periods. In April 1921, when GHQ restructured the three Clare brigades and the two Galway brigades into the 1st Western Division (with Michael Brennan as commandant), Frank Barrett was reluctant to accept the position of vice-commandant. Eventually, in November 1921, he was persuaded to accept the position; his brother Joe was appointed adjutant. This arrangement, however, did not last long, because of differences over the divisive and unsatisfactory Treaty. When the civil war broke out on 28 June 1922, Frank Barrett became commandant of the 1st Western Brigade (republican), which included the three former Clare brigades and the East Galway Brigade. Historian Bill Kissane argues that factional rivalries and differences determined Ireland's post-revolutionary line-up, 'These were expressed most clearly in the rivalry between elites over control of the IRA, and in the split between the Barrett and Brennan families in particular in Clare, an example of how territorial jealousy was elevated into high principle.'[119]

Two of the former commandants of the three Clare brigades, Michael Brennan of the East Clare Brigade and Sean Liddy of the West Clare Brigade, supported the Treaty, while Frank Barrett of the Mid-Clare Brigade opposed the Treaty. Furthermore, several experienced officers in the Mid-Clare Brigade, such as Ignatius O'Neill and John Joe 'Tosser' Neylon (Captain of the Ennistymon Battalion), took the pro-Treaty side, while others stayed neutral in the bitter fraternal conflict. Seamus Hennessy of the Mid-Clare Brigade recalled, 'Ignatius O'Neill brought some good lads with him into the Free State army, but all the Battalion O/Cs were Republican [...] The Captain of Miltown Company [Ned Lynch of Breaffa] went Free State. The Inagh Company captain [Patrick McGough], also went Free State.' In west Clare, experienced officers such as Bill Haugh – adjutant and vice-commandant of the West Clare Brigade and leader of the flying column – also supported the Treaty. Patrick McDonnell of the East Clare Brigade, who joined the anti-Treaty side, stated, 'Most of the column went Free State with Brennan.'[120] This was corroborated by Edward MacLysaght, who wrote, 'In East Clare we were spared the horrors of Civil War because almost to a man we followed Michael Brennan's support of Michael Collins, and the anti-Treaty forces were practically non-existent there.'[121]

In his application for a military pension, dated 13 May 1935, Patrick Keane of Kilnamona gave a list of the membership of A Company (Kilnamona), 3rd Battalion, Mid-Clare Brigade as of 11 July 1921, the date of the truce. In all, there were sixty-three Volunteers, of whom, according to Keane, seventeen (27 per cent) supported the anti-Treaty IRA, six (9.5 per cent) enlisted in the government forces, one joined the Civic Guard (later An Garda Síochána), four were dead and thirty-five remained neutral. This division in the company in a rural area of mid-Clare was probably representative of many other companies in the Mid- and West Clare brigades, who were opposed to the Treaty. Significantly, in Patrick Keane's opinion, thirty-five out of sixty-three Volunteers (55 per cent) in the Kilnamona district chose to remain neutral on this very divisive issue.[122]

From the beginning of the dispute over the Treaty, both the pro- and anti-Treaty parties laid claim to being republicans. In January 1922 Patrick Brennan, TD sent an open letter to the editor of the *Clare Champion* in which he stated, 'The term "Republican" is equally the property of Free Staters and anti-Free Staters [...] our aim is the complete independence of Ireland with a republican form of government [...] We differ from the anti-treaty group only in method [...] we accept the Treaty as a means of securing absolute independence for Ireland.'[123]

During the civil war, the government issued censorship guidelines to the national press directing that the anti-Treaty forces should be deemed 'Irregulars' and that the government forces should be called the National Army. Naturally, the anti-Treaty IRA refuted such terminology and always referred to their own forces as the republicans or the IRA, and to the government forces as Free State soldiers.[124] They also gave warnings to papers that they would be attacked if they applied the term 'Irregular' to the soldiers or officers of the IRA.[125] On 15 and 19 July 1922, copies of the *Freeman's Journal* were seized and burnt by armed republicans at Killaloe.[126]

Before the civil war began in Clare, there was much confusion as opposing parties held significant strategic locations in the county after the local battalions of the IRA had taken over from the evacuating Crown forces in January and February 1922. The republicans occupied the former RIC headquarters in Ennis, and military outposts and former RIC barracks in villages and towns around mid- and west Clare, including Ballyvaughan, Clarecastle, Corofin, Ennistymon, Kildysart, Kilkee, Kilmihil, Kilrush, Liscannor, Lisdoonvarna and Miltown Malbay. The government forces held the Home Barracks, the Ordnance Survey building, the courthouse and the county club in Ennis, and almost all the barracks in east Clare, including Tulla, Scariff, Killaloe and Broadford. Once the fighting began at the Four Courts, tensions between the two sides in Clare erupted into warfare. In Ennis, the republican position at the former

RIC barracks was almost in the centre of a triangle of outposts held by the government troops; after some crude fortifications and sniping from both sides, the republicans decided to evacuate and burn the building, moving their arsenal to the workhouse in Corofin. They also occupied Eden Vale, the home of the Stacpoole family, between 4 July and 22 July; it was about a mile from Ennis, and they made it their headquarters.

During the first couple of weeks of the civil war in Clare, there was little military action apart from a few minor skirmishes between the opposing forces, similar to the Phoney War at the start of the First World War. Although most of the more experienced troops of the 1st Western Division were sent to Limerick in February to secure that strategic city for the government, the remainder of the 1st Western Division secured control of Ennis and the former British army barracks at Clarecastle on 1 July. Meanwhile, republicans took advantage of the shortage of government troops to seize control of some towns in west Clare. To reinforce the 1st Western Division troops in Clare, more soldiers travelled from Galway by train, arriving in Ennis; another contingent travelled from Kerry by boat, arriving in Clarecastle and marching to the courthouse in Ennis. They were temporarily billeted in Carmody's Hotel and the Queen's Hotel, and they secured the town of Ennis and Clarecastle barracks. Troops from other counties were sent to Clare, as indicated by the following republican intelligence officer's report from Clare to the IRA chief of staff, Liam Lynch, 'Kilkenny troops have reinforced Ennis [...] We got intelligence two days ago that a further troop train is on the way to Ennis.'[127]

Following the surrender of the Four Courts garrison, Liam Lynch was appointed chief of staff of the republican forces; he established his headquarters in Limerick, the strategic centre in the mid-west, at the beginning of July. Nevertheless, the rival forces did not engage in battle there until nearly two weeks after the civil war began in Dublin. It seems that the government forces were outnumbered and outgunned by the republicans at first, but the republicans chose to negotiate rather than fight. General Michael Brennan apparently bluffed his opponents, giving the impression that his troops were better armed than they were while playing for time and waiting for

CLARE AND THE CIVIL WAR

reinforcements. Staunch Limerick republican Dessie Long told me that 'Brennan fooled the republicans in Limerick.' Meanwhile, General Liam Lynch was reluctant to initiate hostilities. A truce was negotiated between Michael Brennan and Liam Lynch on 4 July and renewed on 7 July, but the government later overruled these agreements, not wishing to make any concessions to the republican forces. Meda Ryan cites Michael Brennan in his witness statement:

> My whole fright was that Lynch would attack me before the guns turned up, because we couldn't last. I had to keep him talking to prevent him from attacking. We met and we met, altogether about a dozen times. We used to meet in the presbytery of the Augustinian church, where we argued and argued.

Finally, General Eoin O'Duffy, general officer commanding of the South Western Division, arrived from Killaloe with extra troops, heavy artillery and an armoured car, and the battle for Limerick took place on 11–20 July, resulting in victory for the government forces.[128]

A *Clare Champion* headline, 'Fall of Limerick', hailed the victory:

> The city is now in the hands of the National army [...] the five barracks held by the Irregulars are now in ruins [...] The Strand Barracks was battered down by shell fire from National army artillery and the New Barracks, Frederick St Barracks and the Ordnance Barracks were burnt by the departing Irregulars [...] the agony of three weeks is now at an end.[129]

The 1st Western Division, composed of Clare and Galway brigades and under the command of General Michael Brennan, had a major role in taking control of the city for the Provisional Government. After the capture of Limerick city, government troops from the 1st Western Division returned by train to Ennis, where they were billeted in the Farmers' Club, the County Club and the Masonic Hall. Brennan sent a message to the victorious troops:

> Fellow soldiers, three weeks ago, a section of your countrymen took up forcible possession of Limerick City. These men had no authority from the people or the government of the Irish people. On the contrary they acted in defiance of the will of the Irish people. You did not desire to make war against these men, but in defence of the Irish people. Your brave efforts have now prevailed and after considerable effort and danger the city is now cleared of those Irresponsibles.[130]

'and give them a deasant walloping'

Some documents seized by government forces, and either published in the local press or kept in the Military Archives (in Cathal Brugha Barracks, Dublin), give us some idea of republican activities and strategies in Clare during July and August of 1922. In a review of the military situation in Ireland, General O'Duffy refers to one such document from Frank Barrett, dated 17 July 1922:

> In Clare the Irregulars only hold Kilrush. Corofin, the HQ of the First Western Division of the Irregulars, was evacuated on our troops concentrating on Gort, Ennis and Ennistymon. Their leader is Frank Barrett, whose despatch to Simon McInerney, leader of the West Clare Irregulars was published yesterday. An Official Statement issued by GHQ, Irish Army, says that the following document was captured on a prisoner [Simon McInerney]:
>
> 1 – Whereas the Truce has now been violated by the Free State Army in Limerick, you are requested to begin operations at once. 2 – Operations of every description are to be taken against the Free State army immediately. 3 – Send to Eden Vale tomorrow 20 fully equipped men, also one dozen .45 revolvers for use in Ennis. 4 – Ensure a boat always in readiness between Kildysart and Foynes. 5 – Do not spare any officer or man in the Free State army.[131]

Some of the captured documents refer to organisational matters, such as setting up dispatch centres and communication lines. Volunteers were instructed to set up lines of communication (making use of road, rail, river, etc.), and to arrange dispatch centres, dispatch riders and addresses. The following is a pertinent example, 'To Miss Hogan, Cratloe: It is absolutely essential to establish a line of communication between Corofin and Limerick [...] make arrangements for supply line to Limerick and from Limerick via Newmarket arrange with Ml Murray, Newmarket. Contact Dr May Molony, County Infirmary Limerick.' Brigade quartermasters were instructed to establish safe dumps so that food, including tinned meats, flour, sugar, biscuits and bacon, was within easy reach of flying columns. Other captured documents indicate how the republicans sought an arms inventory from all the battalion leaders and advice on intelligence gathering. Several documents refer to disciplinary matters, such as dealing with lawlessness and cattle drives in the brigade area.

Besides such organisational matters, the republicans also stole nine motor cars and five motorcycles in July in an effort to improve their communications. In one report, the intelligence officer to the IRA headquarters in Clonmel, Co. Tipperary states, 'We have opened a line of communications between Foynes and Clare [via Kildysart].' This was in response to an earlier report from Limerick republicans, dated 11 July 1922, which stated that 'Our communications from the Clare side is completely cut-off.'[132]

In late July 1922, Seamus Hennessy, commandant of the republican 4th Battalion in north-west Clare, sent several letters to General Frank Barrett in which he outlined several challenges facing the republicans in his district. In the first letter, which was dated 21 July, he wrote:

> VII. Re attack on garrison at Ennistymon – what we intended to do is to get some other column with us on some particular day and give them a deasant walloping; in any case, we have only six reliable rifles here and except sniping, we could not do a great deal with them here. However, we will see at Battalion meeting this evening what we can do and we will send you all particulars of the different depts. VIII. I had a small part of the ASU [active service unit] of the battalion having taken up a position opposite a trench in the road from Inagh to Ennistymon a few days ago. Just as the car came on the trench Ignatius O'Neill came off the car, so any of them did not fire, as I will tell you the truth, they find it hard to fire on Ignatius or Tosser. IX. I also sent seven men from here on last Saturday to report for duty in Corofin, but some of them 'kicked-up' on the road when one of our own officers was not with them, with the result that none of them did get to Corofin. I hope to discuss difficulties at battalion meeting this evening. X. I am enclosing for you a despatch I received from the company capt. at Inagh as to the cattle drive at Tottenham's of Mount Callan. Kindly let me know if I am to take any steps in the matter.[133]

In another letter dated 22 July, Hennessy reported how raids were carried out to acquire explosives; he also relates how some former Volunteers were neutral and refused to help:

> I was in the western part of the area for the past four days trying

to get a good few fellows in Miltown Malbay working as best they can. We got a good deal of stuff at the chemists and hardware shops for the engineering dept. We also raided the Miltown Malbay railway station, but we did not get much of any importance there. I have arranged to have it all sent to Corofin tomorrow, Saturday [...] Re. the arrest of the FS officer, Capt. P Kerin is in touch with the FS officer Commdt. Frawley. He has promised to do all he can for us, eg, helping to get the fellows desert from the Workhouse and bring out some stuff. The company captains at Miltown and Lahinch are neutral and have refused to take arms or assist the flying squad commandant.

In a letter dated 24 July, Hennessy stated that several of his best officers were arrested, 'You must have heard that three of our best officers of the battalion, A. Malone, Pat Kerin and S Gallagher were arrested by F.S. soldiers on Sunday morning 23 July.'

In that last letter of 24 July, Hennessy outlined how he had set up a republican police force to keep law and order in Miltown Malbay:

Owing to disgraceful outrages and serious crimes committed in the town and parish and insecurity of life by a certain band of hooligans, who do not belong to my political party, I, with the Vice-Commdt and the Capt. of Glendine, formed a committee; we arranged to pick six steady good men from all corps to be stationed in Miltown, not to take part in military operations – Fr Malley and Dr Hillery are delighted with the idea to keep law and order [...] they are not to be attacked by FS troops.[134]

Interviewed by Ernie O'Malley between 1948 and 1954, Seamus Hennessy made some general observations about the civil war. He referred to an ambush at Moy in August 1922:

There was a great mix-up for some of the Free State troops were in civilian clothes and they became mixed up with our own men [...] The Free State however behaved badly and the result was that they turned the people against them. The Free State got a low crowd from the towns to join up with them [...] I was never captured during the Civil War. There was one dug-out in our area but it was caught in the end. The first sweep the Free State made was early in the morning, and they whipped some of my best men.[135]

A *Saturday Record* report from April 1923 corroborated Hennessy's story about the dug-out, recording an occasion in the Miltown Malbay area in which a dug-out was discovered:

> Troops from Miltown discovered a dug out at Mountscott, containing beds, bedding and cooking utensils. As the troops were burning the dug out they came under heavy fire for about one and a half hours from Irregulars firing from a hill about 800 yards away. The troops succeeded in driving off the attackers, no injuries were reported.[136]

Tension in Clare

In early July 1922, Clare republicans took advantage of the absence of Michael Brennan and the 1st Western Division by launching attacks on enemy strategic positions, destroying bridges, trenching roads, disrupting railway lines and taking over the towns of Kilkee and Kilrush for a few weeks. Communications by road and rail were severely disrupted for a couple of weeks. The *Saturday Record* and *Clare Champion*, carried reports that highlighted the tense stand-off between the rival forces in the county during the first weeks of the civil war. At the end of July, the *Saturday Record* noted:

> Corofin Workhouse was occupied by Republican forces for some weeks past [...] It was rumoured to be the battleground in Clare, but the workhouse was vacated by the Irregulars and most of the building was destroyed by fire, along with the former police barracks destroyed by the Irregulars [...] For the past fortnight Kilrush has been completely isolated, there have been no trains or any communications with the outside world, while boats ceased to trade with Limerick during the crisis there.[137]

The attack on Corofin was also noted in a republican intelligence report, '11.30 pm, Free State troops from the Home [Barracks] reported going to surround Corofin [...] 12.30 pm, reports from a reliable source that an attack is contemplated on Corofin through Corofin area.'[138]

The *Saturday Record* dramatically recorded a growing crisis in Ennis during early July:

> Sensation in Ennis following the news of the desperate and deadly conflict in Dublin between Free State and Republican forces, which will be deeply mourned by all true Irishmen the world over. The tension reached us in town when the symptoms were made evident of an impending battle between the Free State and

Republican forces, both of whom were actively engaged in providing fortifications for their respective positions. The old police barracks was in possession of the Republican forces, who also commandeered the adjoining house belonging to the Howard family, as well as the Masonic Hall. The quarters of the Free State forces almost resembled a triangle in relation to the Republican position, their forces being in possession of the Courthouse, the Ordnance Survey House and the County Club, which is the GHQ. The house belonging to Mr TJ Hunt, solicitor, beside the County Club was also commandeered by them.

Consternation prevailed all over the town because of the war-like preparations; the old police barracks being the centre of attention in this regard. Its entrance was blocked by tree trunks and tangled barbed wire. The County Club and the other quarters of the Free State forces were also fortified, with sandbags and steel shutters in the windows.

There was no official information as to whether there was a demand for the surrender of the old police barracks, but, certain hours were mentioned at which the battle was to ensue, which created a considerable shock through the town, so serious were the consequences of a conflict regarded. Saturday [1 July], however, brought considerable relief to the people, who saw that the movements of the Republicans manifested that any idea of a battle, which might have been entertained was abandoned. They acted prudently, for they must have obviously realised that their retention of the premises in the event of a battle would have been an inevitable death-trap, having regard to the exposed part of the building.

During the day, the Republicans were actively occupied in the removal of their equipment from the old barracks, from where they took large quantities of ammunition, guns, rifles and revolvers. Saturday night sealed the fate of the old barracks. Between ten and eleven o'clock it was seen to be on fire and the main portion of the building was destroyed. There were bomb explosions near the National School and the Post Office, fortunately no one was injured.

Some exciting incidents are reported from Clare Castle. The old police barracks there was occupied by Republicans, who left the building on Saturday night, 1 July. The premises are reputed to have been badly wrecked and this operation was followed by rifle fire through the village. It is stated that a motor boat in the quay was occupied by Free State soldiers. The boat was attacked, and its occupants returned fire and it is reported that there were some casualties, on which side it was not ascertained. The telephone apparatus forcibly taken from Clare Castle PO recently has been restored.[139]

The *Clare Champion* report of 8 July also vividly described the volatile military situation in Clare during early July:

The Coast guard station in Kilrush was occupied by Republicans. A report states that this building was destroyed by fire. Other barracks in West Clare were also destroyed. Serious reports are made of extensive blocking of roads and considerable damage to buildings across the county. Roads are rendered impassable by large trees felled across them, while bridges, even in the suburbs of the town [Ennis] have been so seriously destroyed as to prevent vehicular traffic.

Ennis, like other towns, is completely isolated from Dublin, Limerick and other commercial centres for the past week as telephone and telegraph wires have been cut, while the train services are irregular and uncertain. Dublin newspapers have not reached the town for the past week, the only paper arriving, a day late, is the Cork Examiner. In the absence of these sources of information, there is no reliable news as to the state of affairs in Dublin. The enormity of the conflict is appalling and will be deeply mourned by every Irishman at home and abroad with a spark of love for his native land.

During the week, Free State troops commandeered bicycles, while for the past few days, the Republicans are engaged in commandeering bicycles, motor cars and motor cycles as well as provisions and clothing, for which it is said, they are giving receipts.

Edenvale House, the residence of Mr RJ Stacpoole, who is away, is taken over by the Republicans. The Republicans also have taken over Corofin Workhouse, in which they have concentrated many of their forces, stores and other equipment. They have the building strongly fortified [...] Crusheen Bridge has been blown up and some injury was also done to the West Clare Railway.

On Saturday evening 1 July, Republican troops evacuated Ennis police barracks and set fire to the building. Similar evacuations and destruction of the buildings formerly occupied by Republicans took place at Ennistymon, Lisdoonvarna, Kildysart, Liscannor, and other places in the county. On Saturday, GHQ forces commandeered the house of Mr TJ Hunt, Solicitor, Abbey St. Ennis. An attempt was made to destroy by explosives two telegraph poles in Ennis. During the week obstructions were placed on roads all over the county and several are impassable, bridges were blown up in various districts also; railway lines were cut and there were only irregular services on the West Clare railway. Kilrush Coastguard Station was evacuated and burnt by Republican forces on Saturday evening 1 July. Kildysart workhouse was destroyed by fire during the weekend. Republican forces commandeered provisions from Messrs Knox, Ennis and clothing from Mr Mitchell. Motor cars and bicycles have been commandeered by both sides during the week. A large contingent of troops arrived in Ennis by train from Galway, while a brigade from Kerry came by boat up the Shannon to Clare Castle, whence they marched to the Courthouse, Ennis. There was a good deal of interest in the temporary requisition of Carmody's Hotel and the Queen's Hotel by the National forces. The military are now busy throughout the town, where at certain points they are stationed and will not permit people to loiter or stand about corners, such as the Square and the Cathedral crossing. For part of the week we had a curtailed train service, there was disruption at Limerick and goods from Limerick cannot get to Ennis. It is stated that Republican troops are in possession of Kilrush and Kilkee railway stations. Ennis is still cut off from Dublin, Cork and other centres, resulting in no newspapers or mail, except a casual delivery, one on Tuesday evening with 34 bags of mail. All postal services were suspended on Thursday – no mails, telephone, telegraph etc. Trouble was reported in Kilkee on Thursday 6 July where Republican and Free State soldiers came into conflict and a fight is now in progress between them.[140]

A captured republican intelligence report of 13 July 1922 noted significant losses in Ennis:

four of our scouts with five civilians were arrested at Ennis overnight. Three other troops engaged in obtaining food supplies for the ASU have been arrested. The Masonic Hall was raided and three Fianna were arrested.[141]

The *Clare Champion* of 15 July carried the following report:

Early on Friday morning [14 July], the people of the town were startled by the sound of gunfire, causing considerable anxiety. Major Neylon, Ennis and some military companions were fired at near Drohidnagower on the road from Ennistymon to Ennis. An obstruction was placed on the road and the officers were fired upon, two lorries of Free State troops arrived and returned fire. Two men were captured, Capt F. Butler, Parnell St, Ennis and T McNamara, Cloughleigh, Ennis, they were lodged in the Home barracks and were reputed to be on hunger strike. Shots were fired at the Courthouse and GHQ during the night.

The captured republican intelligence report of 13 July from Ennis confirmed that Captain F. Butler was indeed on hunger strike:

> An armed escort of about 20 Free State troops in two cars left the Home [Barracks] Ennis for Limerick, taking Capt. F. Butler with them, he is on hunger strike since Sunday.[142]

The *Clare Champion* of 15 July also included the following:

> There were no postal or train services for the past week, all railway workers are thrown out of employment, many of them have families and there is considerable hardship. There are nightly armed patrols by National army forces in Ennis [...] The West Clare line has been damaged by removal of sleepers [the timbers under the rails] at Roxton, near Corofin [...] More bridges have been destroyed around the county [...] Destruction of public property is rampant in the county [...] distressing news from all over the county complaining of the impassable conditions of the county roads, while bridges are reported to have been extensively damaged, causing a ruthless paralysis of trade in the county [...] Drehidnagower Bridge has been damaged twice by explosives, while bridges in Corofin have been destroyed, barricades were erected at Cragmoher Cross.

> In Clare Castle village quarters are established for the National troops, for whose accommodation some houses have been commandeered, including houses in Thomond Villas. This was considered a military necessity for the protection of the bridge on the main road, which is frequently used for the conveyance of troops, whose movements would be inconveniently impeded and endangered in the event of the bridge being destroyed. The houses acquired by the troops are adjacent to the bridge and they displayed the usual precautionary measures for their protection, with sand bags and steel shutters. Troops have arrived by boat in the village from Kerry.[143]

The captured republican intelligence report of 13 July stated that a dispatch was sent by the commandant of Ennis column No 3 to the commandant of the Mid-Clare Brigade, asking if the latter would destroy Clarecastle bridge. They were detailed to do so but found it impossible, as the local barracks commanding the bridge was occupied by government forces.[144]

After the fall of Limerick on 20 July, the government forces consolidated their presence in Clare. Between 21 and 30 July, they were greatly augmented, and they drove the republicans from the towns of Kildysart, Kilkee and Kilrush with limited losses. According to republican sources, on 22 July government forces made a surprise morning attack against the republicans occupying Eden Vale and drove them out:

> Re attack at Edenvale on morning of 22 July, the following has come from the Home [Barracks], Ennis, from which the attackers came: The attack was instigated by Bill Mack and company in Kennedy's [...] Griffey took armed part in the attack with other unknown 'civilians.' Attackers went with machine gun which jammed after four rounds. McGrath was in charge and Haugh states that he came into armed conflict with P O'Loughlin. Note, Bill Mack is Batt. O/C and resides in Ennis, his company is a no of Volunteers, spies and ex-soldiers. McGrath is in charge of the Home. Haugh is O/C West Clare Brigade, for some time in the Home.

Captured intelligence reports from Clare, dated 24–25 July 1922, also included the following:

> The Home barracks has 150 men, 100 rifles, 6 machine guns, 30 cars including one charabanc [motor bus].

> Lorries moving between Ennis and Clarecastle bringing supplies of petrol. A boat with petrol arrived at Clarecastle.

> Three men of our ASU were captured near Ennistymon on morning of 23 July, they were captured at home.

> On Friday last, 250 troops left Templemore for Killaloe.

> On 24 July about 400 Free State troops equipped with rifles and machine guns have just arrived in Ennis and occupied all prominent points – the Labour Hall, Masonic Hall, Howard's

[69]

and County Club. They have the town surrounded and nobody is allowed leave except on foot [...] Their total strength in Ennis is given at nearly 700 men.

Free State troops from the Home barracks reported going to West Clare tomorrow [25 July].

Thirty Free State troops patrol in Cratloe every night, the movement of republicans is closely watched [...] Tulla is re-occupied by enemy garrison of between 50 and 60 troops.

A second batch of captured republican intelligence reports, dated 27–29 July 1922, had the following information:

At 7.30 pm on 26 July about 20 Free State troops in a Crossley and armoured lorry with rifles and a machine gun were proceeding from Ennis to Kildysart, they came on four men on the Kilrush Road at Darragh. In a sharp fight one of our men was captured and one enemy wounded. A party who were mobilised to attack them on their return from Kildysart was attacked by four cars from Ennis, a few shots were fired, leaving two dead and one wounded on the enemy side. Three more members of Fianna captured in Ennis. An attempt to round-up some of our men in the Crusheen area failed as our men had received information in time.

There is a permanent Free State force in Kildysart since 25th, numbering c. 30 men [...] 150 Free State troops left Ennis for Kilrush on 29th July – fighting is reported from that area [...] Several members of Fianna have been arrested in Ennis, only one dispatch rider and a few girls remain of any use.

This was the last captured intelligence report sent from republican sources in Clare to IRA headquarters in Clonmel. There was, however, a report that related to Kilrush which came from republican sources in Kerry among some captured documents. It was sent by Humphrey Murphy, commandant of the Kerry No 1 Brigade, to the IRA headquarters at Clonmel. The report, dated 19 July 1922, referred to communications in the Shannon Estuary and plans to commandeer ships from Kilrush for the republican cause:

With regard to the E.J.D. [a ship plying on the River Shannon], I understand Ryan of Kilrush who has large shares in her is, and always has been friendly to us and that another merchant named

Glynn, who is not friendly, has two boats – the Corunna and the Turk. Will you arrange with the bearer that if the E.J.D. is not of any great use to us that she be returned as soon as possible and make arrangements that one of the others are to be taken.

Murphy also urged his troops to attack English navy ships and provoke a new war against the British:

If an English destroyer or sloop comes within rifle range of your shore, snipe it and if possible, have rifle grenades dropped on deck. Possibly they may shell the coast or make a landing, the very thing we want them to do. Then we will have the old enemy back and that will alter the whole aspect of the present war.

Historian Paul O'Brien, in his study of the Glynns of Kilrush, the most prominent merchant family in west Clare, records that the civil war had a direct and negative impact on the Glynn businesses in west Clare. Two of their ships, the SS *Corona* and the SS *Turk*, were requisitioned by government forces for the transport of troops, military supplies and prisoners for the duration of the war. C.E. Glynn claimed damages of £5,000 for the loss of the ships from July 1922 to July 1923, but the milling company was only awarded the paltry sum of £75.[145]

Some of the difficulties experienced by the republican forces can be gauged by pessimistic reports from Frank Barrett, commandant of the republican 1st Western Division, written in late July and early August 1922. His letters, a reliable republican source, highlight military reverses; they also show how the division suffered the loss of experienced officers, and how the majority of the general population were opposed to their actions. On 26 July, Barrett reported to the chief of staff, Liam Lynch, 'Our columns are experiencing considerable difficulty owing to the hostile attitudes of great numbers of the civil population. Spies are continually keeping the enemy informed of our movements.' Two weeks later, on 10 August, Barrett reported the 'heavy loss of senior officers'.

Another republican source, an intelligence report on the developing military situation in Clare on 13 July 1922, corroborated Barrett's view on the locals' hostility toward republicans, 'In Meelick and Cratloe Free State troops have been active in clearing roads and blocking roads diverting traffic through Sixmilebridge. Practically the whole population of Meelick and Cratloe areas are reported as hostile [to republicans].' Con Moloney also corroborated this view when he wrote to Ernie O'Malley, commandant of the 2nd Southern Division, late in July, 'Although the First Western Division was well-organised and a tremendous amount of work was done there, it was very hard to do anything effective there as the people generally are hostile and convey intelligence to the enemy.'[146]

Liberation of Kilkee and Kilrush

An *Irish Times* report described the capture of Kilrush (the largest town in west Clare – a major industrial centre and port) from republicans on 28 July. Kilrush had been occupied by republicans since 1 July:

> The National troops entered Kilrush on Friday evening about 4 o'clock by two roads and the Irregulars vanished. About 150 men were engaged in the operation. The Irregulars had been making feverish preparations for a defence of the place, but when the National troops arrived they found that the Irregulars, who had seized great quantities of food the day before, had vanished. They captured one of the leaders, Brody Lillis, in a boghole with his head just above a clump of rushes. He had two revolvers, 45 rounds of ammunition and bombs. Five other prisoners were captured in Kilrush. As the lorries entered the town of Kilrush the people clung on to them and cheered wildly. They feted the troops and were lavish in their hospitality. The welcome that the troops got in Kilkee was even greater.[147]

According to the *Irish Times*, the town of Kilkee in west Clare, the premier seaside resort of County Clare, was liberated on 30 July. The town had been captured by republicans on 1 July:

> The whole of Clare is now entirely cleared of Irregulars, who made a hurried departure, much to the relief of the urban and rural population, late on Saturday night, according to a visitor speaking to an Irish Independent representative. In Kilkee there had been no National troops, they being engaged at operations in Limerick. In their absence, the Irregulars did pretty well what they pleased, and seized everything in the way of foodstuffs, vehicles etc. On Saturday night, 29 July, they burnt the Kilkee coastguard station, their chief centre in West Clare and the police barracks. About midnight on Saturday the Irregulars started to evacuate the town in batches of 12, leaving behind the chief

leader in West Clare, Mr Simon McInerney. At 2pm on Sunday, the National troops unexpectedly arrived, to the great joy and relief of the population. The troops were surrounded by a wildly cheering crowd, waving napkins, handkerchiefs and hats [...] The troops searched a house in Albert Road and found Mr McInerney unarmed.

Already, six barracks have been burnt in West Clare, there are now no Irregulars in any barracks in the county and the remnants have taken to the hills, or else returned home. For almost five weeks there were no newspapers in Kilkee, with the exception of isolated copies from Limerick visitors [...] during that period there was only one delivery of mails [...] Old age pensioners have been left without dole for 3–4 weeks, the tourist season has been very bad in Kilkee this year. Butter and agricultural produce have been left unsold due to the absence of fairs and markets with the result that there was hardly any money in circulation.

Doonbeg bridge was destroyed last week [...] The West Clare railway runs one train per day between Ennis and Kilrush [...] an attempt was made to blow up the bridge at Ennistymon [...] there is a shortage of petrol [...] motors and large numbers of bicycles were seized by irregulars before leaving Kilkee. There was an ambush at Cooraclare on Monday night, one National soldier was slightly wounded.

Recruitment during the civil war

After the civil war began, the government launched a massive recruitment drive all over the country to defend the newly created state from the republicans. By the end of the conflict, the government forces amounted to about 50,000 soldiers. The following advertisements were inserted in the local papers. These advertisements appealed to property owners, especially farmers, who were allowed to join a separate Farmers' Battalion.

Wanted, Men of Grit. Get 40 men in each parish to defend your properties. Form the Parish Guards immediately.
M. Brennan, Commandant General, 1st Western Division
Clare Champion, 12 August 1922

The First Western Never Surrenders, Join the Farmers' Division at once.
Clare Champion, 4 November 1922

Farmers' Battalion
Don't hesitate be men play the game you will be released on 1
March 1923 to return to farm work. The courthouse will be your
HQ. Join at once. Rates of pay: NCOs 3/6 per day+ 4/- wife+ 5/6
wife and 1 child, 5/6, 2 children; 7/3, 3+ children.
Saturday Record, 4 November 1922

Ennis Public Safety Committee established

In July, because of the crisis in Ennis due to transport difficulties and
military actions by government forces and republicans, some
concerned citizens of the town set up a Public Safety Committee.
They organised a house-to-house collection to raise funds. A
deputation consisting of F.F. Cullinan, John B. Lynch, Rev. Fr
Considine and J. Carmody interviewed the military authorities at
the Home Barracks to secure the release of flour; it was supplied to
bakers each day from Monday, 17 July. Another deputation
comprised of John D. Moloney, P.J. McNamara, P. Hogan and J.
Bredin was sent to Dublin on the morning of Sunday, 17 July to
secure the orders of Ennis merchants and charter a boat to convey
the foodstuffs to Limerick and thence to Ennis via Clarecastle. The
mission of the deputation was successful, and a shipload of
provisions arrived at Clarecastle about a week later to the joy of the
merchants and the public. The *Clare Champion* reported:

> Included in a cargo of the SS Edern which arrived at Clare Castle
> last week were 1,000 barrels of stout and 30 tons of foodstuffs
> for Messrs Bredin and Son, Market St., Ennis. The stout has been
> distributed throughout the whole county by Messrs Bredin much
> to the relief and joy of many persons who feared that pussyfoot
> had come to stay.

Though there was a large amount of Guinness stout available for
the general public, the opportunity for drinking Guinness, or indeed
any other alcoholic beverage, in Ennis was curtailed by a
proclamation issued by General Michael Brennan on Thursday, 23
July, 'All pubs to close at 7 pm until further notice!'[148]

Death of Michael Collins

General Michael Collins visited Ennis on Sunday, 13 August. At this
time, Collins was the supreme political and military leader in the

Free State. After the acceptance of the Treaty by the Dáil on 7 January, Collins became chairman of the Provisional Government – effectively prime minister. He was also Minister for Finance. On 12 July Collins assumed the role of commander in chief of the National Army. Meanwhile, he was still president of the IRB. He visited the headquarters of the 1st Western Division and was met by General Michael Brennan, the divisional staff and brigade officers. He then called on Bishop Fogarty at his palace, Westbourne House, and had an interview with him. When news of his visit spread around the town, hundreds of people thronged the streets close to the divisional headquarters, and when he appeared 'he was greeted with enthusiastic cheers and his car was surrounded.' He and his party spent about three hours in Ennis and then departed in an armoured car. Nine days later, on 22 August, Michael Collins was shot dead during an ambush at Béal na mBláth, Co. Cork.[149]

The government suffered two major blows in August 1922. Arthur Griffith, the president of Dáil Éireann, died suddenly from a stroke on 12 August; this was followed ten days later by the tragic death of Michael Collins, who had succeeded Griffith as president. Despite these losses, which affected the morale of the pro-Treaty party, the government under President William T. Cosgrave was determined in its resolution to carry on and establish its military authority over the country.

Bishop Fogarty, who was concelebrant-in-chief of the Mass for Michael Collins at the Pro Cathedral in Dublin, paid a fulsome tribute to the slain leader while denouncing the assailants:

> He was the father of Irish freedom and died the honoured president of the first national Government Ireland had for 700 years. He could have never wrecked Ireland, because she turned him down, he loved her too honestly for that. His passion was to re-animate the soul of Ireland and make her independent. Never had Ireland a more successful leader. When he signed the Treaty he knew he was interpreting the mind of the country. His early death is a sad bereavement to Ireland, he found her manacled, he set her free.

One week later, at a Mass in Ennis, Dr Fogarty stated:

> If he had fallen at the hands of an external enemy we could have borne it, that such a man should be slain by a spiteful faction of

our own country is a chagrin, a bitterness and a shame. They are not men who shot the noble life from behind a hedge, sooner or later, the people will get going in earnest and they will make short work of the wreckers.[150]

Around this time many people were genuinely seeking to bring an end to the civil war in Ireland, which was causing such death and destruction. In reply to a letter from the chairman of Roscommon County Council advocating the formation of a peace party, which was circulated to county councils in early September 1922, Michael Brennan, the chairman of Clare County Council and commandant of the 1st Western Division, stated that the people's will must be respected:

> There is no one more anxious for peace than I am. I have worked as hard as anyone else for peace during the past six months. One result of that work, and of my intimacy with practically all of the Irregular leaders up to two months ago has convinced me that there is no hope of peace in Ireland until the will of the people is accepted by everybody as the final court of appeal in all matters concerning the people, not the bullet and the bomb.
>
> Recognition of the rights of the people necessarily means control of all arms in the country by the people's government. A truce now would be utilised, as before, to provide more material 'for wading through the blood of the Irish people.' When the Irregulars admit the rights of the people, the same people who faced and beat the British Empire when some of their present-day dictators were skulking in safety, Clare County Council will demand peace.
>
> In the meantime, the Council remembers what the people did for it, when 23 out of its 31 members were serving in columns against the English in real columns, not the present-day comic operas. The people stood by us, we stand by them. The government is the people's government, therefore, we stand by that government in its efforts to bring peace and order to our country.[151]

War on communications

The republicans carried out a communications war, conducting many attacks on the railway network in the county – mainly on the West Clare railway line and the Limerick–Athenry line. Their strategy was to paralyse communications, as they had done during the War of Independence. There were more than a dozen attacks on the network and railway services between July 1922 and February 1923. Rails and sleepers were torn up, land mines were placed on tracks, telephone and telegraph lines were cut, rocks were strewn on railway tracks, railway bridges were blown up, signal boxes were damaged, shots were fired at train drivers, and trains were held up by armed men. Railway workers employed to repair the rails and remove obstructions were fired upon by republicans. The line between Doonbeg and Craggaknock was destroyed several times.

The most extensive destruction occurred on Saturday and Sunday night, 13–14 January 1923, when the republicans orchestrated a co-ordinated attack on the railway system. Apart from tearing up rails along many stretches of the line, the station houses at Ardsollus, Craggaknock, Corofin, Kilmurry Ibricane, Lahinch, Miltown Malbay and Quilty were wrecked. The damage was estimated at between £5,000 and £6,000, which was imposed on the ratepayers of Clare. During the attack on Quilty station, the father of the stationmaster allegedly died of shock. A military summary for 13 January states the following with regard to the attack on Ardsollus station, 'About 40 rails on the GS&W Railway [the Great Southern and Western Railway] were torn up. The signal cabin posts were cut and several wagons were burnt.' On the following night, 14 January, the station at Ardsollus was again attacked by republicans. The report states, 'A large number of men entered the station and they removed all stationery and cash from the office together with a quantity of other goods. One signal pole and two telegraph poles were cut and about 120 yards of railway line torn up.'[152]

Frustrated in their military ambitions, the republicans also attempted to paralyse road transport in the county, as they had done during the last few months of the War of Independence, as well as disrupting telecommunications. From July 1922 to April 1923, they resorted to tactics such as trenching roads, blowing up bridges and cutting down telephone and telegraph poles. The Clare Champion of 22 July reported, 'Destruction of public property is rampant in the county, there is distressing news from all over the county complaining of the impassable conditions of the county roads, while bridges are reported to have been extensively damaged, a ruthless paralysis of trade in the county.' Apart from some attacks around bridges near Ennis in July, most of this activity (as in the attacks on the railway network) took place in west Clare. Bridges were damaged in Drehidnagower and Claureen in July; in Clonderlaw, Crusheen and Doonbeg in August; in Cooraclare, Cree and Miltown Malbay in October; in Miltown Malbay, Quilty and Kilmurry in November; in Annagaorach (Cooraclare) and Mountscott (Miltown Malbay) in February 1923; and near Miltown Malbay in March 1923. Besides the bridges, there was trenching of the Miltown Malbay–Kilrush road in August; on roads in Cooraclare and Cree in October; on the Miltown Malbay–Mullagh road in December 1922 and January 1923; on the Ennis–Miltown Malbay road in February; on roads around Kildysart in March; and on roads around Miltown Malbay in April 1923.

These tactics caused great inconvenience to the community, many of whom got fed up with the interruptions to trade and communication. During October, government forces compelled some men in Miltown to repair a bridge about 2 miles from Miltown Malbay, but it was damaged again that night. The parish priest of Kilmurry McMahon, Fr Hayes, organised a group of about sixty parishioners to repair Clonderlaw bridge, which had been damaged in August. The republicans were not happy with this and people were warned not to repair the roads. In October a young man named J.F. McNamara of Ballynagun, Cooraclare was fired at and wounded as he attempted to lay some flagstones across a trench on the road. The Ennis–Miltown Malbay road was again blocked on the night of Thursday, 15 February by a large stone wall; a notice was posted on the wall, reading, 'This is mined, civilians beware, signed the IRA.' Despite the warning, farmers coming to town removed the stones. A *Clare Champion* report of 28 August stated, 'the civilians are the only parties hardest hit by these obstructions, the people in many parishes in East Clare are, we are glad to say, seeing that the roads are being made passable for them.'

One enthusiastic motorist, Georgina Stacpoole of Eden Vale, whose family had experienced several raids and thefts of motor cars during the War of Independence and the civil war, described, in an article in *The Motor*, the difficulties of motoring in Ireland during these times:

> One of the worst features of the raids on private owners is that if for any reason the cars cannot be removed, they are immediately set on fire or otherwise destroyed [...] Last summer, when the car thefts were at their height, the writer happened to witness one of these and a very unpleasant experience it was [...] Irish motorists have also frequently to face the possibility of disaster from trenches and felled trees across roads, which are a continual menace, especially when driving at night; and numerous cars have been brought into repair shops with broken axles and other damage as a result of such encounters [...] Drivers in the remoter parts of the country are particularly badly off when the roads are blocked; for they must make either very considerable detours, or else take their cars long distances across fields to reach their destinations [...] Bridges have also been demolished and one man in a western county has made a small fortune in half crowns by placing planks across a broken bridge in order that cars may pass. In addition to his wealth, he has gained much local celebrity, being known through-out a wide district by the appellation of 'Paddy the Plank'.

Ironically, while the republicans in Clare were destroying road and rail communications around the county, the republican executive were issuing instructions to divisional commandants to keep the lines of communication open. Among the Joe Barrett Papers at Mary Immaculate College, Limerick are letters from headquarters complaining that 'communication routes were unsatisfactory and that there were inexcusable delays'. Commanding officers were instructed to procure two motor cars – preferably Fords – for conveying despatches to and from command headquarters. If possible, these were to be driven by 'reliable women', as it was not safe for men to do so. Commanding officers were also requested to provide lists of garage owners, car owners and drivers. Furthermore, they were to save addresses for postal communications and the names of reliable railway workers and the railway stations where they worked. The following 'reliable' railway workers were named: at Crusheen – J. Molloy, signalman, and Michael O'Dea, milesman; at Ennis – Jack Kerin, relief signalman (who would work Clarecastle as well), Michael Daly, signalman, Jack Cormack, porter (who would work at Ardsollus and Quin) and Michael Roberts, relief signalman; at Cratloe – John Trehy, stationmaster, and Tom Foley, porter.[153]

Frustrated in their plans to blow up the bridge at Clarecastle, the republicans tried to blow up the strategic bridge at Latoon on the main Ennis–Limerick road about 3 miles from Clarecastle on 15 July. The bridge, however, was also being protected by government forces, and the attack was repulsed. There was a gun battle that lasted between one and two hours; this was, apparently, the first major engagement between the rival forces in mid-Clare. A *Clare Champion* report related the story of this attack:

> The most sensational occurrence which has yet happened in the county a direct engagement between the two opposing forces, was that which was enacted on Saturday night in the defence made for the protection of the bridge at Latoon. The safety and preservation of this bridge is of paramount importance to the National troops in the present crisis. Late on Saturday night [15 July], anticipating an ambush at the bridge, National troops were waiting. Later, a body of men arrived at the bridge fully armed and with equipment ready for the demolition of the bridge. They proceeded to carry out some demolition work when they were fired upon by the National troops. Thus, ensuring for the first time, a direct engagement between the two opposing forces in the county. A desperate conflict is reported to have taken place for hours, during which an intense fire was vigorously maintained. This violent conflict created a feeling of alarm and terror among the local inhabitants. It was quite impossible to ascertain if there were any casualties, but the bridge was protected, a large pool of blood was found next morning. The bridge will now be kept under vigilant observation to ensure its protection.[154]

The shooting was heard in Dromoland Castle, as indicated by Lord Inchiquin in a letter to his son, Donough O'Brien, in late July 1922:

> Latoon Bridge was attacked a few nights ago and they started to make a hole in it to put in a big land mine, but luckily the Free Staters were watching it and firing went on for over an hour with the result that the enemy retired. We heard the row about three or four in the morning.[155]

On Tuesday, 3 September, Martin Slattery, a prominent republican from Darragh, was captured and he had in his possession a diary.

Extracts from this diary were published in the *Clare Champion* and the *Saturday Record* in early September under the heading, 'Extracts from the Diary of Martin Slattery, Darragh, a prominent Irregular'. The following extract relates to the attack at Latoon bridge:

> We left Corofin on Friday morning [...] On Saturday, we came on to Stacpoole's [Eden Vale] at 1 pm. We had to do guard duty all day as we had the wind up the Free Staters. At 9.30 pm we left fully fitted out for a great fight. We had with us a wonderful engineer named James Guinane, who was to blow Latoon Bridge out of the face of the earth. The advance party under J Barrett proceeded to the bridge and J Barrett and P Mack went into Healy's house [Manus South] to get some tools for to make holes to put down the extensive explosives. P Costello, J Griffin, Tom Frawley and me, being rear-guard, halted a little above the gates of the house to keep watch for lorries coming from Ennis. After a few minutes a great volley of rifle fire was sent along to us. We then had to creep along the road to a gate leading into a field. Some of the boys that time were praying. J Barrett and P Mack came the same way after us. We then crossed a very large trench and every man went up to his waist in it. T Frawley had low shoes and long stockings, and you can imagine how he took his bath.

The rest of the diary was disparaging to the republican cause, implying that the republicans were engaged in brigandage after they retreated from Latoon bridge:

> After some time, we came to a big house in Spancilhill, we went in, but it being vacant, and nothing in it to steal we left it and came on to Con McMahon's [...] We arrived at Sir Michael O'Loghlen's house [Drumconora, Barefield] about 7 o'clock. The house seemed to be rather desolate looking, the blinds were drawn on every window, and we were very windy [apprehensive], expecting it to be occupied by the Free State army, and they would fire on us, so we kept under cover for at least an hour [...] After a time, P. Costello, who was at that time our O.C., asked a very handy man by the name of J. Darcy to go to the house and see if he could find the caretaker, and tell him, P. Costello wanted to see him. If Darcy was shot, it would not make much difference, as we could easily spare him, and all the boys knew that.

> When we got in we at once prepared to search the house for anything that might be of use to us. I broke the first lock and got

a very fine evening dress suit, the property of Mr O'Loghlen. J
Quin put on the coat and vest and looked lovely. T Hogan and
Pat Harte were very busy at that time looking for money, or its
value in silver. They took as much as they could. At 12 noon on
Tuesday, we had decided to take another visit to Edenvale House,
so Tull Considine went for the car to take away all the mines and
our loot. P Mack returned tonight from Corofin in great cheer,
his pockets full of money and his belly full of beer. P Mack, who
was at this time getting sober, looked on at Pat McCarthy's windy
defence with a very peaceable smile. P McCarthy and D Murphy
fired four shots at a big stone and missed them all. They were so
windy they never even ranged their sight for 500 yards range.[156]

There seems to have been some truth in the contents of the diary; in
August 1923 Sir Michael O'Loghlen of Drumconora, Lieutenant of
County Clare, made a claim for compensation for damage to his
property by republicans, 'Occupation of house and damage to house
and furniture at Drumconora House, Drumconora, County Clare
by armed men in August 1922.'[157]

Another source for the attack on Latoon bridge is Volunteer
Patrick Kearns. In his military pension application, Kearns, from
Kilnamona, describes some of his republican activities, and how he
and others were involved in several attempts to blow up bridges near
Ennis, including Latoon bridge:

I was in charge of Lisdoonvarna Barracks in March 1922 with
sixteen men. In the middle of June 1922 I was appointed O.C. at
Ennistymon. The barracks at Ennistymon was destroyed by us
on 1 July 1922. I then went to Corofin Barracks, the Divisional
HQ, and from there I was taken to go out with a column of
about sixteen men under Captain Joe Barrett. When destroying
a bridge near Ennis [probably Drehidnagower bridge] we were
ambushed by Free State forces. On that occasion I was in charge
of six men and was also in charge of a small number on outpost
duty when our HQ at Edenvale was attacked by Free State troops
in July 1922. I was in charge of an advanced guard of seven or
eight men when proceeding to destroy Latoon Bridge about
August 1922. We were ambushed by seven or eight [government
soldiers], who were lying in wait for us, one man was wounded;
Captain J. Barrett was in supreme command on that occasion.
About the end of August I was sent by my commander, Captain
J. Barrett to plan an attack on Ennistymon National Army HQ.
I was captured when making a map of the grounds and barracks.

I was subsequently imprisoned at Ennis and Limerick prisons, on a prison ship at Dunlaoire, and at Gormanston Camp to December 1923.[158]

Assaults on Clarecastle

At Clarecastle, there were several official reports of attacks committed by both sides in late July and August 1922. It must be remembered that the press was heavily censored. In one attack, a prominent local republican named Tommy Kinnane was seriously wounded:

> National troops were searching for Mr Kinnane and some troops saw him coming towards them on a bicycle. He refused to halt, one of the soldiers caught him by the coat and Kinnane drew his revolver [...] he was shot in the head [...] he is in intensive care in Ennis and in danger of dying or permanent blindness and suffering intense agony. He was in possession of a revolver and two rounds of ammunition.

In an article in the *Irish Times* on 3 August, it was stated that a report reached Galway that Kinnane had been shot dead in Clarecastle on Tuesday evening, 'he endeavoured to shoot a sergeant of the National Army, who the report states was too quick for him and fired first.' But reports of his death were premature, as Tommy Kinnane did lose the sight of one eye but lived until 1947. A Celtic memorial cross was erected in his memory at Clarehill cemetery, Clarecastle on 22 July 1950. At the unveiling ceremony, Bernard Power, secretary of the memorial committee, who delivered the oration, described Tommy Kinnane's career as a soldier in the First World War, in the War of Independence and in the Irish Civil War. He hoped that the aspirations, the bravery and the deeds of men such as Tommy Kinnane, who suffered greatly in the cause of Irish freedom, would not be forgotten by the Irish people.[159]

In a second attack, Sergeant Neville, serving with the government forces, was wounded at Clarecastle by a party of republicans who fired at him. A government report castigated the republicans:

> Sgt Neville served in the East Clare Brigade and took part in every action of that brigade. His home was burnt by the Black and Tans and he was one of the men 'to be shot on sight' by the British troops. Now, he comes under the same heading with the Irregulars, nine of whom attacked him, while alone, on the public

street at Clare Castle on Sunday night. Not being as well accustomed as the Irregulars to running, he remained where he was, lying on the ground and fired about 15 shots at the nine 'heroes', who beat a retreat [...] Clare Castle, it may be remembered was the happy hunting ground of the Irregulars all through the war with the English.

This government report also mentioned an attack on a patrol boat on the River Fergus:

The little patrol boat containing a small party of National Army troops at Clare Castle was simultaneously attacked on Sunday night, 6 August by the Irregulars. A vigorous rifle fire was opened on it and one of the troops was wounded in the face. The National troops returned fire, but with what effect is not known. The boat, under the charge of Lieutenant O'Donnell, is used to patrol the river.[160]

About a week later, the *Clare Champion* reported that Clarecastle army barracks was attacked by a large group of republicans:

About midnight on Saturday [19 August] a report from GHQ, stated that Clare Castle barracks was attacked by a party of about forty republicans. Two army officers were crossing the bridge when the attack occurred. They were fired upon from both sides of the road. Simultaneously, a grenade was thrown at the sentry in front of the barracks, but it fell short of its target and exploded harmlessly, without doing any injury. The two officers on the bridge saw the attackers moving towards the front of the barracks and opened fire with two revolvers at about 60 yards range. They emptied their revolvers and got safely under cover. After an exchange of shots lasting about two hours, the attacking party were dislodged from their position and compelled to retreat. The noise of the shooting could be heard in Ennis and reinforcements were dispatched from the Home Barracks. Some of the reinforcements met the republicans retreating in the direction of Ballynacally. A brief engagement ensued, but the attackers succeeded in escaping owing to the darkness of the night. It was not possible to ascertain if any of the republicans were wounded. Next morning, however, pools of blood could be seen in the vicinity where the attacks took place. The government troops sustained no casualties. There was another attack on Clare Castle barracks on Monday 21 August, when it was sniped at from about 2 am to 4 am. There were no reports of casualties.[161]

There were at least two other reported attacks on the military barracks at Clarecastle. The *Clare Champion* noted an attack in November:

> Alarm at Clare Castle as some firing and explosions were heard on Tuesday night 14 November about midnight [...] some parties passing near the bridge tossed some bombs at the barracks and the guard replied with shots.

And the *Saturday Record* mentioned an attack in December:

> On Monday night [11 December] there was considerable alarm in Clare Castle, with many shots being fired at the old barracks, and the sentries replied [...] also, during Sunday night several shots were fired at Harmony Row and at the County Club, Ennis, HQ of the National forces [...] no one was injured.[162]

Events in west Clare

There was significant republican activity in west Clare in early July, a fact that was noted by an article in the *Freeman's Journal*:

> Irregular activities and agrarian agitation have been the cause of much destruction and distress in West Clare during the past three weeks. The roads leading to Miltown Malbay from Ennis, Kilrush and Kilkee are blocked by large stones and trees for the past three weeks. The food supply is running out, the railway in some parts has been destroyed and there have been no postal or telegraphic communications.

A message from a local correspondent in Miltown Malbay gives the following account of republican activities in this part of west Clare during July:

> 5 July, Barrack and Courthouse burnt at Miltown by Irregulars after vacating the building, estimated damage, £4,500.

> 9 July, Mrs Anderson's dwelling house was burnt by armed and masked men, damage, £3,000, fearing its occupation by Free State troops.

> 10 July, Quilty Coastguard Station burnt to the ground by masked and armed men after National troops evacuated the building.

> 12 July, the gates protecting the sandhills at Spanish Point were torn down, owned by Local Government Board and Mr Reid of Miltown House.

13 July, Irregular troops seize foodstuffs at Lahinch and Ennistymon.

15 July, the house of Mr E A G Ellis of Spanish Point was broken into and two bicycles taken.

The Protestant Church at Miltown Malbay was completely destroyed by fire. The outrage is widely and strongly condemned. Irregular and National troops deny any involvement with the burning of the church. Damage estimated at £2,500.

John O'Connor, (50), of Moy was shot dead by armed men concealed behind a wall. The affair is stated to be in connection with agrarian trouble.

16 July, at both Masses the priests denounced the murder of Mr O'Connor and the recent burnings, especially that of the Protestant Church.

17 July, HQ issued a statement that Capt B Lynch and Lieut E Roche, were fired upon on returning from Ennistymon to Ennis, they were uninjured, but the car was damaged by bullets.

18 July, the house of John Crehan of Dunsallagh, was visited by armed and masked men, who compelled him to take back a horse he had sold last winter.

Pat Hehir of Dunsallagh, was visited by armed and masked men, who cautioned him to hand over land about which there is some dispute.

20 July, Col Tottenham of Mount Callan, was visited by armed men, who ordered him to divide his lands. It is stated that he has since complied with the request.

21 July, John Vaughan and his brothers entered the house of Mrs James Vaughan, Main St, Miltown Malbay and took possession of part of the house, claiming it as part of their dead father's assets. They also cut down part of the woman's meadow.

22 July, the house of Christy Gallery, Dunagan, Miltown Malbay, was burnt to the ground. This is attributed to an agrarian dispute, damage, £1,000.

23 July, National troops from Ennistymon arrested P. Kerin, A. Malone, and S. Gallagher, Irregular leaders from Miltown Malbay.

24 July, Commdt Martin Frawley, of the National forces was kidnapped from his home at Miltown Malbay, by armed and masked men.[163]

Round-ups

The *Clare Champion* reported in August:

> The National Army are actively engaged day and night in effecting arrests of Irregulars throughout the county, troops are despatched from Ennis and other parts of the county to unexpectedly swoop down upon the Irregulars [...] recently a nocturnal visit was paid to one of the islands off Kildysart and several were arrested.[164]

Having secured all the main towns following the capture of Kilrush and Kilkee at the end of July, the government forces began their 'mopping-up' operation by carrying out many searches and sweeps in several parts of the county. This was especially the case in west and north Clare, where searches for republicans on the run were carried out over nine months. After a fight at Moy on 22 August, the government forces captured eight republicans, who were found to be in possession of rifles and about forty rounds of ammunition each. Early in September, the sweeps began in earnest in the Kilmaley district, where sixteen republicans from Barefield, Ennis, Inch and Darragh were arrested. The round-ups continued as the attacks and ambushes on government forces persisted. Between September 1922 and April 1923, sweeps and round-ups occurred in Ballynacally, Ballyvaughan, Barefield, Carran, Corofin, Cranny, Darragh, Doonbeg, Ennis, Ennistymon, Feakle, Kildysart, Kilkee, Kilmaley, Kilmihil, Kilrush, Knockerra, Labasheeda, Lahinch, Liscannor, Lisdoonvarna, Miltown Malbay, Moyasta, Spanish Point, Scariff, Tulla and Tullycrine. By the end of April 1923, dozens of Clare republicans had been rounded up, arrested and sent to prison. In September 1922, the *Clare Champion* reported:

> On Tuesday morning 3 September, a big number of arrests was made, the number of men captured was the biggest yet, sixteen Irregulars from Ennis, Inch, Kilmaley, Barefied, and Darragh,

including W. Barrett, Tull Considine and Martin Slattery, were arrested, other republicans were arrested in sweeps from Ballyvaughan to Kilmaley and in Moy and Corofin.[165]

Attacks on the Big Houses

Historian Tom Garvin notes that many of the Protestant gentry were attacked during the civil war, just as they were during the War of Independence:

> The cost of the war was disproportionately borne by the Protestant community in country areas, who were sometimes murdered, commonly physically threatened, often hounded out of Ireland by the republicans, or by local agrarian opportunists; the bills were put on the ratepayers.[166]

There was some truth in Garvin's observation, as attacks on the Big Houses of the county gentry continued during the civil war. The first of these to be destroyed was Roslevan House, the residence of the Hon. Edward O'Brien and Lady Beatrice O'Brien; it was destroyed in the early hours of Sunday morning, 23 July 1922. The owners had been absent for some weeks, and the house was occupied by the elderly gardener Mr Conway and his sister. Early on Sunday morning, a party of armed men raided the house. The senior couple were locked in a shed, and the raiders spilt petrol all over the house and it was burnt in a short time. The *Saturday Record* of 29 July reported:

> this wanton and disgraceful outrage can in no way be attributed to, or described as a military necessity, for according to the reports, the dastardly act is attributed to agrarian greed. Disgraceful robbery and looting took place all day Sunday, every portion of moveable property was burgled, the entire place presented a scene of desolation.[167]

Lord Inchiquin of Dromoland was O'Brien's brother. He described the destruction of his brother's house at Roslevan in a letter to his son Donough on 25 July:

> On Saturday night Roslevan was burnt to the ground, only the walls left standing. All furniture, linen, blankets, nic-nacs etc were destroyed and now everybody in Ennis is looting the place. Women with perambulators collecting odds and ends, all the potatoes and vegetables are being taken out of the garden. We got the carriages away and I have sent five carts to get whatever is left such as electric light engine, corn bins, water barrels,

horses, mowing machines, if there are now any of them left, which I doubt. I [...] think it was the work of a lot of Free-booters and robbers who looted the place and then burnt it to hide traces of their work. Poor uncle Eddie and Aunt Bea, I don't know what they will do. I don't suppose they will ever live in County Clare again.

In a second letter, dated 5 August, he wrote:

Uncle Eddie and Aunt Bea are terribly distressed about the burning of Roslevan, as they were both very fond of it, and had done so much to improve it. But I fear it will have to be sold. I shouldn't wonder, if they spent from £3000–£4,000 a year there and they also employed seven men.[168]

Other Protestant-owned houses in the county besides Roslevan House were attacked by incendiaries and land-grabbers in an attempt to drive out the owners and gain possession of their lands. Several homes were attacked during the civil war while law and order was in disarray: between the withdrawal of the Crown forces and the setting up of the Civic Guard, and while the government was striving to assert its authority over the republicans. On Sunday, 30 July 1922, Kilmore House, Knock, 'a beautiful mansion' and the home of Francis William Gore Hickman, was burnt to the ground. Gore Hickman was a solicitor based in Ennis and a legal advisor to the British Army Southern Command during the years 1918–21; his home had been attacked several times before this incident. Volunteers surprised incendiaries at the 'splendid' home of James Wakely at Mountshannon on Wednesday, 23 August 1922. They opened fire on the arsonists, who retreated under cover of darkness. On Monday, 14 August, the Lakeside Hotel, Killaloe was burnt by republicans. Ballyalla, the home of Vere O'Brien, was under threat in May 1923; Lieutenant Hanrahan and a party of three government soldiers went to O'Brien's house at Ballyalla and remained on guard duty until 4 a.m. on 19 May 1923. Luckily, there was nothing to report on that day.[169]

Among republican documents captured by the government forces was a letter from Captain M. Molony, Inagh Company to General Frank Barrett outlining how the home of Captain Tottenham of Mount Callan, an old gentleman and a retired British army officer, was attacked in July 1922:

Last evening *c.* 30 men calling themselves 'labourers' went to Capt Tottenham's at Mount Callan and drove his cattle up the mountains and laid a boundary across the land and took possession of the place [...] intending to divide it up, they had no authority to do this. Some were armed with shotguns, Tottenham's farm is a property. He is keeping six herdsmen there with large families and paying at least 28 workmen. Some of the men who went to see him have farms of their own and the greater part of them were not heard of when men were wanted when the Tans were here. Some of them belong to my company. I offered to leave the case to the priests, but they refused. The leader is Thomas Keane of Brownsleave, a farmer who also works on the roads and has not paid his rates [...] he wants more land. This should be looked after and put the cattle back on his own land. Capt. M. Moloney, Inagh.[170]

The home of the McAdam family, Blackwater House, near Parteen, was damaged by republican forces, along with the mills at Blackwater, between 14 July and 31 July 1922. Although the home of Major William Hawkins Ball, Fortfergus House, was extensively damaged on 27 June 1921, further damage was caused to the garden house and boiler house when the property was seized by republicans on 15 July 1922. The home of Annie J. Gore, Ballinahinch House, was damaged between 1 July 1922 and 5 February 1923. Ardataggle House, O'Briensbridge was extensively damaged by armed raiders between 1 May and 22 November 1922. The lodge at Paradise, Ballynacally belonging to Helen Henn was burnt on 23 December 1922. The windows of Beechpark House, Ennis were destroyed on 18 May 1922. The home of E.G. O'Brien, Cratloe Woods House, was damaged by armed raiders between 28 and 30 July 1922. Robert Parker's house at Castlelake, Sixmilebridge was extensively damaged on 20 August 1922. The properties of Francis C. Sampson located at Moynoe and Kilgorey, near Scariff, were damaged several times throughout 1922. At Mrs Hibbert's property at Woodpark, Scariff – which was burnt on 10 June 1921, during the War of Independence – there was further destruction of the lodge and out-offices; this occurred between 14 July and 1 October 1922. The property of Edith Vereker of White Hall, Parteen was raided by armed and masked men, who damaged the house and stole property on 5 August 1922. The property of Colonel John Massy Westropp,

Doonass House, was attacked and damaged by gunfire on 10 December 1922. Lord Leconfield's property at Kildeema South, Miltown Malbay was burnt on 12 July 1922, and further damage was caused to the property later that year.

Eden Vale, the Georgian mansion of the Stacpoole family, was taken over by the republicans of mid-Clare on 4 July 1922 and occupied until 22 July 1922. During this time, the republicans seized some of the family's property, including farm produce, clothing and jewellery. The Stacpooles of Eden Vale were fortunate that their home, which had been in the family for nearly one hundred and fifty years, was not destroyed by the republicans after they were driven from the building on 22 July. In his memoir of life at Eden Vale, written in 1941, Richard John Stacpoole, JP, DL, described the circumstances of the republican takeover:

> In 1922 when the Free State had come into being and the Republicans had risen against it, we suffered considerable trouble, having both cars stolen and three different raids for arms as well; but these were too well-hidden and were never found. On the advice of the Adjutant of the Free State troops in Ennis, who feared further trouble, we went away for a while to Trefiew in North Wales, leaving the servants in the house; it was promptly occupied by the Republicans, but they left after three weeks there and before we returned home.

The Stacpooles' neighbours, the MacDonnell family, who had been resident in Newhall since 1776, sold their demesne in 1921 to the Joyce family, a wealthy Catholic family from Galway. The demesne was a property of about 400 acres, and it included a Georgian mansion. Some locals resented the purchase of the demesne by outsiders, and the property was damaged. Anastasia Joyce submitted a claim for compensation for 'cattle driven off the land and injured, and destruction of gates at Newhall on 8 April 1922'.

It must also be remembered that these attacks were directed at the landowners, most of them Protestant, in order to force them to divide up the remaining estates in the county that had not been sold despite the introduction of the Land Acts of 1881, 1891 and especially the Wyndham Land Act of 1902. Under these acts, many tenants were enabled to purchase farms from their landlords. Land hunger and land agitation were important factors in the political movement at the time. Many land-hungry farmers took advantage of the political crisis in Ireland, when law and order was difficult to impose.

A statistical analysis of the post-truce Damage to Property (Compensation) Act, 1923, a law relating to compensation for criminal injuries, reveals that, in Clare, at least 85 out of a total of 350 claims for compensation – about a quarter of the total claims – were directly related to land agitation. The types of claims under this heading included cattle driving, knocking of walls and fences, illegal occupation of lands, burning of hay, maiming and killing of animals, destruction of out-offices, seizure of property and destruction of farm machinery.[171]

A sectarian attack

Sadly, the Protestant church at Spanish Point was wantonly destroyed by fire on the night of Saturday, 22 July 1922, the same night that Roslevan House was burnt. The destruction of the church was widely condemned on all sides, as noted in the *Saturday Record*:

> When a House of Worship, no matter to what religion it belongs, is made the object of an outrage, the depravity of the wrong-doers is becoming increasingly alarming and demoralising in its frightfulness. The outrage which deprives the Protestant members of the community of their church at Miltown Malbay is deservedly and strongly reprobated.

The *Saturday Record* also noted that the police barracks in Miltown Malbay, which was occupied by republican forces since its evacuation by the police, was also destroyed at this time.

One prominent local republican leader, James D. Kenny, rejected assertions by Michael Brennan that republican forces were responsible for the burning of the church; while the local commandant Anthony Malone denied any republican involvement, he felt that the outrage was damaging to the republican cause. Among captured documents was a letter from Malone to Frank Barrett, mentioning how the Protestant church at Miltown Malbay was burnt:

> The Protestant Church at Miltown Malbay was burnt down some time late last night [...] I have no information to connect any body with the outrage yet [...] This is the third case of burning of private property in the parish since 29 June outside

the IRA barracks. It is the common belief that the IRA are responsible for these outrages. Of course, members of the IRA may or may not have taken part in them, but without knowledge or consent of the Brigade staff. I want to know if anything can be done whereby these false reports concerning the IRA can be repudiated. I am opposed to these outrages as well and I can see that such things are a blow to republicans.[172]

Though, it cannot be claimed definitively that this sectarian attack was authorised or carried out by republican activists, it was popularly attributed to them.

Arming the republicans

While the Irish government forces were able to purchase weapons from the British government, including artillery, aeroplanes, ships and army trucks, along with hundreds of machine guns, tens of thousands of rifles and copious supplies of ammunition, the republicans found it much more difficult to acquire arms and ammunition and were, therefore, at a huge disadvantage. Although they secured some weapons during the truce period, they were largely reliant on the limited supply of weapons that they possessed during the War of Independence. The Army Executive tried to secure weapons in Europe, from Belgian, French and other arms dealers, but they secured little. Some republicans in Clare tried but failed to secure weapons, as the following items indicate. In the *Saturday Record* on 7 October 1922, there was the following report of attempted arms acquisition:

> Attempts were made to land some weapons from Kerry by boat across the Shannon near Kildysart. The boat contained a Lewis gun, some bombs, ammunition, and some rifles; two men were captured.

About five months later, in the *Clare Champion* on 23 March 1923, the following was recorded:

> Michael O'Donoghue of the Causeway, Ennis, was arrested in Liverpool charged with having 5 revolvers and ammunition in his rooms at Liverpool [...] When charged with illegal possession he said: 'What about the shiploads of ammunition the government are sending the Free Staters?'

Civic Guard in Clare

Following the departure of the RIC from their barracks, especially from towns around Clare at the end of January and February 1922, it took many months before the new police force, the Civic Guard (nowadays known as an Garda Síochána), was established, trained and dispersed in stations around the county. This was a difficult task, as the government was simultaneously combatting the anti-Treaty forces in the civil war. Naturally, most members of the new police force were supporters of the Treaty, as the republicans were opposed to the Free State government. Many Clare men joined the new police force; the two pro-Treaty Clare TDs, Patrick Brennan and Sean Liddy, resigned from the Dáil and had prominent roles in the formation of the new police force in the first years of its establishment.

The republicans were opposed to the Civic Guard, and they made it difficult to establish the new unarmed police force in Clare. Nevertheless, the police were eventually accepted by the majority of the people; as the first commissioner Michael Staines prophesised, 'The Civic Guard will succeed not by the force of arms or numbers, but on their moral authority as servants of the people.' Garvin states that Clare was one of the counties that was most resistant to the new police force:

> Like the Free State army, the Civic Guard, after a shaky start, gained acceptance, except in areas where the surviving remnants of the IRA persisted in long-term resistance, often fuelled by agrarian passions or by criminality. Leitrim, Clare and Kerry were the most recalcitrant counties from the point of view of the police.[173]

The first members of the Civic Guard arrived in the county towards the end of September 1922; twenty-five policemen under Superintendent O'Dwyer arrived in Ennis to undertake duties in the town and district. The *Clare Champion* noted that the new Civic Guard 'were welcomed by the majority of the people as the military had no time to deal with the petty criminals and thieves active in Ennis'. About a month later, a party of fifteen guards and two sergeants under Inspector Cronin took up duties in the old RIC barracks in Kilrush. By the end of October, the Civic Guard were deployed in stations in Broadford, Ennistymon, Kilkee, Killaloe, Kildysart, Lisdoonvarna, Newmarket-on-Fergus, Sixmilebridge and Tulla. A year later, in October 1923 – six months after the civil war had ended – the Civic Guard were established in thirty-nine barracks throughout the county. The new Civic Guard had 1 chief superintendent, 3 superintendents, 3 inspectors, 63 sergeants and 181 guards based in thirty-nine stations. By contrast, the old RIC had 2 county inspectors, 8 district inspectors, 88 sergeants and 382 constables based in sixty-seven stations.[174]

Members of the Civic Guard experienced hostility in some parts of the county, which was fomented by the republican forces. In February 1923, a sergeant and a guard were held up en route to Tulla; they were robbed by three armed men and stripped of their uniforms. Similar incidents occurred in Killaloe and O'Briensbridge. In March 1923 the Civic Guard station in Broadford was burnt to the ground by a party of armed men. In April the Civic Guard were held up in the Kildysart area; their car was fired upon at Ferguson's Hill, and they were stripped of their trench coats by armed men. This was the second time that the Civic Guard had been attacked in the vicinity of Kildysart. In June, midway between O'Callaghan's Mills and Broadford, two members of the Civic Guard stationed at Broadford, Mulroy and Donnellan, were attacked by two armed and masked men carrying a shotgun and a revolver. One of the men fired the shotgun and struck Donnellan on the head. Mulroy grappled with the man holding the revolver and disarmed him after the revolver failed to shoot. The attackers escaped, leaving the revolver. A house newly occupied by the Civic Guard at Strand Line, Kilkee was damaged during an armed attack by republicans on 29 November 1922. A house occupied by the Civic Guard at O'Briensbridge was destroyed on 27 December 1922. In July 1924 twelve armed and masked men raided the Civic Guard station at Loughraney, Feakle; after threatening the police they stole four police bicycles.[175]

Besides the new police force, the government also established a new courts system to replace the British judicial establishment of resident magistrates, justices of the peace and petty sessions courts. New district courts were established in each county. In Clare they were established in Ennis, Ennistymon, Kilrush, Killaloe, Scariff, Sixmilebridge and Tulla. The resident magistrates of the twenty-six counties of the Free State were informed at the end of August 1921 that their tenure of office was ending in January 1922. The first new district justice to be appointed in Clare was Justice Dermot Gleeson from Tipperary. Gleeson was a distinguished historian and lived at Carnelly House, Clarecastle. He held a revolver for his own protection during the early years of his office. The first court under the new system was held in Sixmilebridge in late January 1922. The new courts were not welcome in all districts; for example, a premises used as a courthouse at Broadford was destroyed by fire on 16 March 1923.[176]

During the War of Independence and the truce period, there were few instances of non-political crimes. However, matters deteriorated after the treaty was signed; in the period before the deployment of the Civic Guard, there were many instances of petty and more serious crimes, such as armed robberies and murderous agrarian outrages. There were also many attacks on private individuals. Many of these crimes were attributed to anti-Treaty republicans. There were at least fourteen cases of armed robbery at post offices and other locations in Clare between July 1922 and April 1923. One case that was highlighted in the local press was the attempted boycott of a prominent Ennis auctioneer and estate agent, Michael McMahon. There was a suggestion that republicans were involved in the boycott, and Frank Barrett made a rare public statement to the *Clare Champion* refuting the allegation:

> Letter to Mr Michael McMahon: Re attempt to boycott your practice as auctioneer: 1. In connection with the above I can assure you that the ruffians responsible have no connection whatsoever with the Republican movement. To my mind it is the work of some cowardly individual or individuals, who have some private spleen against you, or who wish to further their own ends by this cowardly method of intimidation. 2. The Republican forces in this area shall make every effort to trace the culprits.[177]

During the civil war, there were many instances of politically motivated intimidation and outrage in the county beyond attacks on government forces. Government supporters were attacked and their properties were damaged, allegedly by republicans. Some individuals were also violently assaulted. On Saturday, 13 September 1922, 25 tons of hay belonging to Joseph Hehir, a supporter of the government forces, were destroyed at Labasheeda. On Thursday, 11 January 1923, 50 tons of hay belonging to Thomas Malone of Labasheeda, who was described as a National Army supporter, were destroyed. The family home of Lieutenant Tim McMahon from Miltown Malbay, who was killed while serving with the government forces in Tralee, was also attacked by republicans in September 1922, and 15 tons of hay were burnt 'because of his connection with the army'.

Bart Crowley, a Clare county councillor from Tullagower, was taken from his home in September 1922 by armed men and questioned about matters relating to the Free State. They asked him did he assist Kerry troops to come to Ennis; when he replied 'yes', he was fired at and wounded by pellets. There was also a repetition of the despicable practice of cropping women's hair. In what was described as a 'ruffianly act', two women, Mrs McMahon and her daughter, who were living in a house between Crusheen and Ballinruan, were visited by four masked men; they treated the women shamefully, cutting the hair off each of them. The culprits were not identified or arrested. The motive for the outrageous attack was not mentioned.

At 9 p.m. on 29 December 1922, the home of Patrick Callanan of Dromellihy, Cooraclare was raided by a party of republicans, and his daughter, Mai Callanan, was shot in the foot. The republicans, while on the run, had billeted themselves in Callanan's home for several nights. Mai Callanan was suspected of informing the government troops at Kilrush of the whereabouts of the republicans. This may have been the motivation for the shooting, even though she denied this. One of the perpetrators, William Campbell, was later arrested for the crime.

Among the Joe Barrett Papers is a letter dated 14 February 1923 from GHQ of the Army Executive to Frank Barrett, commandant of the 1st Western Division (republican). Contained in the letter is an inquiry into why the house of Conor Hogan, a Farmers' Party TD supporting the government, was not blown up. The letter also instructed that civilians were to be cautioned against supporting the government, and that the new Civic Guard must not be allowed to function in an area where they have no military support – they were 'to be hampered as much as possible'.[178]

Claims made under the Damage to Property (Compensation) Act, 1923 show that there were at least forty-eight instances of armed robbery undertaken by republicans looking for provisions such as food, drink, milk, boots, shoes, clothing, fuel and cigarettes. When the republicans occupied Eden Vale as their headquarters between 4 July and 22 July, they procured provisions and other supplies from local businesses, as indicated by the following compensation claims:

Callinan, Sinan, Clarecastle – seizure of provisions and shop goods by armed men between 3 May and 6 July 1922.

Hogan, Anne, Mill St., Ennis – commandeering of bacon by Irregular forces in occupation of Edenvale House, on 21 July 1922.

Honan, Stephen, O'Connell St., Ennis – seizure of bread and flour by Irregular forces in occupation of Eden Vale House, between 6 and 22 July 1922.

McSherry, Ellen, Clarecastle – destruction of house and premises at Clarecastle Police barracks on 1 July 1922.

Minihan, John, Tiermaclane – commandeering of flour and stout at the above address by Patrick McNamara, Quartermaster of the Mid Clare Brigade of the Irregular forces on 15 July 1922 (receipt provided and signed by B. Barrett, Quartermaster, Barracks, Edenvale). Burning and destruction of former RIC Barracks at the same address [Tiermaclane] by persons unknown on 13 April 1922.

O'Dea, John, Clarecastle – commandeering of beds, bed clothing, petrol and property by Irregular forces from 3 July 1922 to 6 July 1922; occupation of houses at same address by National Army forces and damage to said houses during an attack on National Army by Irregular forces on 24 August and 27 August 1922.

Bredin, John, Market St., Ennis – seizure of bacon and shop goods on 7 July 1922 by Irregular forces.

Butler, James, Parnell St., Ennis – meat supplied to Mid-Clare Brigade of the Irregular forces, Ennis from 23 May 1922 till 27 June 1922.[179]

The records of the Damage to Property (Compensation) Act, 1923 show that most of these stolen goods and provisions were seized by republicans during July 1922. These records also reveal that while robberies occurred throughout the county, most of the thefts occurred in the greater Ennis area. Significant numbers of thefts also occurred in Kilrush, Kilkee and Mullagh. These documents also highlight the fact that the republicans in the Ennis area were commandeering goods as early as April 1922, when they took over several public buildings in the mid-Clare area. There are only two instances in which the claimants state that the republican forces provided signed receipts:

> Seizure of motor cycle at Ennistymon on 6 May 1922, receipt provided and signed by P McNamara, Quartermaster.

The following is the second instance:

> Tiermaclane – commandeering of flour and stout at the above address by Patrick McNamara, Quartermaster of the Mid Clare Brigade of the Irregular forces on 15 July 1922 (receipt provided and signed by B. Barrett, Quartermaster, Barracks, Edenvale).[180]

The vast majority of the seizures or destruction of property were carried out by unidentified armed and masked raiders. They were usually described in the compensation claims as 'armed Irregulars' or 'persons unknown'. However, there were six instances in which the people who had allegedly carried out the armed raids were named:

1   seizure of cigarettes and goods from M Carmody, Labasheeda, by armed Irregulars under command of Connors on 15 December 1922.

2   seizure of drapery goods at Culligan's Kilrush, by two Irregulars, James Mahony of Knockerra, Kilrush and Martin Shanahan, Doonbeg, on 28 July 1922.

3   Occupation and damage to house at Castle Lloyd, Merton Square, Kilkee, belonging to Stephen Duggan, by Irregulars under command of Joseph McNamara, and commandeering of

motor cars at Kilkee by Irregulars including Mr McInerney of Kilferagh and Thomas Lillis of Tarmon up to 30 August 1922.

4   seizure of boat by armed men, one of them was Sonny Connors of Kildysart village, between 1 and 5 July 1922.

5   seizure of household effects etc. at Kiltannon, Tulla, by Irregulars under command of Brigadier General M Moloney on 3 May 1922.

6   seizure of hardware goods at Francis St Kilrush by Irregulars in occupation of Kilrush between 2 June 1922 and 6 July 1922 under the command of Martin Shanahan, Simon McInerney, P Cooper and John Hogan.[181]

While the vast majority of the compensation claims for damage to property (excluding land agitation) were attributed to 'Irregular forces', there were seven instances where the offences were allegedly caused by the 'National Army'. John Egan of Athlunkard claimed for the occupation of, and damage done to, a cottage by the National Army between 11 and 31 July 1922; Mary Goodwin claimed for the seizure of a car by the National Army at Parteen on 15 July 1922; Frank Lyons of High Street, Ennis stated that the National Army commandeered his car on 7 July 1922; John McMahon of Cragbrien claimed for the seizure of a bicycle by the National Army on 27 September 1922; Ellie O'Callaghan of O'Briensbridge claimed for the occupation and destruction of premises by the National Army on 15 September 1922. Ironically, Marcus Patterson of Clifden House, Corofin claimed for the destruction of the former RIC barracks in Ennis by the National Army on 1 July and 3 July 1922. This was clearly a mistake, as the building had been burnt by the evacuating republicans. Finally, Leonard Wilson of Miltown Malbay claimed that his premises was damaged by gunfire from National Army forces on 17 November 1922.[182]

The Damage to Property (Compensation) Act, 1923 also gives us a comprehensive insight into the wanton destruction of public buildings by the republicans during the civil war. A total of twenty-four public buildings were destroyed by the republican forces during the civil war, the majority of them during July and August 1922.

Frustrated by the success of the government forces, the republicans destroyed the public buildings, allegedly 'to prevent them being used by their opponents'.

Local administration

With the government focused on survival and more than half of its revenue allocated to raising and funding an army, local administration suffered. Clare County Council had major difficulty in raising revenue to fund its activities, such as road repairs and paying for the support of patients and the salaries and wages of staff at the mental hospital in Ennis and the workhouses in Kilrush, Ennis, Killaloe and Ennistymon. Some members of the public refused to pay their rates for political reasons. In response to this major financial crisis, Michael Brennan, chairman of Clare County Council, issued the following warning:

> Clare County Council – demand for payment of Rates. The Council has received information that certain persons are objecting to and refusing to pay their rates, thereby evading their legal responsibilities. Notice is given that all outstanding arrears must be paid by 25 March 1923. Any person failing to comply with the terms of this notice will have the rates collected by force, M Brennan, Chairman.[183]

One prominent Kilkee farmer, T. Falvey, the president of the West Clare Executive of the Clare Farmers' Union, was arrested for making a speech in Kildysart in which he allegedly told the audience not to pay any rates. He was sent to Limerick Jail for a few weeks. Another difficulty in raising funds for the council was that rent and rate collectors were being intimidated and robbed. For example, J. Kett of Kilkee was held up and robbed of a large amount of money by armed and masked men after Mass at Cree. Because of the threats to rate collectors, they had to have an armed army escort while carrying out their collections. Corporal Green and four soldiers accompanied J. Kett on his visits to places such as Kilmihil and Mullagh to collect the overdue rates on 19 May and 22 May 1923.[184]

As a consequence of the shortage of local revenue, the council had to introduce cutbacks in services. They had to lay off many workers, especially the lowly paid road workers who faced great hardship because of the funding crisis. An issue of the *Saturday Record* from March 1922 criticised the non-payment of rates:

> The roads in the county are in a deplorable state, apart altogether from the malicious damage to them for so-called strategic purposes, practically all the road workers in the county have been laid off as there is no money to pay their wages as people refuse to pay their lawful rates, more than 600 men are now idle and on the dole.

The *Saturday Record* of September 1923 reported that the rate warrants for the year 1922–1923 were £204,000, of which only £99,000 had been lodged by Thursday, 18 September 1923, leaving a deficit of £105,000. The *Saturday Record* stated that because of this debt nurses had not been paid for nine months and labouring work could not be provided for poor labouring men.

It seems that the farmers, by far the largest body of ratepayers in the county, were the main culprits. Richard J. Stacpoole of Eden Vale wrote an open letter to the Clare Farmers' Union in January 1923 appealing to them to pay their rates:

> As an old member who helped to establish your Union in Clare [...] I appeal to you to re-consider your decision to withhold payment of rates. You say that there is an enormous amount of old unpaid rates outstanding and that you have taken this step to compel the County Council to enforce payment of these [...] I hold no brief for the Council, but we all know the difficulties they have to contend with. Will what you are doing make it easier for them to collect those unpaid rates?

The Catholic Church and the civil war
The Catholic hierarchy in Ireland had strongly supported the Treaty as the best possible deal, and they condemned the anti-Treaty republicans when they took up arms against the Provisional Government. Patrick Murray states:

> In the division on the Treaty, it is not surprising that the Catholic Church leadership upheld the more moderate point of view, which was also the majority one. There could never be any question of the Church using its authority in support of a political minority, or of denying legitimacy to those who expressed the national will. Even before the Treaty was approved by the Dáil on 6 January 1922, it was clear that a substantial majority

favoured this view [...] There was considerable emphasis on the need to ensure that the national will, or what Bishop Fogarty called 'the considered judgement of the nation,' be taken into account by Dáil deputies when they voted. Dr Fogarty argued that rejection of the Treaty by the Dáil in the face of the massive public demand for its ratification would be 'morally wrong' and a 'negation of representative democracy.'[185]

In August 1922, the Catholic primate of Ireland, Cardinal Logue, issued a warning that threatened the republicans with excommunication:

> The country welcomed the terms of the Treaty but then a faction arose and flouted the Government. This faction had now developed into brigandage until there was no law or order in many parts of the country. Outrages had been committed on retired policemen, I deplore this conduct. I give an excommunication warning against anyone committing outrages. In the name of God I appeal to the armed minority to ground their arms.[186]

In October 1922, the Irish Catholic hierarchy issued a pastoral letter appealing for peace, denouncing the republicans for taking up arms against the democratically elected government and threatening them with excommunication:

> Carrying on a system of murder, assassination and destruction in defiance of the law of God and of the state, without any legitimate authority to justify it [...] is morally only a system of murder and assassination of the National forces [...] No one is justified in rebelling against the legitimate Government set up by the nation and acting within its rights [...] Such being Divine Law, the guerrilla warfare now being carried on by the Irregulars is without moral sanction; and therefore the killing of National soldiers in the course of it is murder before God. The seizing of public and private property is robbery [...] all those who participate in such crimes are guilty of grievous sins, and may not be absolved in Confession, nor admitted to Holy Communion if they persist in such evil courses.

Cardinal Logue and twenty-six bishops signed the pastoral letter. The letter was published in all the national and local newspapers, and read at all Masses on Sunday, 22 October 1922.[187]

C.S. Andrews recalled that republicans had contempt for the bishops' pastoral:

We regarded the pastoral as pointless because it was based on the premise that the Staters were the legitimate government – a premise which we did not accept [...] The pastoral had no practical effect in diminishing IRA resistance. I heard of only one prominent IRA man who was also a leading light in one of the great Limerick Confraternities, who submitted. I know of no member of the rank and file who did. But I know of a great number of the rank and file who left the Church and I know of a great number of both leaders and rank and file who never went back.[188]

Bishop Fogarty, formerly an enthusiastic advocate of de Valera, Sinn Féin and the Volunteers during the War of Independence, became one of the most bitter ecclesiastical opponents of de Valera and the anti-Treaty republicans. Murray opines, 'Fogarty's post-Treaty anti-Republicanism tended to focus on de Valera to an almost pathological degree.'[189] Pádraig Óg Ó Ruairc, a historian, takes a strong anti-clerical view of the role of the Catholic Church during the period of the Treaty debates and civil war:

the pastoral now asserted the moral authority of majority rule under the Free State government as a tenet of Christian morality [...] but the majority of republicans resented the corrupt use of religious authority for political purposes [...] the Catholic Church still sided with the rich and powerful against those who had fought for Irish freedom.[190]

On Monday, 18 December 1922, Bishop Fogarty, in his annual address to the pupils and parents of St Flannan's College, was quoted as saying:

These are sorrowful, but wonderful days [...] The Irish people must obey the Government [...] Ireland is your own, the Government set up here is your own, and do your best to see that the Government will do what is right. But, treat any assault or attempt to smash the government as a sacrilege and an outrage upon the sacred altar of national freedom.[191]

Bishop Fogarty's pastoral letter, issued in February 1923, strongly denounced the republicans as fanatics, not patriots:

The lamentable condition of our country, hacked to pieces by some of its own people, has overwhelmed us with shame and sorrow [...] patriotism for some people seems dead and the vile passions of revenge and hatred have taken its place, Ireland is now threatened by the tyranny of crime. What is the motive? Is it the establishment of an Irish Republic? Why, it is on record that their own leaders do not believe that it is possible. But to wreck Ireland because we cannot get everything we would like to have is fanaticism, not patriotism. What can be gained by this horrible and horrifying campaign of violence? Is it mere revenge and personal ambition? If we believe in government by the people, let us bury our weapons and pay our debts to society and help to maintain law and order. Let us rise and renounce violence and faction and love our country.

Countess Markievicz, TD, a republican socialist and a convert to the Catholic Church, denounced Bishop Fogarty for his support of the government. Markievicz had been sentenced to death for her role as a captain in the Citizen Army during the 1916 Rising, she had canvassed in East Clare for de Valera during the by-election of 1917, she was elected as an MP in 1918 but refused to take her seat in the House of Commons, she was appointed Minister for Labour in the First Dáil, and she strongly opposed the Treaty as a betrayal of the republic. In a letter to the *Irish Independent*, she castigated Dr Fogarty and criticised him and the Catholic Church for opposing the republicans:

> When a priest descends from his high altar to try and lead his flock on one side or the other in a political election, he puts himself in the position of being a politician and every layman has the right to criticise him as a politician and to protest against dragging the Church we all love and revere down to the hustings for the purpose of influencing voters [...] Dr Fogarty states that the government has raised Ireland from anarchy, I challenge that statement as untrue. Anarchy was created in Ireland when the 'Pact for Peace' was broken, the mandate of the people ignored and directly after the election [of June 1921], before any parliament at all had been summoned, the clique of the Free Staters took over the English guns and attacked the Four Courts under orders from England.

> Dr Fogarty goes on to tell the people that if they want peace and ordered government they will only get it by setting up a strong government, i.e., the present Murder Government [...] No bishop has raised his voice against the shooting of prisoners [...] They have refused the Sacraments to men and women because they stood true to their principles.

Bishop Cauchon of Beauvais and other French aristocrats joined with the English to excommunicate and to burn St Joan of Arc. Our bishops are very little removed form Bishop Cauchon [...] We regret these actions of theirs, for a long-suffering people have not lost their faith, although Fr Murphy was excommunicated in 1798, although the bishops helped to pass the Act of Union, broke up the Young Ireland Movement, hounded Parnell to death and excommunicated the Fenians.

I write this letter fully understanding the responsibility I take when I speak in critical terms of a bishop. I speak as a Catholic, with regret, but as a simple duty, believing that the Church is best served by her children standing for truth and honour, and forcing their clergy to conform to the principles laid down by the Holy Father during the Great War.[192]

Mortality in the civil war

Despite Michael Hopkinson's assertion that Clare played a small part in the civil war, at least thirty-five people associated with the county were killed, either in the county or outside of it, during the ten months of the conflict; many others were wounded during the war and subsequently died prematurely. At least nineteen government soldiers were killed; thirteen republicans were killed, five by execution. Also, several combatants died at a relatively young age after enduring hardships during the War of Independence and civil war, including some who suffered poor health from the effects of hunger strikes. At least one civilian, Albert O'Brien from Kilfenora, was killed during the conflict. Also, on 25 November 1922, there was an armed raid by republicans on Ballyvaughan post office. During this raid, the postmistress, Ms Grant, collapsed and died. During the republican attack on the West Clare Railway station at Quilty in January, the father of the stationmaster allegedly died of a heart attack.

Two Clare men died during the early days of the conflict in Dublin. One was Joe Considine of Clooney, who was among the republicans occupying the Four Courts; he was seriously wounded by the shelling on the first day of the conflict and died of his wounds at Jervis Street Hospital later that day. He was the first casualty of the war. Some days later, Captain Michael Vaughan of Moughna, Ennistymon, who worked for the Ordnance Survey Department of the government forces, was shot dead in an ambush on Leeson Street, Dublin on Wednesday, 4 July.[193]

Four republicans died in the early phase of the conflict in Clare, between July and August 1922. Sean O'Halloran, from Crusheen, was wounded in an engagement with government troops between Ennis and Gort; he died of his wounds on Friday, 17 July. Patrick O'Dea was seriously injured in an attack a mile outside Kilrush while repulsing government soldiers on 14 July; he died of his wounds in Kilrush hospital on 15 July. His last words reputedly were, 'I am glad I am dying for the Republic, lads.' His interment took place in his native parish of Doonbeg. Kildysart barracks was attacked by republicans on 6 August. According to an official government report published in the local newspapers, 'under cover of darkness a bomb was thrown at the sentry, who threw it back and injured four of the attackers who were arrested at the scene.' One of the republicans, John O'Gorman of Doonbeg, died as a result of his injuries on 11 August; a second republican, John (Sean) McSweeney, died a few weeks later in hospital. Pádraig Óg Ó Ruairc states that the republicans crept towards the barracks to plant a mine, but it exploded prematurely, seriously wounding the two men. However, Maurice 'Moss' Twomey, an ex-IRA chief of staff, writing in the 1930s, states that John O'Gorman and Sean McSweeney were blown up by a 'trap mine' set close to the barracks. Ó Ruairc also records that a government soldier named Patrick Kelly was killed by the IRA at Kilrush on 22 August.[194]

Besides these victims, John Neville from Lisdoonvarna was shot dead in Killester, Dublin. His head and body were riddled with bullets; his body was found in a graveyard. On Monday, 9 April 1923, a farmer's son named Martin Moloney, 21 years old, from Cloontymara, Inagh, a captain in the local battalion during the War of Independence, was shot dead in controversial circumstances. A party of government soldiers surrounded the farmhouse and tried to arrest two brothers, Martin and Thomas Moloney. Both men ran away, and several shots were fired; Martin Moloney was hit and fatally wounded. The dying man accused a soldier named Collins of shooting him, but Collins denied it, stating that a soldier named Foody had fired the shot. At the inquest, Captain Touhy stated that he had fired a shot at the fleeing men. His brother Thomas refused to give evidence but said, 'Enough has happened and I am not going to say anything. It might have happened by accident all that did happen.' The jury at the inquest returned a verdict that Martin Moloney had been shot by government troops. Ó Ruairc states that Captain Martin Moloney was 'murdered' by government troops.[195]

One republican attack that was widely condemned occurred when a Red Cross ambulance transporting a patient from Kildysart to Ennis was fired upon and the driver, Private Patrick Comer from Ballinasloe, was mortally wounded. The *Clare Champion* described it as follows:

> a desperate, cowardly attack was made on unarmed soldiers in a Red Cross van by a party of about 20 irregulars on 20 August. The driver, Private Comer, aged about 25, from Ballinasloe, was fatally wounded. This attack provoked universal abhorrence and condemnation, an exceptional brutal and in-humane act, which must disgrace those cowardly men who took part. It is the custom in every army that members of the Red Cross do not carry arms. They were ambushed about 6 miles from Ennis on the Kildysart Road. About 20 rifle shots were fired at about 6 p.m. in the afternoon. The attackers wore trench coats and some had hats, they were cowardly men to fire upon an ambulance, a callous act. it was about 10 p.m. by the time Fr. Considine arrived from Ennis. Private Comer was admitted to hospital in Ennis about 10.30 p.m., but he died next day. The jury returned a verdict of wilful murder of Private Comer by a person or persons unknown, who fired upon him while driving a Red Cross ambulance on 21 August.[196]

In another controversial killing, Lieutenant Michael Considine was fatally wounded by republicans while carrying out operations at Lickeen in the Ennistymon district. The *Saturday Record* stated, 'one of the republicans raised a white flag, indicating that they were going to surrender, and then they disgracefully opened fire fatally wounding the officer [...] the Irregulars also fired upon the Red Cross ambulance proceeding to the scene, a despicable act.' Lieutenant Considine died in Ennis hospital. He was a native of Lisdoonvarna and was commandant of Ennistymon district. Seán Enright mentions the controversial killing of Nicholas Corcoran, a republican prisoner who was shot dead in Clare by Sergeant Boyle of the government forces. Corcoran was part of a prisoner work party that was assembled to clear barricades from roads. The prisoners apparently declined to work, and after some warning shots, Boyle hit and mortally wounded Corcoran. Boyle was tried at the Green Street courthouse in Dublin, and he was unanimously found not guilty of murder by a jury.[197]

Several Clare-born men who were members of the government forces were killed in actions outside of the county during the civil war. One of the first to be killed was Private P.J. Walsh, a native of Bodyke; he was killed during the fighting in Galway city on 4 July. Private Thomas Hartigan of Moymore, Ennistymon was killed in an ambush while serving with the government forces at Ballinasloe. He was shot and seriously wounded at 1.45 a.m. on 15 July and died of his wounds in a Dublin hospital. Another young casualty of the conflict was Private Joseph McEnery of Clonroadmore, Ennis, who was killed while serving with the government forces during the battle of Limerick. The body of Lieutenant Lee, a native of Kilrush, was buried at Glasnevin; he died as a result of injuries received at Clondrohid, Co. Cork in September. Private J. Moloney, who died at Limerick from wounds received there in October, was buried at Kilmurry Ibricane. Also in October, Corporal W. McNamara of Bunratty was shot dead by a sniper at Meelick, Co. Galway. Finally, Sergeant Denis Minogue, from Scariff, was killed in the fight at Ballineen, Co. Cork; he was buried in Scariff.[198]

Following the government's success in Limerick, and having secured military control in the main towns of Clare by driving out the republicans from Kilkee and Kilrush, the battle-hardened soldiers from the 1st Western Division helped to end the war in Kerry. At 3 a.m. on 3 August, the SS *Corona* and three small boats sailed from Kilrush to Tarbert with 240 soldiers drawn from the 1st Western Division, joining with other government divisions to help defeat the republicans in Kerry. At least six Clare men serving with the government forces were killed in military engagements with the republicans in Kerry. Private John Quane, from Meelick, was killed at Listowel on 17 August 1922; Private P. Connors, from Ennistymon, was killed by a landmine at Ballyseedy Woods on 28 August; and Captain Donal Lehane, from Lahinch, was killed during the siege of Killorglin on 27 September. Captain Lehane was the last male member of his family; his father and brother were shot by the Black and Tans after the Rineen ambush. In late August two other Clare men were killed by a landmine in Kerry: Lieutenant Tim McMahon, 25 years old, from Miltown Malbay, and Sergeant Michael Roche, from Connolly. On 29 December 1922, Private John Talty of Lisdeen was shot dead at Castlegregory, Co. Kerry. Though they suffered ten casualties in Kerry (including four accidental deaths), the 1st Western Division were not associated with the controversial reprisal massacres in Kerry, such as the Ballyseedy massacre of 7 July 1923, which was attributed to the Dublin Guards Brigade.[199]

Four other government soldiers were killed in Clare between November 1922 and April 1923. Lieutenant Michael Keane, from Kildysart, was mortally wounded while the government forces were carrying out a sweep in the Tullycrine area on 6 November, and he died at the scene. According to the *Clare Champion*, 'his comrades were refused admittance to bring the dying soldier into a house.' His body was brought by motor launch from Cappa to Kildysart. In Killaloe, at a dance held on the night of 18 November, shots were fired from a Catholic chapel about 33 yards from the hall; at 12.30 p.m. a Thompson machine gun and about thirty rifles poured a hail of lead into the ballroom, killing Sergeant Manaphone. An *Irish Independent* reporter noted sarcastically, 'The hall was attacked because six Free State soldiers were dancing there [...] For two years during the terror, this same hall was used by the Black and Tans and military for dances once or twice a week, but never a shot was fired.' On Tuesday evening, 16 January, the government army garrison at Kilmihil was sniped by republicans and Private Pat Nugent of Bodyke was shot dead. One report in the *Saturday Record* alleged, 'Kilmihil is said to be the hot-bed of the Irregular movement in Clare. The sympathy of the people is completely against the troops, who have often been refused for a drink of water. Even a pillow to put under the head of the dying soldier, Pat Nugent was refused.' Finally, Private Stephen Canty, 21 years old and a native of Causeway, Co. Kerry, was part of a military detachment patrolling the town of Ennis on Saturday night, 21 April, at around 10 p.m.

When the patrol reached the junction of Carmody Street and Drumbiggle Road, at least three revolver shots were fired at them, one of which fatally wounded Private Canty.[200]

Meanwhile, old scores were still being settled and new wounds were festering that long outlived the War of Independence and the civil war. One victim was Patrick Clancy, from Clare. He was a member of the RIC until June 1921 and was shot dead in Cork in October 1922. Another ex-RIC man from Clare was lucky to escape with his life after he returned to visit his relatives in west Clare in September 1923. Michael Hennessy, from Moy, came home to visit his family and friends, and, according to the *Clare Champion*, was cautioned several times to quit the country. He was fired at from behind by a party of men armed with revolvers as he entered a pub in Lahinch; several shots were fired, and he was wounded five times. He had not resigned from the RIC until the force was disbanded in April 1922. It is also stated that he had a narrow escape in Miltown Malbay on Race Night. No one was arrested for the attack. He was a brother of Seamus Hennessy, a prominent officer in the republican forces. Seamus denied that Michael had been cautioned to leave. Tragically, a Clare-born member of the Civic Guard, Sergeant James Woods, was shot dead during an attack on the Civic Guard station at Castleisland, Co. Kerry on Tuesday, 3 December 1923. He was a native of Lisdoonvarna, only 22 years old.[201]

Executions

Perhaps the most controversial aspect in this fratricidal war was the government policy of executing republicans, which was introduced in November 1922 and continued until April 1923. Over the course of these months, seventy-seven men were executed. After the execution, under emergency legislation, of the first five republicans, including the leading republican propagandist Erskine Childers in November 1922, the IRA issued a warning to all government TDs that they would take drastic measures if the policy of executing republicans captured with weapons was not ended. Matters escalated when the government introduced even more severe legislation on 30 November, issuing a 'shoot to kill' policy on anybody found in illegal possession of weapons. Following the assassination of Seán Hales, TD by the IRA in Dublin, the government responded by executing four leading republicans who had been seized after the surrender of the Four Courts garrison in July. This illegal execution of four leading republican prisoners, Richard Barrett, Joseph McKelvey, Liam Mellows and Rory O'Connor, was carried out 'as a warning and as a reprisal' for the killing of Seán Hales. The executed men were clearly not responsible for the death of Seán Hales, TD, as they were incarcerated at the time. These executions sent a strong message that the government was determined to end the rebellion; the government introduced even more draconian emergency legislation in the new year, giving the army emergency powers to execute people for relatively minor offences.

Historian Breen Timothy Murphy states:

> the executions policy had a significant impact on the dynamics of the Civil War making it a far more ruthless and divisive affair, moreover it left an enduring legacy of bitterness [...] evidence suggests that the official policy of executions achieved its primary objective and expedited the end of the conflict [...] The public, for the most part, supported the Government and the executions policy. The executions were accepted as a necessary evil to defeat the Irregulars, but if victory was not achieved quickly the support for these executions and the Government would dwindle. Though the executions did in fact achieve its objective, it was not the only factor which hastened the end of the Civil War.[202]

Between August and December 1922, the government introduced tougher measures against the republicans, eventually setting up military tribunals with powers to impose the death penalty on republicans captured with weapons. In August General Eoin O'Duffy, general officer commanding of the South West Command, issued the following communiqué:

> I give notice that the troops under my command have definite orders to fire upon any person destroying bridges, railway lines, telegraph or telephone lines, obstructing public roads, felling trees or cutting trenches, looting or destroying private property, and to place under arrest for trial by court martial all persons aiding or abetting such wanton destruction and looting.

Judge Seán Enright contends that the government's execution policy under the guiding principle of *suprema lex, salus populi* (the safety of the people should be the supreme law) when civil law had failed was of dubious legality and a major debasement of the trial system.[203]

C.S. Andrews recalled the deteriorating military position in August 1922 from a republican perspective:

> Apart from the terror, the military situation went from bad to worse. As early as August de Valera realised there was no possibility of winning the war. He wanted to call it off but Liam Lynch made it clear to him that any public action to this end would be repudiated by the Executive and the fighting would continue. By now, the bitterness and hatred the Republicans had towards the Free State regime had reached a point when nothing short of total defeat would have induced them to give up the struggle. It required an accentuation of the terror which in turn heightened the motivating forces of bitterness and hostility before that defeat was accomplished.[204]

Around this time, many were arrested during round-ups in Clare. They were offered their freedom if they signed an undertaking to renounce violence against the government. The following *Clare Champion* report from west Clare suggests that many of those arrested did take up the government offer:

> In Clare, there has been little doing except rounding up. In Cooraclare district nine members of a road cutting party were arrested. A large number of prisoners have been released upon signing undertakings not to take part in further actions with the irregulars against the government. The undertaking read as follows: 'I promise that I will not use arms against the Parliament elected by the Irish people or the Government responsible for the time being to that parliament, and that I will not support in any way any such action, nor will I interfere with the property or persons of others.'[205]

One of those arrested was Con McMahon of Clooney, who was captured on 11 September 1922. According to a report issued by the military authorities in Ennis, McMahon gave an undertaking not to escape from hospital, where he was being treated for injuries. However, as the following published report suggests, he allegedly dishonoured this undertaking:

Statement from Div HQ, Ennis: On 11/9/22 Con McMahon of Clooney, Ennis was arrested and conveyed to the Home Barracks. At the time of his arrest it was found that he was wounded in the leg. On 12 September he was removed to Ennis District Hospital after signing the following undertaking: I pledge my solemn word of honour that I will not attempt to escape, or allow others to take me from hospital without the permission of Commandant General Brennan. No guard was placed over Con McMahon while being treated in the district hospital and on Sunday night he took his departure. As a result of the prisoner dishonouring his undertakings, wounded prisoners will in future be sent to military hospitals only.[206]

Early in October the government offered a full amnesty and pardon to all who had taken part in armed rebellion against the state who surrendered their arms on or before 15 October 1922. They also established military courts to deal with republicans captured with firearms. The order was signed by General Richard Mulcahy of the Army Council on 2 October.

On 4 November 1922 at a meeting of Clare County Council, Councillor Denis McMahon proposed the following motion, which was seconded by Councillor Thomas McGrath:

That we, Clare County Council, again reiterate the terms of peace of the people of this country-

1 the handing in of all arms by the Irregulars on the call of the National Government.

2 Renunciation of the principle of armed resistance to the will of the people.

3 Absolute and unswerving allegiance to the People's Government and the acceptance of the national constitution implemented under the Treaty.

We call on the Government to speed-up their methods of restoring law and order in the country, and save us from economic, social, and political ruin.

It is quite apparent to us that the Government has not used its powers to the full in meeting the armed attack, which has been made on the elemental right of a people to choose its own methods towards achieving independence. In the coldness of a well-considered judgement, we say, 'get on with the work, or get out!'

The motion was adopted, with two councillors dissenting, Councillor James D. Kenny and Councillor John O'Dwyer.

In December the government introduced sterner legislation and issued the following proclamation, threatening death to any person found in possession of arms without proper authority:

> A conspiracy exists to assassinate the members of the nation's parliament and has already claimed two victims. To safeguard the lives of the people's representatives, to safeguard the life of the nation itself, the sternest measures are necessary and will be adopted. Any person found in possession of a bomb, dynamite or gelignite, any gun, revolver, rifle or lethal weapon without the proper authority shall be liable to suffer death or other such punishment as a committee of army officers shall think fit. The confirming authority will be two members of the Army Council.[207]

In response to these draconian laws, General Liam Lynch, chief of staff of the IRA, issued a letter to all battalions instructing them to shoot on sight all Provisional Government ministers who voted for the 'Murder Bill'. The letter also advocated for the destruction of houses belonging to government supporters and for all active and aggressive Free State officers who supported the bill to be shot on sight.[208]

In December several prominent republicans were arrested during round-ups in Clare. Among them was Bernard Barrett of Bearnageeha, 'one of the leaders of the Irregulars in Clare' and a brother of Frank Barrett. Another was Pat 'Pappy' Costello, 'a well-known Irregular and brother-in-law of Frank Barrett arrested during a round-up in Darragh'. Eleven republicans were arrested in early January in places such as Kilmaley, Ballinruan, Feakle, Liscannor, Kilfera, Cahermurphy, Tulla and Moyasta. Significantly, the *Saturday Record* report stated that two of the men were captured with arms: Denis McGrath, from Kilferagh, who was found to be in possession of a rifle, revolver and ammunition; and Joseph Egan, from Cahermurphy, found in possessions of a revolver and ammunition. These men were lucky not to have been sentenced to death under the new legislation.[209]

On the weekend of 13–14 January 1923, there was widespread destruction of the railway network in Clare. Government forces carried out extensive searches in the Clooney–Carrahan district on 15 January – Ardsollus railway station, which was in that district, was one of the stations that had been extensively damaged. The soldiers found a dug-out near Carrahan, which held four republicans: Con and Vincent McMahon, Paddy Hennessy and John Darcy. The military report of the arrests on 15 January states:

> Search in Clooney–Carrahan district [...] Troops searched districts and found four Irregulars in a dugout. 52 rds amm[unition] found nearby. One of the prisoners attempted to escape. He was fired at and wounded and re-captured. Arrests, Clooney and Carrahan, Con and Vincent MacMahon, Carrahan, Patk. Hennessy, Clooney and John Darcy, Cooraclare, all active Irregulars, were arrested in a dug-out with 52 rds of .303 ammunition.[210]

The charges against the four captured republicans were extremely serious, as all four of them could have been sentenced to death for possession of arms. Though they were unarmed in the dug-out, fifty-two rounds of ammunition were found in a nearby haystack. The discovery of the ammunition was the tenuous evidential factor that led to their conviction. It seems that the government decided to make an example of two of the men, Con McMahon and Paddy Hennessy. Rather than execute two brothers, they chose to shoot one of them, Con McMahon. One reason for this may have been his departure from Ennis Hospital after allegedly signing an undertaking not to do so without the permission of Commandant General Michael Brennan.

John Darcy may have been spared because two of his brothers had already died during the War of Independence: Michael was drowned while fleeing from the RIC after an ambush in February 1920, while Patrick was shot as an alleged spy by the IRA in June 1921. According to Seán Enright, John Darcy attempted to escape and was seriously injured. He was sent to the medical officer at Limerick prison and was then kept in the main prison compound. Knowing that Darcy could be executed, the other prisoners hid him in a clothes press. In the late spring of 1923, John Darcy escaped from the prison, via a tunnel, along with about thirty other prisoners.

Thus, only Paddy Hennessy and Con McMahon were charged, tried and found guilty by a military court in Limerick. They were executed on 20 January 1923. The government issued an official statement on the matter:

> Cornelius [Con] McMahon and Patrick Hennessy, both of Clooney, Ennis, were arrested on Tuesday 16th January at Carrahan, they were tried on a charge of being in possession of arms and ammunition without proper authority, being implicated in the destruction of the railway at Ardsollus station on Sunday 14th and further, with being in possession of articles taken from Ardsollus station on the same date. Both prisoners were found guilty and sentenced to death. The sentence was carried out at Limerick this morning, 20 January 1923 at 8 am.[211]

The death of these two republicans, the first Clare men to be executed by the Irish government, was controversial. The executions were carried out as an exemplary deterrent to encourage other Clare republicans to give up the military campaign and show that the government was determined to carry out the severe policies to end the war. The military trial, like the trials that the IRA held before they executed the three 'spies' during the War of Independence in Clare, was unsatisfactory, to say the least. The men would hardly have been found guilty in a normal criminal court. On the night before his execution, Paddy Hennessy wrote several farewell letters to his family and friends in which he declared his innocence but forgave his enemies, 'even those who swore my life away':

> County Jail, Limerick,
> Friday night [19 January 1923]
>
> Dear John and all the boys,
>
> You hardly know that Con [McMahon] and I are to be executed at 8 o'clock on tomorrow morning. We were tried by court martial, found guilty and sentenced to death [...] We were tried at midnight on Wednesday night, called from our cells where we were asleep, got no chance to defend ourselves. Found guilty on frivolous evidence, of course our lives are sworn away. But we are dying for Ireland, still true to the Republic to the last; money could not buy us [...] As for me I am in the best of cheer and expect to face death like a soldier; a true Irish one.
>
> I forgive my enemies, even those who swore my life away. I

forgive them from the bottom of my heart, for as well as me, there is a God to judge them [...] I am in right good cheer, knowing that I am going to Heaven [...] They can only kill my body, my spirit will still live [...] do not shed tears for me. If you do, let them be tears of joy. For there is joy in my heart tonight, knowing that I will be with God tomorrow night [...] Patrick Hennessy.

In another letter to his sister Theresa, he wrote, 'When arrested there was nothing on us, but afterwards the military found some stuff in a cock of hay and charged us with it but we are innocent [...] I have never fired as much as a shot at anybody and that is a great consolation going before my God.' And in a third letter to his girlfriend, Jenny, he wrote, 'We are dying as martyrs for Ireland [...] and I expect to face death like a soldier and a true Irishman.'[212]

Liam Deasy's appeal

General Liam Deasy, deputy chief of staff of the Army Executive, was captured on 18 January 1923 and sentenced to death. However, he requested an interview with the commander-in-chief of the government forces, General Richard Mulcahy. Following this meeting, Liam Deasy's life was spared, as he agreed to make the following statement in a letter sent to each member of the Army Executive, urging them to end the conflict:

> I accept and I will aid in immediate and unconditional surrender of all arms and men as required by General Mulcahy. In pursuance of this undertaking, I am asked to appeal for a similar undertaking and acceptance from the following: E de Valera, P Ruttledge, A Stack, D O'Callaghan, L Lynch, C Moloney, T Derrig, F Aiken, F Barrett, T Barry, S McSweeney, S Robinson, H Murphy, S Donovan, and F McCarthy, and for the immediate and unconditional surrender of all those associated with them together with their arms and ammunition.

This appeal was published by the government in the national and local papers. The republican prisoners at Limerick and Clonmel also signed a statement seeking an end to the conflict, 'It has gone far enough and ought to stop now [...] we are unanimously resolved that the present struggle has developed into a war of extermination and a waste of blood.'[213]

Frank Barrett received the confidential letter from Liam Deasy at the end of January and, having considered Deasy's request, made the following reply to his appeal:

> I received on 31 January 1923 your confidential communication of 30 January 1923, with a copy of your undertaking to General Mulcahy and the promise by you to help in securing the immediate and unconditional surrender of all arms and men. The receipt of your communication came to me not alone as a surprise, but had a most bewildering effect on me [...] I have to say here that whatever I may think about the prudence of your action in giving your guarantee to General Mulcahy, I have the most profound respect for your material display of absolute contempt for death. None of your comrades can deny your extraordinary physical courage, now I believe that no one on earth can deny you are possessed of extraordinary moral courage [...] You had an enviable career and record as a soldier of the Republic, you have made tremendous sacrifices for the sacred cause of freedom, but to my mind, you have in this action, made a sacrifice more supreme [...]
>
> In pursuance of this undertaking you appeal amongst others for a similar undertaking of acceptance. My reply is: (a) As an officer of the Irish Republican Army I will act as a soldier with his army and not act as an individual. (b) As a member of the Executive of the Irish Republican Army, I have no right whatever, in view of the terms of our constitution; in view of the terms of certain resolutions passed by the Executive from time to time, to give such an undertaking on behalf of the Army, or any unit or portion of the Army and I will not do it [...] signed, Frank Barrett, O/C 1st Western Division.

Remarkably, General Michael Brennan also praised Liam Deasy's moral courage, 'Liam Deasy's moral action after his capture was the greatest act of moral courage I have known in my life.'[214]

Also in response to Deasy's appeal, Frank Barrett, as commandant of the republican 1st Western Division, corresponded with General Liam Lynch, on the matter:

> Until recent developments [Deasy's surrender appeal and the end of the hunger strike in Limerick Jail] I had no doubt but we could have defeated the Free State army and compelled the Free State army to capitulate. My hopes of doing this are not all that bright. Anyhow, to do so will exhaust all our last resources and England

is there always. We cannot now join the Free State army in anything. What then is going to defeat England?[215]

In succeeding letters, Frank Barrett conveyed the response of the Volunteers of the republican 1st Western Division to General Liam Lynch. In these letters, he stated that the ranks were demoralised by Deasy's appeal, yet he expressed a hard-line view and was highly critical of, and dismissive of, de Valera's Document No 2:

> The publication of these documents, coupled with the action of the Limerick and Clonmel prisoners has produced a very demoralising effect on all ranks [...] There has been no surrender, as far as I know, of a single man or weapon [...] As result of what appeared in Saturday's Irish Independent from de Valera's Document No. 2 and from Miss McSwiney [an uncompromising republican and sister of the hunger-striking martyr Terence MacSwiney] I feel a bit at sea regarding what the Government [the republican government led by de Valera] stands for [...] You know that it is not for Document No. 2 or compromise between parties that men are in the field. If the republic is to be compromised in any way I will immediately surrender unconditionally and order all ranks in the area to do likewise.

Ten days later, in another letter, Frank Barrett suggested that the republicans were demoralised and should make an orderly retreat from the field of battle:

> The publication of the President's interview [de Valera's Document No. 2] together with Miss McSwiney's letter was doing our cause more harm than any of the other events [...] the people have a frightful contempt for Document No. 2 [...] The country is demoralised and its resources almost exhausted [...] I believe that great numbers of our men will avail of the amnesty and hand in their arms [...] the population generally are in a kind of a 'fog', in expecting peace but not knowing where it's going to come from [...] We cannot compromise under any circumstances [...] you cannot have any agreement other than complete victory or unconditional surrender with the Free State [...] We must attain that objective [achieving a republic], or leave the issue as clear and uncompromised as Pearse left it in 1916. It is soldierly and manly in a given set of circumstances to admit defeat [...] If we are to quit, we must do so as a unit; if our political leaders are to wage a political fight the retreat from the field must be orderly and concerted.

On 2 February 1923, Frank Barrett wrote to General Liam Lynch opposing the policy of burning houses belonging to Free State supporters as reprisals for acts against the republicans, 'The people who supported and kept us during the Anglo-Irish War at such terrible risks, and those who support and keep us now, will all be left homeless, not a just recompense for all they have endured.'[216]

Early in January Bishop Fogarty privately believed that the government was winning the war. Writing to Monsignor Hagan at the Vatican, he stated:

> The Irregulars, as far as the rank and file are concerned, are fast breaking up, and they are dwindling into a mere assassination club, with a few clumps of desperadoes scattered through the country. The rank and file are most anxious for peace, but their leaders are holding out for some trick of their own, which they are hardly likely to get. We may have some troubled months ahead of us, but the worst is over, in my opinion.[217]

After Liam Deasy's appeal to the republicans to call off their campaign, the government issued a proclamation on 8 February, signed by General Richard Mulcahy, announcing a second amnesty:

> Bearing in mind the acceptance by Liam Deasy of an immediate and unconditional surrender of all arms [...] the Government are prepared to offer an amnesty to all persons now in arms against the Government, who, on or before Sunday 18 February 1923 surrender with arms to any officer of the National forces, or through an intermediary surrender before 18 February.

In response to the government proclamation, the GHQ of the Army Executive issued the following statement on 12 February 1923, which suggests that General Liam Lynch was either delusional about the military situation in the country at the time or a hopelessly optimistic, irreconcilable diehard:

> The enemy is making the most of Liam Deasy's document to bring about a split in our army. All officers, will by word and by example do their utmost to prevent unauthorised actions by any Volunteers or sections of Volunteers.
>
> We have the enemy on the run at present and it is very certain, if we present a united front now that our ideals will be fulfilled in a very short time. At the moment, so bad is the enemy position that he is banking all on bringing about a split in our ranks.

I do not wish to issue a definite instruction to you at the moment, but I would ask that you do all in your power to bring off a successful operation. At the moment a few successes all round will counteract the effect of Liam Deasy's Document and will be a fitting answer to the enemy Amnesty offer.

However, about a month later, the Army Executive, growing more desperate, issued General Order No 17, dated 8 March 1923, which instructed each divisional commandant to treat any republican who surrendered himself or his arms to the enemy as a traitor, 'Treachery – From date of this Order, any Volunteer who surrenders himself or any arms to the enemy will be tried by court martial constituted according to usual procedure, on the charge of treachery, and if convicted will be shot.'[218]

Following Liam Deasy's capture and his appeal to the other members of the Army Executive, Bishop Fogarty praised Deasy for encouraging the republicans to lay down their arms in the interests of Ireland:

It is no use appealing to some of the prominent leaders, they listen to nobody and to nothing except themselves. The Limerick prisoners have also appealed for a cessation of violence till nothing is left but blood and ashes. I appeal to the young men in arms with Irish hearts to listen to the prayers of the people and renounce violence, which if persisted in can only ruin Ireland.[219]

The shock execution of Paddy Hennessy and Con McMahon followed by the offer of a second amnesty after Deasy's capture may have prompted some republicans in Clare and elsewhere to give up the struggle. A *Saturday Record* report in early March indicated that republicans in Clare were becoming less active:

For some time past, there has been a marked lull in Irregular activity in South and West Clare. However, it is learnt that none of the Irregulars surrendered any arms or ammunition [this may have been in response to General Order No 17], but it is known that some of them have returned to their homes, with the intention of not taking any action against the Government. One of them informed our correspondent that he was fed up with the whole situation and it was high time to draw the line.[220]

Besides the military casualties on both sides, at least one civilian was killed during the civil war. Albert O'Brien of Kilfenora – an ex-lieutenant in the First World War – was shot dead at Lemanagh on 10 February 1923 while motoring from Kilfenora to Ennis. The *Clare Champion* stated that O'Brien was shot by a government soldier, but Pádraig Óg Ó Ruairc states that O'Brien was accidentally killed by republicans, who mistook him for an officer of the government forces. Ó Ruairc also states that Corporal Martin O'Loughlin, a government soldier, was shot dead on 4 April 1923.[221]

Tragedies in Ennis

Up to April 1923, the people of Ennis had been spared the worst horrors of the civil war; however, in the space of twelve days in late April and early May, the community of Ennis was shocked when four young men were killed in tragic circumstances. One was a government soldier from Kerry, and the three others were young men from Ennis who were blamed and executed for the death of that soldier. These were the last executions during the civil war – though two of the young men were executed on 2 May 1923, two days after the republicans suspended their offensive operations in the country. At every Mass in Ennis cathedral on Sunday, 22 April, the shooting of the soldier was vigorously condemned. Rev. Fr Meade, administrator of Ennis parish, stated that his death had been 'cold-blooded murder!'[222]

This tragic end to the civil war in Clare began on Saturday night, 21 April, when a military patrol was fired upon, and a young soldier, Private Stephen Canty, 21 years old and a native of Kerry, was shot dead on Carmody Street, Ennis at around 10.30 p.m. Apparently, he was due to marry within two weeks. Three revolver shots were allegedly fired at the soldiers, one of them fatally wounding Private Canty. He was the last member of the government forces to be killed during the civil war.[223]

Two Ennis men, Patrick Mahony and John O'Leary, were arrested near the scene and suspected of being involved in the killing. They were present under armed guard at the inquest, which was held at the Home Barracks on Monday, 23 April. John Hunt, a solicitor, represented John O'Leary, but Patrick Mahony was not professionally represented. After some time in the barracks, the jury repaired to the Town Hall, where they recorded their verdict at

3.30 p.m. Patrick Lynch, Kings Council for the state, described the killing as 'the most cruel murder ever committed in this county'. Crucial evidence was given by two key witnesses, Corporal M. Sexton, who was in charge of the patrol, and Sergeant McGillycuddy of the Civic Guard. Corporal Sexton testified that he saw the defendants across the street after hearing two shots fired. He arrested and searched them, but no weapon was found; however, a revolver was found nearby. Corporal Sexton stated that he saw Private Canty smoking a cigarette after the two shots were fired. Then another shot was fired. He said that some of the soldiers had revolvers.

Sergeant McGillycuddy and Guard Hayden, another member of the Civic Guard, were patrolling in the neighbourhood at the time of Private Canty's death, and the sergeant testified that he saw Private Canty alive after the first two shots were fired. Then he stated that he heard other shots fired by the military. During this time, Sergeant McGillycuddy said that both Patrick Mahony and John O'Leary were being held in military custody. Following this crucial evidence, John Hunt, the solicitor, said that the evidence given at the inquest by Corporal Sexton and Sergeant McGillycuddy completely exonerated the two young men and proved that they did not kill Private Canty. Both Pádraig Óg Ó Ruairc and Sean Spellissy state that Private Canty was shot dead by the republican Miko Casey; however, neither of these historians gives a source for this assertion.[224]

At the inquest, the following document was produced, which caused a sensation. It was found near where the two men were arrested:

HQ 1st W/D
19/4/23

Dear Paddy,
Herewith enclosed £2. I received your message re. petrol for the jobs. The other £1 you can have for personal expenses. I was disappointed to learn that ye were not successful in burning up that show, the other night, better luck the next time. Try to finish it off asap. I trust you got those rifles you asked for and I expect to hear something from you in the near future. I'm sure there are many handy jobs in the town. It needs something in that way and of course you are the only one we expect anything from that way.
Mise,
Sean

This document was used to imply that Patrick Mahony was involved in armed robberies and, according to Sergeant McGillicuddy, the attempted arson of the *Saturday Record* offices. After deliberating for several hours, the jury found 'that Stephen Canty, a Private in the National Army, was unlawfully shot by some person unknown on Saturday 21 April [...] from the evidence, we find that neither of the prisoners, Mahony, nor O'Leary, could have fired the fatal shot.'

However, the inquest was not a trial, and the jury's verdict could not legally influence the deliberations of the military court held later, on the same day. At the military court, the two defendants, Patrick O'Mahony and John O'Leary, were accused of the murder of Stephen Canty. The GHQ in Dublin issued an official report, which was published in the local press and stated that the two men were tried before a military tribunal held at the Home Barracks on 23 April 1923. The men were charged with being in possession of a partially loaded revolver and were implicated in an attack on the patrol that included Private Canty. The statement added that both Mahony and O'Leary admitted to being in possession of a loaded revolver at the time of the attack, and that O'Mahony had admitted to ownership of a document found on the ground near where he was arrested. Both of the accused were found guilty and sentenced to death, but John O'Leary's sentence was commuted to a ten-year penal prison sentence. The execution of Patrick Mahony was duly carried out at 7 a.m. on the morning of Thursday, 26 April at the Home Barracks in Ennis.[225]

A record in the Military Archives at Cathal Brugha Barracks states:

> A picquet of 6 men under Corp. Sexton were fired on at Carmody St., at 10.30 pm on 21/4/1923. Two of the attackers were captured. Information received which resulted in the arrest of 4 others involved in the attack – 2 revolvers found – Mahony and O'Leary swore that the revolvers belonged to them. Other prisoners were Shaughnessy, Quinn, White and Fahy. Private Stephen Canty killed in the attack. Capt A de Beacan, 23 /4/1923

This military file also records that Patrick Mahony was executed for armed robbery at the Ennis Home Barracks on 26 April 1923. It is remarkable that the 'official' notice which was published in the papers linked Mahony with the death of Private Stephen Canty, whereas the record in the Military Archives states that Paddy Mahony 'was executed for armed robbery at Ennis', despite the fact that he was not accused of any specific robbery. These contradictory statements only serve to highlight the injustice of the execution of Patrick Mahony – and of the other two republican defendants, William Shaughnessy and Christopher Quinn.[226]

Patrick Mahony, from Market Street, Ennis, was 25 years of old; he was an ex-soldier, having served in France between 1915 and 1917. After his army service, he entered the motor trade in Clonmel for a couple of years and returned to Ennis in 1919. As a republican, he took the anti-Treaty side and was captured by government forces near Darragh in September 1922. He was interned at Hare Park internment camp in the Curragh until about three weeks before his arrest in Ennis on the night that Private Canty was killed. The official notice also mentioned that Patrick Mahony had been arrested on a previous occasion but was released on signing the usual form of indemnity. Mahony's last letter to his brothers was published in the *Clare Champion*:

> My dearest brothers [...] I am to die in the morning [...] I have made my peace with God [...] I am innocent of the death of the poor soldier; I am sorry for his fate; but I forgive my enemies, if I have any – from the depths of my heart [...] May God bless Ireland and may her sons be united once more in love with one another [...] Good bye to all of you and pray for me.[227]

The execution of Patrick Mahony did not satisfy the military authorities, and, sadly, there were two more controversial executions in Ennis. Christopher Quinn and William Shaughnessy were executed at the Home Barracks on 2 May for firing at Private Canty with revolvers, causing his death. On 3 May, GHQ issued the following statement:

> Christopher Quinn, Turnpike, Ennis and William Shaughnessy, Old Military barracks, Ennis, were each separately charged on the 25 of April before a military tribunal in the Limerick Command with – (A) taking part in an armed attack on National forces on the night of 21 April at Ennis, in that at about 10.30 pm did feloniously and with malice aforethought, slay and kill a member of the National forces, to wit, no 42,820, Private Stephen Canty, of A company 12th Batt. (B) Being on the night

in question in possession of a loaded revolver. The evidence shows that following some shooting in Carmody Street on the night of Saturday 21st, Private Canty with other troops was holding up and conducting a search. While discharging this duty, Private Canty held up the two prisoners. He was searching William Shaughnessy and had located a revolver on his person, when Christopher Quinn drew a revolver and fired at the soldier point blank. William Shaugnessy then drew the revolver in his possession and fired also at the soldier. Private Canty fell mortally wounded in the head and expired a short time later.

Shaughnessy and Quinn, it was clearly shown, had set out with others on the night in question with the object of carrying out a raid for money on the home of a resident in the district. William Shaughnessy had been arrested by the National troops on 15 July 1922 and was released on 2 September 1922 after signing the form undertaking not to take up arms again against the Government. Both the accused were found guilty on the separate charges made against them. The findings were confirmed in each case and both prisoners were sentenced to death. The executions were duly carried out at Ennis at 7.30 am on Wednesday morning.

On the eve of his execution, Christopher Quinn wrote a final letter to his father, John Quinn:

Father, I know it is hard on you, but I am dying for Ireland, the land that I love. My last letter to you, I know it's hardly but welcome be the will of God. I am to be executed in the morning. Well father, I am taking it great because better men than I ever was fell. You have a son that you can be proud of, as I think I have done my part for the land that I love. Dear father, I will now say goodbye. Goodbye till we meet in Heaven.

The bodies of all three men were interred, in accordance with military regulations, in the grounds of the Home Barracks. It is remarkable that none of the allegations against O'Shaughnessy and Quinn were mentioned at the public inquest into the death of Private Canty on Monday, 23 April 1923. It seems that the military authorities were determined to inflict an exemplary punishment on some young men who were unfortunate to be arrested near the scene of Private Canty's murder. The public, even their families, were not allowed to attend their trials; the press was also forbidden to attend.

Certainly, the burden of proof at these secret military trials was far short of the normal standard for conviction in criminal cases nowadays – that is beyond a reasonable doubt. The evidence given at the inquest clearly indicated that Patrick Mahony and John O'Leary were innocent of the murder. We have no military court records to corroborate the charges against the other two young republicans from Ennis, William Shaughnessy and Christopher Quinn, whose families only learnt of the tragic fate of their 18-year-old sons on the day after their execution. They were the last republicans executed by the government during the civil war.[228]

Following representations to the government, the bodies of all republicans executed during the civil war were released to their relatives for reburial in consecrated ground on Tuesday, 1 November 1924. The bodies of the three men executed in Ennis, Patrick Mahony, William O'Shaughnessy and Christy Quinn, along with those of Con McMahon and Paddy Hennessy, who were executed in Limerick, were accorded huge public funerals in Ennis and Clooney. After lying in state at the Town Hall in Ennis, the bodies were then brought to Ennis cathedral for Solemn High Mass. The remains of the three Ennis men were brought to the republican plot in Drumcliffe graveyard, while Paddy Hennessy and Con McMahon were buried in Clooney graveyard after military salutes and the playing of 'The Last Post'. Thousands of republicans from all over Clare attended the funerals, and the oration in both cemeteries was given by Brian O'Higgins, TD (de Valera was in prison at the time). O'Higgins stated that the young men had died for the cause of Irish freedom:

> The flag which now covers their coffins has been defiled, I am sorry to say, by Irish slaves. But all the same it is sacred to us and we must wipe out that stain that presently rests on the Irish tricolour [...] It is as sacred to us as the memory of our young soldiers, and both we shall hold dear.[229]

Nine years later, on the tenth anniversary of their deaths, Brian O'Higgins spoke in bitter terms at the unveiling of a monument in memory of the IRA Volunteers from Clooney:

> When the abomination known as the Irish Free State came into existence by force and corruption, Con McMahon, Patrick

Hennessy and Joseph Considine and their comrades found their English enemies reinforced by Irish slaves who had sold themselves for the wages of Judas [...] One died in battle, fighting against the dragging down of his proud country to the status of a partitioned Dominion of the British Empire; the other two were slaughtered by the mongrel 'Free State' set up in the country by English cunning and Irish treachery.

O'Higgins even denied that there was a civil war:

You have been told that there was a Civil War in this country in 1922, and they took up arms against the established government. That is a lie, but like many another English-made falsehood, it has become settled in the minds of many people as if it were the truth. There was no Civil War in Ireland in 1922 and these men whom we honour today were not 'Irregulars' or 'rebels,' but loyal Volunteer soldiers fighting in defence of the established Republic of Ireland.

O'Higgins appealed to the young men of Clare 'to destroy this mongrel Irish Free State [...] a usurpation, a fraud and an insult to the patriot dead.'[230]

'Being hunted as animals'

Though General Frank Barrett was commandant of the republican 1st Western Division, there are few references to him in the local papers between the start of the war in June 1922 and his capture, along with other republican leaders, in April 1923. Ernie O'Malley briefly mentions him in his memoir (the reference is undated):

Frank Barrett came down from Clare to Lynch's HQ [in the Knockmealdown Mountains], mud-splashed to his hips as the meeting began after 6 o'clock [...] Clare was in a bad state, or according to Frank Barrett, he made a poor mouth, I thought. His men had to dump their rifles in some battalions, as they had no ammunition.[231]

C.S. Andrews also mentions Frank Barrett's report on the state of Clare, 'Frank Barrett of the First Western reported [to General Liam Lynch] that his Division had been badly hit by arrests.' Andrews also describes, in detail, the circumstances of Barrett's arrest, along with that of several other members of the Army Executive, on 17 April, following the death of General Liam Lynch, who was shot while retreating over the Knockmealdown Mountains on Tuesday, 10 April 1923:

> With Liam Lynch's death I knew the end of the Civil War had come. Only his iron will had kept it going for the last few months. After his death, the members of the executive scattered over the hills. Austin Stack, Frank Barrett, Sean Gaynor, Dan Breen and Humphrey Murphy, arrived with several other commandants at Arraglin [...] Stack called a meeting which was attended by Frank Barrett, Sean Gaynor, Dan Breen [...] about ten of us gathered to hear Stack's statement [...] All those present, with the exception of Dan Breen, agreed with Stack that it was neither politic nor wise to carry on the war [...] We decided to move across the Knockmealdown Mountains towards the Comeraghs [...] Austin Stack, Frank Barrett, Sean Gaynor and I decided to make our way towards Mullinahone [...] we moved our billets several times, travelling at night [...] At Crow Hill we hid in a dugout, a hollowed out haystack [...] Stack could not take the discomfort and left to go to a house and was arrested [...] next evening we moved again [...] towards the Nire Valley, which might be outside the round-up area. By this time, we were very weary, very dispirited and very wet. We were on the run in the most literal sense, being hunted as animals are hunted from lair to lair. Next morning we were arrested [...] we were kept overnight in Lismore Castle [...] then two nights in Fermoy [...] then to Cork [...] On 27 April, just a week after we arrived in Cork Jail, de Valera and Frank Aiken ordered a 'cease-fire [...] Frank Barrett had the additional worry of being a young married man starting to raise a family [...] after about two months in Cork Jail a group of about 50 of us were released [...] Barrett and Gaynor were not included.[232]

Sean Gaynor's memoir corroborates C.S. Andrews's recollection, 'I was on my way to Arraglin with Frank Barrett and we marched for four or five days when we heard that Liam Lynch had been killed [...] we were surrounded all the time. There was Austin Stack, Dan Breen, Todd Andrews, Frank Barrett and I.'[233] Dan Breen also recalled Barrett's arrest, 'After Liam's death, Austin Stack, Frank Barrett, Daithí Kent, Sean Gaynor and I came up from Arraglen to make for the Nire Valley. We reached Mount Mellary after midnight, before daylight we resumed our journey through the foothills of the Knockmealdown Mountains.'[234]

The national and local newspapers also announced the capture of many of the republican leaders around this time:

> Irregular leaders nearly all captured – The capture and death of Liam Lynch has been followed up by other important captures [...] Mr Frank Barrett and others were also captured [...] Among them Count Plunkett, TD, Miss McSwiney, TD, Miss K O'Callaghan, TD, Mr A Stack, TD, Mr Sean Gaynor, Mr [C.S.] Tod Andrews and Dan Breen.

All of them were unarmed when arrested.[235]

The death of General Liam Lynch on 10 April, the capture of many leading members of the Army Executive on 17 April, the overwhelming superiority of the government military, and the policy of executions hastened the end of the civil war. On Friday, 27 April, Éamon de Valera issued a statement on the conditions on which he was prepared to negotiate for peace, 'As evidence of our goodwill, the Army Command is issuing forthwith an order to all units to suspend aggressive action – the order to take effect as soon as may be, but not later than noon, Monday, April 30th.' On the same day, Frank Aiken, the new chief of staff, issued a statement directing all members of the IRA to suspend all offensive operations from Monday, 30 April:

> In order to give decisions of the Government and Army Council effect embodied in attached Proclamation of this day, you will arrange the suspension of all offensive operations in your area as from, Monday April 30th. You will ensure that – whilst remaining on the defensive – all units take adequate measures to protect themselves and their munition.[236]

Frank Aiken ordered the Volunteers to 'dump arms' on 24 May 1923. Following the suspension of republican offensive operations, de Valera paid tribute to the republican soldiers on 24 May 1923:

> Soldiers of Liberty, Soldiers of the Republic, Legion of the Rearguard: The Republic can no longer be defended successfully by your arms. Further sacrifice of life would now be in vain, and continuance of the struggle in arms unwise in the national interest and prejudicial to the future of our cause. Military victory must be allowed to rest for the moment with those who have destroyed the Republic. Other means must be sought to safeguard the Nation's right.[237]

On 29 June 1923, Sean Casey, divisional adjutant of the 1st Western

Division (republican), reported to Frank Aiken that all the arms had safely been dumped:

> All arms have been securely dumped [...] No arms have been captured in this area by the enemy since above order came into effect [...] The discipline of the men is indeed very good [...] several of the men have gone back to their own areas and are now engaged in work of re-organisation of their respective units [...] The morale of the civil population is good and we certainly have the support and active sympathy of 70% of the population.[238]

From a republican military perspective, the civil war was over. The government forces were gradually reduced and surplus government troops were withdrawn from Clare. After ten months' occupation, the National Army evacuated the Ennis County Club, and also left the Old Ground Hotel, Ennis, which they had occupied for four months. Many republicans were in prison or else were lying low.[239]

'Fair is foul and foul is fair'

A general election was held in August 1923, and it could be seen as a fair barometer of the political opinions of the people of Clare, whether they supported the pro-Treaty parties or the anti-Treaty republicans. The civil war was effectively over following 30 April, and although many republican prisoners were still incarcerated, it was the first free election held in the county since 1918 and the electorate had a very wide choice. After the split over the Treaty, the pro-Treaty supporters set up a new party called Cumann na nGaedheal. In Clare, there were fifteen candidates in all: five anti-Treaty Sinn Féin, five pro-Treaty Cumann na nGaedheal, three Farmers' Party and two Labour Party candidates.

An editorial on the Clare election in the *Saturday Record* was clearly pro-Treaty:

> It is easy to shout for Irish Freedom, it is easy to howl: 'Up the Republic!' But it is not easy to convert the catch-cry into concrete reality. This is a task that requires far more ability and far more courage than all the silly ladies who interrupt meetings [...] If Clare thinks that the wholesale wreckage of Ireland's political and economic resources is the surest way to absolute independence, then let Clare vote for Mr de Valera and his associates, the Anti-Treatyites have no policy![240]

On the other hand, the *Clare Champion* stayed neutral in the election, giving fair coverage to all of the candidates, pro- and anti-Treaty republicans, as well as Farmers' Party candidates and Labour Party candidates.

Canon O'Kennedy of St Flannan's College and eight other prominent clergymen (with the support of Bishop Fogarty) along with county councillors and representatives of farmers and business held a meeting at the courthouse in Ennis to select pro-Treaty candidates for the forthcoming election. Among those who attended were: Canon Clancy, PP, Kildysart; Rev. J. Glynn, PP, Mullagh; Rev. M. Breen, PP, Ruan; Rev. J. Monahan, PP, Crusheen; Rev. C. Culligan, CC, Kilkee; Rev. M. Crowe, CC, Ennis; and Rev. W. Moloney, CC, Corofin. At this meeting, a letter from Fr James Clancy, PP, Kilballyowen, was read in which he promised to do all he could to secure the return of the Free State candidates, 'in spite of the atrocious threats of sanguinary war [...] which one of the present representatives has treated us as his contribution to the feast of the national apostle [a reference to de Valera's speech at Thurles on 17 March 1922, warning of 'wading through rivers of blood'].' The clergy and the other attendees selected the following pro-Treaty candidates: Eoin MacNeill; Patrick Kelly, Cree; James O'Regan, Sixmilebridge; Michael Hehir, Connolly; and Peter O'Loughlin, Liscannor.[241]

Just before the election, Canon O'Kennedy wrote a short letter to the press urging support for the government candidates, 'Steady, Claremen, Steady. Ask yourself in this election why there is no attack on any Irregular excesses – but on the Government's actions? MacNeill is the enemy, de Valera is patted in the head.' He concluded with an incantatory line from the three witches in Shakespeare's play *Macbeth*, 'Fair is foul and foul is fair.'[242]

In the general election of August 1923, Eoin MacNeill's nomination in Clare was supported by several priests, including Canon O'Kennedy and James Monahan. Of the forty-six members elected to regional constituency committees, twelve were priests – as were five of the senior organisers. Canon O'Kennedy was appointed director of elections. Patrick Murray holds the view that Bishop Fogarty 'appears to have imposed his extreme anti-republican views on the great majority of his clergy. Very few Killaloe Diocesan priests openly declared themselves republicans in a diocese with a considerable republican electorate.'[243]

Eleven days before the election, there were sensational scenes in Ennis when de Valera made an appearance for a speech on 15 August. He had secretly stayed overnight at the home of Mr and Mrs Burke of Knockanira House near Darragh, and he made his way to the meeting at Ennis in disguise. The meeting was chaired by T.V. Honan of Ennis, chairman of Ennis Urban Council, who said:

> The war for the past twelve months, much as they regretted it, might be worth it. It was a war of purification, for they now know their friends and those who stood the test. Please God, those true and brave men like President de Valera would carry their flag until they had finished the battle and won complete independence for the country.

De Valera's appearance was anticipated by the government. Shortly after he had made his way to the platform to an enthusiastic reception from the crowd of republican supporters, some shots were fired and he was arrested by a party of government troops. He had spoken only for a couple of minutes before pandemonium broke out. The *Clare Champion* reported on the circumstances of the arrest:

> Mr de Valera was arrested in Ennis on Wednesday 15 August during the course of an anti-Treaty meeting, about 3,000 people attended [...] soon after he commenced speaking troops began to arrive and take up positions in the vicinity of the platform. The crowd resented the presence of the troops and in order to clear the Square, the troops fired some shots in the air. Immediately, the crowd stampeded in all directions, many being injured in the rush. Two military officers then approached the platform, Mr de Valera came forward and he was arrested. He was taken to the Home Barracks and then to Limerick.

Before he was arrested, de Valera was reported as stating:

> Men and women of Clare, when we could not come to you and tell you the truth, they spoke to you and said that we were anarchists and that we were out for destruction. We come here today, and I come here as one of you, to tell you that I have never stood for destruction. I have never stood for brother's hand being

raised against brother's. I have never stood for playing the
enemy's game, and the enemy's game is to have one part of the
nation fighting the other part. I have always preached only one
gospel and that is the gospel I preach to you here today. That
gospel is: if the nation kept together and was united it could
achieve independence.[244]

During his incarceration in Cork Jail, Frank Barrett was nominated
as a republican candidate for the new constituency of Clare, which
replaced the former East Clare and West Clare constituencies in
1923. Among captured documents stored in the Military Archive
were letters from an anonymous correspondent to Frank Barrett
making observations on the forthcoming election. The first letter is
dated 12 August 1923:

> Election work is causing a buzz everywhere. De Valera is going
> to appear publicly in Clare on 15 August. If I get any news as to
> reception etc. I shall let you know. It's like the old days outside.
> Enthusiasm of crowds everywhere at meetings. The change of
> opinion is very marked. Of course, you know that all the papers
> are censored.

The second letter is from 22 August 1923, 'The Ennis meeting on
15 August was a great success. The arrest of the President was a
great drawback to us as his extraordinary personality would work
wonders for us.' Frank Barrett's reply, dated 24 August, was also
intercepted by the authorities, 'Republicans will of course be the
most eager and enthusiastic workers in the contest as they alone
have a cause worth fighting for [...] I will consider Clare having
done very well if the President and Brian O'Higgins are returned
there.'[245]

The election took place on 26 August, and it was an
extraordinary success for de Valera and the republicans of Clare.
There were 59,433 people within the electorate, and 40,629 of them
voted (about 68.36 per cent). According to estimates provided by
the *Clare Champion*, the voting in some rural areas was as high as
80 per cent, and about 50 per cent of the people in Ennis voted. Of
the total votes, 1,181 were spoiled, so the valid poll amounted to
39,448. The quota was 6,575 votes.

There were five seats to be filled under proportional
representation, and the results of the first count were as follows:

Frank Barrett (anti-Treaty), 482; Michael Comyn (anti-Treaty), 219; Éamon de Valera (anti-Treaty), 17,762; Michael Hehir (pro-Treaty), 1,809; Conor Hogan (Farmers' Party), 1,914; Patrick Hogan (Labour Party), 2,083; T.V. Honan (anti-Treaty), 114; Patrick Kelly (pro-Treaty), 588; P.J. MacNamara (Labour Party), 2,140; Eoin MacNeill (pro-Treaty), 8,196; Brian O'Higgins (anti-Treaty), 114; Peter O'Loughlin (pro-Treaty), 237; James O'Regan (pro-Treaty), 918; Patrick Ryan (Farmers' Party), 1,313; Bart Skehan (Farmers' Party), 1,556.

The aggregate results of the valid poll were as follows: anti-Treaty Sinn Féin, 18,691 (47.38 per cent); Cumann na nGaedheal, 11,748 (29.78 per cent); Farmers' Party, 4,783 (12.1 per cent); Labour Party, 4,223 (10.7 per cent). Éamon de Valera, Brian O'Higgins, Eoin MacNeill, Conor Hogan and Patrick Hogan were elected.[246]

Despite the civil war tensions, the election was apparently conducted in a free and fair manner, and there was a huge choice of candidates. According to the local press, 'there was a conspicuous absence of disturbance and intimidation in the county, armed military and civic guards were on duty at the booths and on the streets, and there were only two attempted cases of impersonation.' Nationally, Cumann na nGaedheal under W.T. Cosgrave won 63 out of 153 seats in the Dáil (around 41 per cent of the vote), while the anti-Treaty republicans under de Valera won 44 seats (around 27 per cent). The republicans, of course, would not take their seats in the Dáil because of their refusal to take an oath of allegiance to the English monarch; therefore, Cosgrave was elected as president of the Irish Free State.

Éamon de Valera received 45 per cent of the valid poll in Clare. This was an outstanding result, proving that he was hugely popular despite all that was said about him and his rejection of the Treaty. His controversial arrest in Ennis just eleven days before the election had outraged many people. Despite losing the civil war, the number of votes in favour of the republicans was surprisingly high in Clare – probably the highest vote percentage in the country. Another factor behind this high level of support for de Valera and the republicans may have been the shock and outrage caused by the government's execution of five Clare republicans between February and May

1923. The Clare electorate clearly favoured the republicans over the pro-Treaty side. The republicans of Clare may have lost the military battle in the civil war, but they won the political battle in the general election of 1923.[247]

Hunger strikes

Though the civil war effectively ended after the republican suspension of offensive activities on 30 April 1923, there were many outstanding issues to be resolved. Among the most important was the matter of the thousands of republicans, including many Clare men and several Clare women, who were incarcerated in jails and internment camps around the country, having been arrested in round-ups over the previous ten months. Some of these republicans had been in custody since the start of the civil war in June 1922. The government was reluctant to release the internees early in case they resumed their military activities. They did offer early release to prisoners who signed an undertaking to renounce violence, but committed republicans would not, on principle, sign such a pledge. Therefore, thousands of republicans were interned for many months after the suspension of their military campaign. Michael Hopkinson estimates that there were over 12,000 republican internees in April 1923. Many of these republicans were still interned more than a year later. Frustrated at the prison conditions and seeking an end to their incarceration, they resorted to a mass hunger strike in October 1923.

James Barron of Newpark House, Ennis, better known as 'Aimee', was one of the republicans who was arrested and interned very early in the war. He was newly married and then residing in Claremount House in the parish of Clarecastle. He was arrested in July 1922 at Claremount and was interned in various prisons until he eventually ended up in Gormanston internment camp. Aimee was interned for more than a year, until he was released after the hunger strike in October 1923.

While he was interned, Aimee was allowed to write and receive a letter once a week. However, there were very strict limitations on what Aimee could write; his letters were censored, and he was not allowed to comment on prison conditions or political matters. Likewise, his wife Evelyn was curtailed in what she could write to

Aimee. In one of her early letters, dated 29 September 1923, she did not even know where he was being kept and asked, 'Aimee, where are you at all?' Evelyn was critical of the fact that Aimee had been arrested without being charged, but she supported his decision not to sign any incriminating documents:

> My God it is heart-breaking to think that you my husband have been arrested on no charge and that the paper they would have you sign would be an admission of your guilt. That you have right on your side in refusing to sign anything at all that they have in refusing to give you the trial you demand.

In another letter, which is undated, she wrote, 'Aimee we want you to sign no papers, we want no concessions for you.' On 2 February 1923, she wrote, 'More than half of your letter is cut away by the censor.' Because of the writing restrictions and the fact that her letters were being scrutinised by military censors, much of what she wrote only dealt with family matters, such as the birth of their son Ernie. She also wrote about some local gossip, such as weddings and farming matters. She mentioned that there was a meeting in Ennis for the release of prisoners. She was also allowed to send her husband some gifts, such as cake, butter and cigarettes.

In his letters to Evelyn, written from K Hut in Gormanston, Aimee always told her that he was 'in the best of health'. In a letter dated 7 June 1923, he wrote, 'I have very little to write about, I wouldn't write at all only I know you will be happy to see the envelope, I am in the best of health.' Naturally, Aimee wanted to be released from his internment, and one Clare TD, Conor Hogan, asked a question in the Dáil on 31 October 1923 about his incarceration, stating that 'Aimee Barron had not borne arms in the Irregular campaign.' In reply, Richard Mulcahy stated, 'The release of Mr Barron had been ordered and was about to be effected when he went on hunger strike. As a result of his action it will be necessary to reconsider the question of releasing him later.'

Aimee Barron, like thousands of other republican prisoners being held in prisons and internment camps around the country, went on hunger strike in mid-October 1923 to protest against their continued incarceration, even though the republicans had called off their offensive campaign on 30 April 1923. Writing to his wife on 26

October 1923, Aimee reassured her that he was well, 'Dearest Evelyn, this is the sixth day of the hunger strike and of course we feel a bit weak, but taking everything into consideration, I must say that we are all well. I hope, Evelyn, that this will not worry you, I believe it won't, you were always so brave.' Following this hunger strike, Aimee Barron was released in November 1923, along with some other Clare republicans. After his release and joyous return home to his family, Aimee Barron went to Australia for about six years and then returned to Newpark. He refused, on principle, to apply for a War of Independence pension, as it would acknowledge recognition of the Free State.[248]

The mass hunger strike began on Sunday, 14 October 1923 in Mountjoy Jail. From there, the strike spread to all the prisons and internment camps in the country. According to republican sources, more than 8,000 prisoners went on hunger strike. But the strike was poorly organised and many of the hunger-strikers were unsuitable for this ordeal. Morale and leadership among the strikers were poor, and the strike began to collapse within a couple of weeks. Hopkinson states that there was immense confusion in the various jails before three weeks were out, and many strikers started taking food again. After a considerable number of protestors in Mountjoy had broken off the strike, it was decided on 13 November to end it. Prominent leaders such as Con Moloney, Frank Barrett and Dan Breen signed the pledge ending the hunger strike. The collapse of the hunger strikes had a demoralising effect among republican prisoners. The government did increase the rate of prisoner releases after the hunger strike, but it would not contemplate a mass release policy, as this would have been seen as giving in to the strike. The gradual release of prisoners was not completed until the summer of 1924.[249]

In Clare during late October 1923, a mass political campaign was organised to secure the release of the republican prisoners. Prayers for the release of prisoners were held at services in Ennis cathedral, which were followed by a rosary and a procession led by the band of the Ennis United Labour Association. During these processions, which lasted for seven days, the local cinema was required to close down. It was claimed at one of the meetings, and reported in the

Clare Champion, that Frank Barrett and twenty-nine other Clare prisoners were in a low state on hunger strike. A prisoner's release campaign was organised in Clare, and a countywide petition was also held. One report stated that 30,542 persons from every parish in Clare had signed a petition calling for the release of prisoners, including Brian O'Higgins, TD, who was reported to be dying. During November motions were passed by Ennis Urban Council, Ennis Rural District Council, Kildysart Rural District Council and Clare County Council calling for the release of the hunger-striking republican prisoners. At the meeting of Ennis Urban District Council, chaired by T.V. Honan, the following motion was adopted, 'That we, the members of Ennis UDC, call for the immediate release of the political prisoners, being convinced that this course of action will prove the shortest course to peace within our land.' [250]

Sean Gaynor, commandant of the 3rd Tipperary Brigade during the War of Independence and commandant of the 1st Southern Division (republican) during the civil war, was captured, along with General Frank Barrett and other senior republicans, in mid-April 1923. Gaynor described the organisation of the hunger strike in Mountjoy Jail and explained why he resigned from the IRA in disgust following the collapse of the strike after twenty-five days:

> General Barrett, himself of higher rank and member of the Executive successfully organised a general strike of fellow prisoners in Mountjoy. The slogan insisted by Barrett was 'death or release!' We held out for 25 days [...] Frank Barrett and a Clohessy man from Clare were most vigilant agitators for the hunger strike[...] On Sunday morning, 14 October 1923, Frank Barrett made a very strong appeal to the men to 'persevere till death!' Of about 250 men in Mountjoy, 211 declared in favour of strike and on the same day General Barrett gave us the strike pledge: 'Death or release!'
>
> A week later, on Sunday 21 October some of the men were beginning to abandon the hunger strike, General Barrett characterised them as traitors and deserters, who were no longer worthy of being members of the IRA. On the 23rd day of the strike, General Barret sent for me and told me that there was a grave danger of the men going off the strike in big numbers and that he would prefer to call it off in an organised way, rather than have a mass stampede. On the 25th day of the strike I was told

that General Barrett had gone off the strike. General Barrett sent a message to me saying that a doctor from outside had examined him and could hold no hope for him if he persisted on the strike and in view of the disgraceful manner in which the camps abandoned the strike and when he considered his home responsibilities, he decided he was not prepared to die on the strike and had given it up [...] I would never have gone on strike if I thought our leaders were not sincere in their protestations [...] in view of General Barrett's action, I decided to go off the strike, sign the form of undertaking and resign from the IRA [...] I notified the Chief of Staff, Frank Aiken, of my actions on 15 November 1922 [...] The insincerity of the leader of the hunger strike in my wing of Mountjoy in urging young men to sacrifice their lives if necessary on the strike and then going off it himself on the 25th day so disgusted me, that immediately I heard of his action I decided to go off the strike, sign the form of undertaking to the Free State and resign from the Army.[251]

The court martial of Frank Barrett

In mid-November 1923, after more than eight months in jail, and following the collapse of the hunger strike after twenty-five days, Frank Barrett was anxious to get out. But in order to secure his release, he had to sign a document promising to keep the peace. He decided to sign the document, believing that he was not compromising his republican principles. He sent a note to his brother-in-law, the Free State army officer Colonel Paddy Mulcahy, a brother of General Richard Mulcahy, stating his wishes. He was released shortly after the strike ended.

Following his release from Mountjoy, Frank Barrett went to a Dublin nursing home to recuperate. From there, he wrote to another brother-in-law, Pappy Costello of Darragh, who was arrested in early December 1922 and then interned in Newbridge, advising him on a means of getting out of jail:

> If you are anxious to secure your early release adopt the following suggestion and you will be released immediately. On a slip of paper write the following and send it to Paddy Mulcahy via the camp governor: 'It is not my purpose to oppose in arms the government elected by the Irish people.' In doing this you do not involve a breach of principle as both military and political leaders have definitely agreed not to continue armed resistance against the government. If any of the men in the camp from the

First Western Division are anxious to secure their release, let them adopt the above scheme.

Simon McInerney, commandant of the republican West Clare Brigade, who had been imprisoned since his arrest at Kilkee in late July 1922, took umbrage at Frank Barrett's action and reported the matter in a letter to Frank Aiken in February 1924. McInerney and three other republicans, S. Madigan, T. Lillis and M. Falshee, all west Clare republicans imprisoned in Hare Park internment camp in the Curragh, stated that Frank Barrett and J.J. Clohessy had signed a document to secure their release from custody in Mountjoy. They alleged that, in signing this note, Frank Barrett had breached Order No 8 of the IRA code (issued by the chief of staff General Liam Lynch on 28 September 1922), which directed that prisoners were not to sign any form of undertaking as a condition for release from custody.

Upon receipt of this letter of complaint, Frank Aiken ordered that Frank Barrett be suspended from his position as commandant of the republican 1st Western Division and court-martialled by the officers of the 1st Southern Division on a charge of breaching Order No 8.

After being notified of the charge, Frank Barrett wrote an apologia to Frank Aiken to justify his actions:

> I don't feel downhearted after going off the strike, although I feel disappointed with myself at not having the generosity to give the little that was left of me for the freedom of our beloved land, especially when I know that I was sure of victory, within a few days [...] That I insisted on launching the strike in an organised manner and participated in it for the purest motive and fully confident of my going through the gates of death if necessary, are also considerations that help to ease one's mind.
>
> What worries me most is the knowledge that as a result of what has happened I must sever my connections with the Army, which I have done my part in organising, training and equipping during my eleven years in the organisation.
>
> No printed or typed form was signed by me [Barrett just wrote a few words on a slip of paper stating that he would not oppose the government with arms]. The Republican cause will not suffer by my actions. My allegiance is unaltered and unalterable. I realise that my action constitutes an act of indiscipline aggravated on account of the fact of my responsibility.

[142]

Following the court martial, and as a means of resolving the issue, Aiken suggested that Barrett write another letter to Colonel Paddy Mulcahy repudiating his earlier note, stating that it 'was written while he was in a weak mental and physical state after twenty five days of hunger strike'. Aiken added that Frank Barrett was not to resist if he was re-arrested after Mulcahy received the letter.

However, Frank Barrett decided to resign from the IRA:

> Having very carefully reviewed and considered the whole position, I have arrived at the conclusion that the best course to be adopted in the interests of the future of the Army is for me to resign my position both from the membership of the Executive and from the command which I held at the time of my capture, and I now respectfully beg to do so. May God grant speedy victory to the splendid efforts of yourself, your committees and loyal associates, Frank Barrett.

Simon McInerney, having repudiated the actions of Frank Barrett and others, was released on 10 July 1924. The next day, he wrote a letter to Frank Aiken, wondering what he was to do and stating 'my difficulty in reporting back to Clare if the Barretts were still in control'. The decision to subject Frank Barrett to a court martial was apparently unpopular among the officers and men of the republican 1st Western Division. An IRA reorganisation report regarding Clare from May 1925 states, 'The situation in Mid-Clare is very difficult [...] in and around Ennis, the vast majority of the officers were dis-satisfied with the decision regarding Frank Barrett and it would be next to impossible to secure new officers who would be outside the Barrett influence.'[252]

Republican women prisoners – members of Cumann na mBan – also went on hunger strike. Ann Mathews states that 645 republican women were interned during the civil war, including two Clare women, Annie Hogan of Moyhill, Cratloe, who was imprisoned for 141 days, from 13 February 1923 to 4 July 1923, and Sinead McInerney of Kilkee, who was held for 150 days, from 20 February to 20 July 1923. Annie Hogan wrote to her mother about the hunger strike in Kilmainham Jail and how the striking women were treated:

> At midnight, a large force of Criminal Investigation Department and Free State soldiers rushed into the compound and up the landing where the prisoners were. They caught hold of each girl

in turn, kicking, beating and dragging them along the landing to the top of the iron staircase [...] several prisoners were dragged to the foot of the stairs by their hair, others by their feet, their heads banging on each iron step [...] many girls collapsed [...] the language and behaviour of those men surpasses description [...] this went on from midnight till 5 am.[253]

Annie, or 'Nan' Hogan, a 25-old republican who was arrested for helping some republican prisoners escape from Limerick prison, also went on hunger strike following her internment in Kilmainham Jail and the North Dublin Union. Nan Hogan was an early member of Cumann na mBan in east Clare, and she was commandant of the 2nd Battalion, East Clare Brigade. She died prematurely in early July 1924, allegedly due to the effects of her hunger strike.

Another Clare republican who died prematurely was Section Commander Dan Crawford of Shanaway, Mullagh. He was arrested and interned in Limerick Prison, where although his health deteriorated, he went on a three-day hunger strike. He was released unconditionally, 'a broken man', and died on 16 June 1924.[254]

On 15 August 1924, one year after his sensational arrest, de Valera returned to Ennis to give an address at another huge Sinn Féin rally. This rally was attended by thousands of supporters, including many from outside of the county. Unfortunately, one man, Michael Hartnett, was tragically killed following the meeting. He and a few companions had travelled by car from Tipperary town to attend the republican rally, and while they were returning home, they encountered an army checkpoint at Kerin's Cross, Clarecastle. According to army witness statements, the car did not stop and between six and eight bullets were fired at the car, killing Michael Hartnett instantly. There were no weapons found in the car. At the inquest, the verdict of the jury was that 'Michael Hartnett died of bullet wounds inflicted by the military.' The 31-year-old republican was a member of the 4th Battalion of the Tipperary Brigade IRA. He was buried in the republican plot in Tipperary town. Although the civil war had been over for more than a year, Michael Hartnett could be regarded as another victim of these tragic times in Clare.[255]

Split in the GAA

The Treaty and the civil war also caused a split in the GAA. Fortunately, the division was temporary and largely confined to Clare. According to Seamus O'Reilly, the split was due to the civil war and especially the executions of Con McMahon and Patrick Hennessy, both of whom were prominent GAA figures from Clooney. Many delegates were also unhappy with the county board chaired by Canon Hamilton, who was pro-Treaty. Failing to secure the deferment of a county board meeting, the secretary, Sean McNamara from Crusheen, walked out and many delegates followed him. Some of these delegates then formed an independent county board after a meeting at the Town Hall, Ennis, on 2 February 1924. Delegates from twenty-five clubs (twenty-two hurling clubs and three football clubs) attended a second meeting a couple of weeks later. The officers that were elected included: Sean McNamara as president, Dan Minogue as vice-president, Frank Barrett as treasurer and Gerard O'Loughlin as secretary.

Mike Cronin agrees with O'Reilly, claiming that the split was over the executions:

> The only split that took place within the GAA in the wake of the Civil War was in Clare. The split was over the executions by the state of the Clare footballers and anti-Treatyites, Con McMahon and Patrick Hennessy, and led to the emergence in 1924 of rival county boards. On one side was the official GAA Board led by Fr Michael Hamilton, who was pro-Treaty; the other 'Board' contained the anti-Treatyites.

However, in a letter submitted to the *Clare Champion*, the secretary to the new board, Gerard O'Loughlin, stated that this board 'was being formed by a group of old Gaels, with the main object of preserving the rules of the GAA as they now stand [...] as there seems to be a general move throughout the country that rules 9 and 10 should be deleted and that rugby, hockey, association football etc., should become part of the national pastimes.'

During 1924 both 'official' and 'unofficial' GAA matches took place, and several clubs entered teams in both the official and unofficial competitions. In August 1924 there was an unofficial GAA match between a Tipperary team and a Clare selection. This suggests that there was also some split in Tipperary. For about a year, the two groups ran rival competitions and organisations, but the split seems to have petered out in 1925, as there are no reports of 'independent' GAA games in the summer of that year.[256]

Fianna Fáil (the Republican Party)

In 1925 Frank Aiken, the IRA chief of staff, announced at the IRA convention that, with the backing of de Valera, he and others, including Seán Lemass, were considering an end to the policy of abstention from the Dáil. A majority of Sinn Féin delegates at a special convention in Dublin on 9 March 1926 were opposed to ending this policy, so de Valera resigned as president of Sinn Féin on 10 March 1926. Two months later, in May 1926, de Valera formed a new party, Fianna Fáil (the Republican Party), and he declared that the hated 'oath' to the English monarch was the only factor preventing his entry into the Dáil. He declared outside the Dáil after the general election of June 1927, when Fianna Fáil won 44 seats, that 'as long as I and my party were representatives of the people, we would never take an oath to an English king!'

However, a few weeks later, on 10 July 1927, Kevin O'Higgins, a TD and the Minister for Justice, was assassinated by republicans while on his way to Mass in Booterstown, Dublin. Following this killing (which de Valera unreservedly condemned) and the introduction of the Electoral (Amendment) Act, 1927, de Valera and his fellow Fianna Fáil TDs eventually entered the Dáil on 11 August 1927. President Cosgrave, fearing another IRA campaign against his government, had hurriedly introduced the Electoral (Amendment) Act to force all elected TDs to enter the Dail; if they didn't, they would forfeit their seats. When signing the roll, de Valera famously declared that he wasn't taking an oath to the king and that the oath was only 'an empty political formula'.

It was an embarrassing *volte-face* for de Valera and his republican supporters in Fianna Fáil. As historian Maryanne Gialanella Valiulis notes, 'The Treaty oath, worth a Civil War in 1922, was transformed into an empty political formula in 1927.' De Valera admitted that his action was humiliating:

> I grant that what we did was contrary to all our former actions
> and to everything we stood for, contrary to our declared policies

and to the explicit pledges we gave at the time of our election. It was a step painful and humiliating for us who had to take it, and for those who had supported us.[257]

However, through this significant political act, de Valera strengthened parliamentary democracy in Ireland and confirmed the pro-Treaty supporters in their beliefs that they were right in 1922.

Frank Aiken resigned as chief of staff of the IRA and joined the new party, along with many other republicans. Naturally, this decision caused a bitter rupture with Sinn Féin and doctrinaire republicans. Incidentally, Dan Breen, TD, the legendary Tipperary republican, was the first of the anti-Treaty republicans to resign from Sinn Féin and enter the Dáil on 25 January 1927, about seven months before de Valera and his Fianna Fáil TDs signed the roll.[258] De Valera went on to hold the position of taoiseach on three separate occasions: 1932–48, 1951–4 and 1957–9. He represented Clare as a TD until he retired from electoral politics in 1959, and then he served as President of Ireland for two terms, from 1959 to 1973.

Brian O'Higgins, a Sinn Féin TD for Clare since 1922, announced his intention of standing as a Sinn Féin candidate in Clare in the general election of June 1926, 'to help uncompromising republicans, who against great odds are working for the old policy of Sinn Féin'. Although he received 1,412 first preferences (3.2 per cent), he was not re-elected, whereas Fianna Fáil won two seats in Clare with a total of 15,328 votes (39.76 per cent) out of a valid poll of 38,546. Nationally, Sinn Féin won only five seats, while Fianna Fáil won forty-four. In the second general election of September 1926, after the Cumann na nGaedheal government was beaten on a vote of confidence, three Fianna Fáil candidates were returned as TDs for the constituency of Clare, whereas Cumann na nGaedheal had won one seat and Labour another. The total vote for Fianna Fáil candidates was 42.9 per cent of the valid poll. Sinn Féin did not put up a candidate in Clare on this occasion.

Brian O'Higgins had been in the General Post Office, Dublin during the Easter Rising. He was interned in 1918 and during the civil war, and he went on hunger strike in October 1923. He remained in Sinn Féin after the formation of Fianna Fáil in 1926, and he was a member of Comhairle na dTeachtaí, a republican group composed of former members of the Second Dáil (16 August 1921–8 June 1922) that presumptuously transferred the sovereignty of the republic established by the Second Dáil to the IRA Army Council in 1938. O'Higgins had been president of Sinn Féin between 1931 and 1933 but resigned from the party in 1934. He was a Gaelic League organiser, and under the pseudonym 'Brian na BanBan' he published many songs and poems. He died on 10 March 1963.[259]

Frank Barrett was elected to Clare County Council in 1924 as a Sinn Féin representative. In 1926 he joined de Valera's new party, Fianna Fáil; he did, however, on 7 June 1926, express reservations about the future of republicanism in the new movement:

> The economic conditions prevailing, emigration and unemployment, constitute a formidable argument in favour of a change of policy, and Dev would be entitled to a fair chance on his new scheme, as long as he can guarantee that there is no danger in it to Republicanism. He feels he can guarantee this, but, personally, I have fears [...] We must hope that things will come right in time, in our time.[260]

Following the county council election of 1928, in which Barrett stood as a Fianna Fáil candidate, he was elected chairman of the council, a position that he held until his untimely death in 1931. In 1928 he chaired a convention of former IRA comrades at the Old Ground Hotel, Ennis to help those comrades in poor circumstances. After years of being on the run, and enduring imprisonment on several occasions and a twenty-five-day hunger strike in October–November 1923, his health was undermined, and he died prematurely on 13 April 1931. He was between 38 and 39 years old.[261]

Frank Barrett's military and political opponents Michael Brennan, Patrick Brennan and Sean Liddy pursued successful careers in the newly established Irish police force and the Irish army.

Michael Brennan, from Cratloe and commandant of the 1st Western Division since November 1921, pursued a successful career in the Irish army. He was chairman of Clare County Council from 1918 to 1922. He was appointed commandant of the National Army in Limerick in May 1921; on 24 January 1923, he was promoted to the rank of major general in charge of the Limerick Command. After this service, he was appointed as a general officer of the Southern Command. He held the post of adjutant general of the Irish army from 1925 until 1931. In January 1931 he was appointed inspector general of the Irish army. On 15 October 1931, he became chief of staff, a position which he held until his retirement. He was promoted to the rank of lieutenant general and retired on 29 January 1940 after a distinguished military service of almost twenty years. Lieutenant General Michael Brennan died on 23 October 1986.

Colonel Patrick Brennan, former commandant of the Clare Brigade (1917–19) and Clare TD (1921–2), resigned from the Dáil on 13 December 1922 and joined the newly established police force, the Civic Guard, which was renamed An Garda Síochána in December 1923. He became an assistant commissioner of the new police force.

Commandant Sean Liddy, former commandant of the West Clare Brigade (1919–22) and Clare TD (1921–2), resigned from the Dáil on 18 December 1922 and joined the Civic Guard. He retired in 1953 with the rank of chief superintendent of the Sligo-Leitrim Division.[262]

Dr Michael Fogarty had a long and distinguished career as Bishop of Killaloe from 1904 up to the time of his death in 1955. The golden jubilee of his episcopacy in 1954 was an occasion of great pomp and ceremony at the cathedral in Ennis, with the hierarchies from church and state in attendance. Taoiseach Éamon de Valera, having represented Clare since 1917, attended and spoke at the ceremony. De Valera stated that he had first met Dr Fogarty on the night before the East Clare by-election of 1917. He added that it 'was a great sorrow to me when we went different ways afterwards [...] It was a matter of great regret that the bishop and I did not see eye to eye and that we did not meet for a long time afterwards.' An *Irish Press* photographer took a photograph of the taoiseach and the 95-year-old bishop, and if 'the camera never lies', it would seem from the body language of the bishop, who is looking away from de Valera while shaking hands with him, that old bishop Fogarty did not forget or forgive de Valera for his opposition to the Treaty.[263]

Healing the wounds of war

One Ennis man, Jimmy Mahony, who was born in 1900 and emigrated to America in 1927, reminisced, in radio interviews during 1988, about his time growing up in Ennis during the years of the War of Independence and the civil war. Although he was quite elderly at the time of the recordings, his recollections give a valuable first-hand account of life in Ennis during these tragic times. His father was a pro-Treaty supporter, while his uncle supported de Valera and the anti-Treaty party. His first cousin was Patrick Mahony, who was executed at the Home Barracks, Ennis on 30 April 1923 for the killing of Private Stephen Canty at Ennis. The following is an excerpt from the recording:

> It was very unsettled in Ennis, there was for and against [the Truce]. The bishop of course was pro-Truce [...] I was in the Town Hall when the news came through [...] There was great jubilation and all forces were confined to barracks [...] People were glad to get some kind of relief [...] The dance halls were opened up, we 'struck up the band' and people were beginning to enjoy themselves. Then came the split between accepting or rejecting the Treaty. Those who rejected the Treaty walked out and became more militant.
>
> During that crisis there was a rush for all the places that were vacant. Those who favoured acceptance of the Treaty took the Home Barracks because the stronghold was there and they were handed whatever arms and ammunition they required to maintain law and order and establish the Free State.
>
> The Irregulars occupied the [RIC] Barracks. The Free State forces tried to negotiate peacefully to get the Irregulars out, but they refused to go. They took whatever equipment that was left by the police and they burned the place. These men carried arms against the establishment of the Free State. They formed groups and they became Irregulars [...] They were numerous enough to cause trouble. The men in the streets didn't want the Civil War. The leaders wanted it and they got recruits to do the work for them.
>
> [There was] very slow reconciliation. The town had a very good spiritual leader in Bishop Michael Fogarty. He was very close to the leaders during the struggle for independence. He could not see them separated over ideology and he wanted to get the country back to stability. His opinion was very much respected by all the parties, irrespective of their political feeling. He was responsible for maintaining peace among factions. When the

easing off came, a lot of men had to be reconciled to the Church. The Franciscans were very charitable and kind and they led many of the dissenters back to the Church. This was done very slowly, it takes a long time for the wounds of war to heal.[264]

Summary

The civil war had taken a taken a terrible toll on Clare, with at least seventeen men killed in the county and nineteen Clare men killed outside the county during this tragic conflict. When Commandant Michael Brennan and the 1st Western Division were engaged in fighting to secure the city of Limerick for the government forces, local republicans in Clare took advantage of the absence of the 1st Western Division to take control of the towns of Kilrush and Kilkee and other parts of mid- and west Clare for a few weeks. After the battle of Limerick was won on 20 July, the government forces easily regained control of the towns in west Clare towards the end of the month, with little loss of life. This marked the conventional phase of the war, which the government forces easily won by seizing control of the main towns. For the next eight months or so, until the ceasefire on 30 April 1923, the republicans in Clare resorted to guerrilla warfare tactics. Much material damage was done to institutional buildings and the transport infrastructure in the county. But a far greater impact was the loss of life and the psychological trauma experienced by the whole community.

The struggle was an unequal one, as the government forces were much larger and better equipped than the republicans, and many of the republican leaders were arrested in round-ups. The government also introduced severe measures, including the death penalty for those found in possession of weapons. Besides this, the republican forces were strongly denounced by the Catholic Church and the media at national and local level. Furthermore, public opinion was not generally supportive of the republican military campaign against the government.

Clearly, no one side in this tragic conflict had a monopoly on the suffering, and by the end of the civil war at least thirty-six people associated with the county were dead. Others subsequently died prematurely because of injuries incurred during the war, illnesses caused by unhealthy living conditions while on the run, or ill-health arising from hunger strikes in prison. It must be remembered that several innocent civilians also died because of this conflict.

There were highly principled and sincerely motivated men and women on both sides of the conflict, and although the Free State government secured a military victory, the republicans only accepted defeat in a military sense – not in a political sense. While many took part in the conflict, four people had a significant influence on the development of events in the county and, indeed, in the country at this time: Bishop Michael Fogarty and Michael Brennan, who supported the Free State forces, and Éamon de Valera and Frank Barrett, who supported the republican Army Executive. Their respective roles were hugely important, and they had a great impact on the evolution of events, both inside and outside of the county, during this great national tragedy.

The government forces had won the bitter military struggle against their passionate and very determined republican opponents, who had rejected the Anglo-Irish Treaty of 1921. The republicans had adopted a doctrinaire position and had sworn to stand by the republic declared in the Proclamation of the Irish Republic and by the First Dáil in 1919; it had launched a military challenge to smash the newly established government and renew the war against England.

The victory of the government forces helped to lay the foundations of democracy in the Free State. From a republican perspective, the greatest bitterness, apart from losing the war, was caused by the controversial execution of republican prisoners allegedly captured with firearms, five of whom were from Clare. Sadly, there were significant sectarian activities committed before and during the civil war, some of which were authorised by the anti-Treaty Army Executive. The civil war left a bitter legacy that determined the character of Irish political life for generations. However, if public opinion in Clare was ostensibly opposed to the actions of the republicans before and during the civil war, a substantial proportion of the electorate supported the defeated republicans in the general elections of 1923 and 1926, shortly after the civil war was over.

Speaking at Béal na mBláth in August 2016, President Michael

D. Higgins, whose family in Clare were divided on the civil war, spoke of the 'tragic and bloody Civil War':

> a dreadful human tragedy for so many Irish families [...] no single side had the monopoly of either atrocity or virtue during the Civil War [...] And while we should never under-estimate the challenge that was to build the foundations of a stable democratic state in the midst of turmoil and in the shadow of a great power, we must never forget what a terrible price was paid in divided families and communities, leaving a legacy that was felt for generations.[265]

4

SECTARIANISM IN CLARE

The burning of the Protestant church in Clarecastle in April 1920 and the attempted burning of the Protestant church in O'Briensbridge in June of the same year were denounced by the local communities and by the IRA leadership during the War of Independence. As County Inspector Gelston remarked, the motive for the burning of the chapel at O'Briensbridge 'is to introduce religious strife into the present unrest'.[266] Such sectarian acts only added to the fears of Protestant unionists and their belief that they were not wanted in Clare. The records of the Irish Distress Committee and the Irish Grants Committee, and the records of the Damage to Property (Compensation) Act, 1923 provide lists of people who claimed and were awarded compensation for their sufferings during the years of the War of Independence and civil war. These and other contemporary records indicate that many Protestant people sincerely believed that they and their properties were attacked because of their Protestant religion and their politics. Protestant landowners and businessmen were attacked, and Protestant churches, schools and rectories were destroyed or seriously damaged in the period between the signing of the Treaty and the end of the civil war in acts that can only be described as sectarian attacks.

It has already been mentioned that, according to Bielenberg, the records of the Irish Grants Committee should be used with caution – that claims may have been exaggerated in order to claim greater compensation, though 'the evidence reveals serious difficulties faced by Protestant loyalist households.'[267]

One of those compensated for his sufferings was James Wakely, who has previously been mentioned as a justice of the peace that was targeted during the War of Independence. He was not a landlord, but he could be classified as a 'strong farmer', with about 350 acres of land around Mountshannon. In July 1921 threatening notices were posted calling for a boycott of his meadow lettings. Mill Farm, an outlying farm of 20 acres, was seized; fences were knocked, his cattle were driven off and the lands were ploughed up in November 1921. In April 1922 he received threatening notices to clear out of Mountshannon. His house was attacked on 17 August 1922, his meadows were spiked and his stock were driven off the lands; however, with the help of a few friends the attackers were repulsed. During this time, his wife was dying, and he could not get a nurse to look after her. Shortly afterwards, in September 1922, the house was broken into and he received a threatening letter to clear out within fourteen days or 'he would be treated as the Orangemen treated them in the North.' On 5 July 1923, while returning from Scariff Fair, he was kidnapped by four masked and armed men. He was kept for about eight hours and 'court-martialled'. He was released after he agreed to sell part of his lands. He left Ireland immediately and fled to England almost penniless. He tried to sell his lands after he had fled, but he was unable to do so, as no one would buy them. The lands were compulsorily purchased by the Land Commission, who eventually paid £3,000 for the 350 acres of land at Mountshannon, as well as the house. In his claim, James Wakely stated that the land was worth £5,500.[268]

Many of the Protestant residents of Clare believed that they were targeted because of their religion and their unionism. This was certainly the opinion of Rev. Samuel Waldron King, a Church of Ireland minister at Kilrush who stated in his claim for grant aid that he was knocked off his bike and his shotgun was stolen in September 1922. Although Rev. King made an outrageous claim that the Catholic clergy were fomenting the agitation against Protestants, he was fully convinced that the struggle was a sectarian one:

> Every Protestant or unionist, (which meant the same thing I am happy to say), was a mark in those days, and the priests posted up notices that every Protestant should leave in 24 hours or they would be murdered. We did not know when we went to bed at night if the morning would find us alive.

Rev. King added that if people applied to any court, it would only incur extra persecution. His application was dated 29 May 1928.[269]

Some Protestant businessmen were also attacked and forced to leave the county, even though they stated that they were not involved in politics. Thomas Doyle, from Drumadoora, Feakle and a native of Northern Ireland, was an egg dealer who ran a profitable business for some years. However, during 1920 his business was threatened. In December 1921, he received threatening letters and had to leave for Northern Ireland until February 1922. On his return, he received a death notice, and he went back to Northern Ireland between June and September. On his return to Clare in September 1922, his house was burned and his business was ruined.

He stated that, as a Protestant and a native of Northern Ireland living in a Catholic and nationalist district, he was looked upon as a foreigner and a supporter of the British government, 'Feakle is an isolated town in Clare, with very few Protestants living there and County Clare was a most disturbed county. I, a North of Ireland Protestant, was singled out for attack.' Clearly, he believed that this was a sectarian attack. He was awarded a sum of £1,435.[270]

Another businessman, Charles Strachan Copland of Dunmore, Doonbeg, was born in Scotland and was a Presbyterian. He set up a mineral water factory in Kilrush in the spring of 1916. He said that he was doing well until the Sinn Féin members and republicans started boycotting him because they said he was a loyalist. He stated that he never interfered in politics in any way or gave the republicans any excuse to attack his business. By 1920 he was under threat and felt unsafe going about on the streets. He received two letters that threatened his life. He closed his business in November 1920, a close friend advising him that if he did not clear out, he would be shot on sight by the IRA. A party of IRA took over his premises and destroyed his machinery and bottles, declaring that 'they did not want any Scotch spies around Kilrush and that they wanted satisfaction for what the Presbyterian Orangemen were doing to the Catholics of Northern Ireland'. He stated that he was persecuted because he was a Scotsman and a loyalist.[271]

Apart from the burning of the Protestant church in Clarecastle in April 1920 – probably the worst case of sectarianism from this time – there was also the burning of the Church of Ireland building at Miltown Malbay, which occurred on 14–15 July 1922, shortly after the civil war began. The testimony of Rev. David Albert Elliott,

MA, mentions this outrageous sectarian act, as well as other attacks upon Church of Ireland properties in the district:

> I am Rector of Miltown Malbay, County Clare and in addition I had under my care the outlying parishes of Lahinch and Ennistymon. On the 15th July 1922, the Parish Church of Miltown Malbay was destroyed by the IRA and all my clerical robes etc. destroyed. The bell of Lahinch Church was pulled down from the belfry and taken away and other damage done to the church in 1922. Ennistymon Church was damaged in 1922, in 1923 and subsequent years and many of the requisites for Divine Service were maliciously destroyed or removed. Ennistymon schoolhouse was badly damaged in 1922, as was also the vacant rectory and lands attached thereto [...] I believe the damage mentioned was done because of the political and religious opinions of myself and my small congregation and because of our allegiance to the British Government.[272]

The destruction of the Protestant church in Miltown Malbay was damaging to the anti-Treaty republicans during the civil war, as they were blamed locally for this outrage. James D. Kenny, a leading republican in the area, denied assertions from Commandant Michael Brennan that republican forces were responsible for the burning. The local commanding officer of the anti-Treaty forces, Anthony Malone, stated that he had no knowledge of who caused the outrage and that it was committed without the sanction of the local officers. Nevertheless, he accepted that it was commonly believed that republicans were responsible. He added that such outrages were damaging to the republican cause.[273]

The question of sectarianism was also highlighted in some of the claims made under the Damage to Property (Compensation) Act, 1923, as there are several references to the destruction of Protestant Church properties in the county during 1923 and 1924. The Protestant ministers in Ennis (Rev. J. Griffin), Kildysart (Rev. Henry S.V. Daly) and Miltown Malbay (Rev. A. Elliott) submitted a joint claim for compensation on behalf of the Representative Body of the Church of Ireland relating to damage done to church properties in their parishes. The scope and content of the claim is as follows:

> Destruction of stained-glass church windows at New Quay,

between 13 August and 20 August 1922; the burning and total destruction of church and contents at Legard, Miltown Malbay on 14 July 1922; the seizure of church bell and damage to church slates at Lahinch, besides smashing of doors and windows on 3 June 1922; the seizure and destruction of church property at Ennistymon on 19 June 1922, with every window of the rectory was smashed, while the marble altar piece was broken; the occupation and destruction of Kildysart rectory by Irregular forces on 2 July 1922; and damage to Ennistymon rectory and out-offices between March and October 1922.[274]

William F. Carroll, from Kildysart, also made a claim relating to the burning of a rectory and its contents on 2 July 1922. The destruction of the Protestant rectory at Kildysart, which was owned by Carroll, was caused by 'Irregulars' (anti-Treaty republicans) in July 1922. In June 1922 the republicans took possession of the rectory, and when vacating it on 2 July, they burnt it as well as the out-offices. The rectory was being used occasionally. Compensation of £450 was awarded by Judge Bodkin. There were 11 acres attached to the rectory; the land was sold separately.[275] In addition to these claims, Henry Webster made a claim for damage to the Methodist church at the Causeway, Ennis between 1 June and 30 June 1922.[276]

Several people besides clergymen made claims for damages to property, alleging sectarian motives. Mr Bothwell of Kilkee made a claim for damage to property and seizure of equipment at Kilkee on 22 May 1922. In his claim, Bothwell also mentioned that all Protestants had been warned to leave within twelve hours.[277] Francis William Gore Hickman submitted a compensation claim for 'the destruction of his property and livestock driven off his lands at Kilmore, Knock, in support of Belfast Catholics from February 1922 to March 1923.'[278]

The threats against some of the Protestants of west Clare were also highlighted in contemporary newspapers:

> On Friday morning [28 May 1922] several Protestants in Kilrush received threatening letters warning them to clear out of Kilrush within 12 hours or take the consequences. The notices were posted on their doors. Notices were also posted up in the Market Square. Recipients were very disturbed by the threats.

Ironically, they reported the matter to the anti-Treaty IRA, and the

Brigadier Commandant Simon McInerney 'took prompt action and issued a proclamation denouncing the threats and asking the citizens of Kilrush to help in tracing the culprits. The IRA promised to protect the Protestants of Kilrush'. Very Rev. Fr Dean McInerney, PP, strongly denounced the letters at Mass on Sunday. Fr Culligan, CC, presiding over the district court at Kilrush, also strongly denounced the threats to the Protestant people of Kilrush.[279]

David Fitzpatrick, in his study of the War of Independence period, concludes that the Clare Volunteers were not motivated by sectarianism:

> Overall, Clare Volunteers did their best to suppress anti-Protestant bigotry [...] It is true that six big houses were burnt down in Clare just before the Truce as a regular Volunteer operation of which the Chief of Staff fully approved [18th Infantry Brigade intelligence summary, 20 August 1921], but the houses were unoccupied and the Volunteers seem to have feared that the police or military would commandeer them for barracks. Volunteer officers often proved unable to contain the vengeful fury of their rank and file in the villages and countryside, obsessed with ancestral grievances.[280]

Sadly, sectarianism was also experienced in the period between the Treaty and the end of the civil war, with the worst cases occurring between May and August 1922. Some responsibility for this sectarianism must be accepted by the anti-Treaty republicans in the county, and at least one aspect of it was sanctioned by the highest levels of the republican Army Executive in 1922.

A.T.Q. Stewart gives a Northern insight into sectarian violence:

> One major source of error is the confusion between terrorist violence and sectarian violence. They are not the same, though they appear so. Terrorist violence consists of a deliberately planned campaign of outrages intended to achieve a political purpose and is directly aimed at coercing government. Sectarian violence, on the other hand, is the continuing consequence of environmental and historical circumstances [...] Rage at terrorist murders of members of one community can provide sectarian disorder in another community. Equally, sectarian disorder can provide a convenient cloak for planned terrorist activity [...] The conflict in Northern Ireland has become over the years every bit as sectarian as that which rages in Jerusalem.[281]

Sectarian outrages have been common in the north of Ireland ever since the Plantation of Ulster in the seventeenth century. Nevertheless, since the foundation of Northern Ireland after the passage of the Government of Ireland Bill, 1920, there have been many bitter sectarian clashes in this deeply divided society. These outrages usually flare up during the Orange parades in July and August each year, and around the time of elections. Between 1920 and 1923, hundreds of Catholics and Protestants were killed in these sectarian clashes. These killings were condemned by nationalists and unionists in Clare. Protestant select vestries in various parts of the county met and issued statements on the matter.

The select vestry of the Protestant church in Kilkee held a meeting on Easter Monday in 1920 and passed the following resolution:

> That we, the members of the Protestant community in Kilkee do herby condemn in the strongest possible terms, the appalling atrocities committed in Belfast against our unfortunate Catholic countrymen. We have always lived on the best of terms with our fellow Catholic countrymen and we disassociate ourselves entirely with the brutalities of the North. And we desire that a copy of this resolution be sent to the press.

Also, at a meeting of the select vestry of the united parishes of Tuamgraney and Inishcaltra, a resolution was passed, condemning the outrages taking place in north-east Ulster, 'The victims have our utmost sympathy, and we sincerely hope that the friendly relations existing between the Roman Catholics and Protestants of Southern Ireland, will soon prevail in this unfortunate area.' A protest had already been signed by all the Protestants of the district, and the resolution was forwarded to the government.[282]

Alexander Knox, a Protestant businessman from Ennis, condemned religious persecution and religious bigotry in Belfast. Also, on 20 September 1920, at a meeting of Ennis Protestants chaired by Richard John Stacpoole, DL, of Eden Vale, the following resolution was passed:

> That we, the Protestant residents in the parish of Drumcliffe, Co Clare, view with the gravest concern, the outrages and reprisals which are taking place in Ireland, and deeply regret that while we in our churches are praying for the peace and welfare of our country, our co-nationalists should commit such outrages which

are in direct contravention to our prayers. We desire to record the fact that we live in peace and good will with our Catholic fellow-countrymen, that religious intolerance does not exist in our county; and we sincerely hope that nothing has been done will disturb the harmony which has always existed in this parish.[283]

Ironically, while nationalists and unionists from Clare condemned sectarian outrages by Orangemen and loyalists in Northern Ireland, some republicans in the county were behaving in a sectarian manner towards the Protestants in Clare. On 12 June 1922, Commandant Simon McInerney sent the following letter to the editor of the *Clare Champion*:

A Chara,

Please publish in the next issue of your paper the following explanation regarding the confiscation of the property of Mr F W Gore Hickman, of Kilmore House, Knock:

Acting under orders from GHQ, I, as Brigadier Commandant of the 5th Brigade [west Clare], confiscated the property, effects and stock on above estate as a reprisal for the extermination of the Roman Catholic population in Ulster. A Proclamation was issued at the time to this effect. The cattle on this estate were sold by the officers of B Coy [Kilmurry McMahon] 2nd Batt, on my orders, and the proceeds of the sale were handed over to the Brigade QM [quartermaster] at Brigade's HQ, Cappa, Kilrush. The officers concerned not receiving a penny of the proceeds. This explanatory letter has been written as it has come to my knowledge that certain individuals made grave allegations against these officers to the effect that they sold the cattle on their own authority and kept the proceeds. Signed, Simon McInerney, Brigade Commandant, Fifth Brigade, First Western Division.[284]

Clearly, this was a blatant act of sectarianism, as Francis William Gore Hickman, a Protestant, was being punished in west Clare for the sectarian acts committed against Catholics in Ulster by loyalists and Orangemen. Secondly, and significantly, McInerney stated that he was acting under orders from the republican Army Executive. Moreover, Gore Hickman was not the only Protestant in Clare to receive such sectarian treatment; it seems that several other Protestants were also punished as a reprisal for the sectarian attacks in Ulster.

On June 21, a British newspaper, the *Morning Post*, published an article about the treatment of Protestants and loyalists in Clare, 'A statement of the case of Mr Francis Gore Hickman [Kilmore House], an Irish loyalist, who has been driven from Ireland and ruined by the Free State.' To corroborate this claim by Gore Hickman, the *Morning Post* published a statement by Henry Vincent MacNamara:

> I am an Irish landowner and loyalist, and for 37 years 1883–1920, I resided at Ennistymon House [...] I possess an estate of 12,000 acres, there is also a small town of 1,200 inhabitants and two villages [...] I farmed about 2,000 acres, which I kept in my own occupation.
>
> From the middle of 1919, owing to the weakness of Dublin Castle administration, things in County Clare were getting steadily worse [...] In Dec 1919 I was one of a shooting party of seven [...] we were ambushed and became the centre of murderous fire [...] After this, the state of the country became worse [...] and as the demeanour of the people grew more hostile, I considered it unsafe for my wife and two daughters to remain in Ireland. We left our home at the end of February 1920.
>
> I put my steward in possession of my house, he gradually disposed of my stock and farm implements [...] I must state that there are charges, head rents on my property amounting to £30,000, upon which I pay yearly interest of 5% [...] which costs about £1,500 annually.
>
> After my departure, many outrages were committed on my property. Some of my respectable tenants were driven by threats from the farms they held and forced to surrender them. A large tract of my valuable grazing land was seized and, as was stated recently in the Freeman's Journal, is being administered by a 'Soviet' [...] Two substantial seaside houses and out-offices were destroyed by fire [...] I have obtained decrees for £5,000, but I have not received a penny.

In the *Morning Post* article, Henry Vincent MacNamara states that, in May 1922, he received a letter from Frank Barrett, acting as commandant of the republican 1st Western Division, which outlined the reasons that he was to be forced from his residence. The letter, signed by Frank Barrett, was published in the newspaper:

> As a result of the treatment of the Catholic population in Belfast

and other Northern towns by the Orange gunmen there are thousands of men, women and children homeless and starving.

There is no doubt in our minds that the policy of the Orangemen is to drive all the Catholics from the Northern area.

We are also fully alive to the fact that the British Government is supplying the necessary cash and arms to enable the Orangemen to complete the task of exterminating all Catholics from the north.

Now these homeless people and starving people have to be attended to and all their immediate needs supplied.

For this purpose, housing accommodation is an immediate necessity. Equally immediate is the necessity of food for these people.

In the absence of other resources for this purpose, the Executive Council of the IRA have decided that Unionists and Free Masons [*sic*] in the South and West of Ireland be compelled to supply these needs.

In pursuance of this decision you are hereby ordered to leave your residence at Ennistymon House, Co. Clare, which, with your entire property is confiscated in the name of the Executive Council of the I.R.A.

MacNamara's letter to the *Morning Post* continued:

Reference is made in the notice to me as an Orangeman and Freemason, as a matter of fact I belong to neither of these organisations. Being a Protestant and a Loyalist was quite enough for me receiving condign punishment.

Shortly after the receipt of this notice my Protestant steward was given a friendly hint to make himself scarce and in due course he removed with his family to a safer place. My house was then occupied by members of the IRA, who were subsequently evicted by Free State troops, by a fusillade, which broke most of my windows [...] For the past eight months, the Civic Guard have been in occupation, but no rent has been paid. Moving my family and furniture to London has put me to enormous expense [...] my case is like so many others – the result of loyalty to king and country. What a tragedy that such an utterance should be possible.

In the *Morning Post* article, MacNamara included a copy of a letter that he had received from Gore Hickman:

> I reported the seizure of your property to the Provisional Government troops and have been informed that they are unable to take any action in the matter as they are powerless. I received an intimation yesterday that Kilmore House, Knock, my place and all my goods have also been seized and confiscated. I had about £1,500 worth of cattle there, about £700 worth of hay and a large amount of agricultural machinery and implements and I have absolutely no redress. I got a message late last evening that Kiltannon [Colonel Moloney's property in Tulla] and everything on it had been confiscated. The entire country from New Quay and Ballyvaughan to Corofin has been driven and the cattle are wandering all over the country. This is, of course, quite a different matter from the seizure of your property.
>
> Your property, Molony's, and my property have been seized by the Irish Republican Army who have officially notified us of this. I presume that you will lay the facts before the authorities in London or have the matter raised in Parliament. We can do nothing. We had arranged to collect rents in Ennistymon to-day but of course having received notification of the seizure of your property had to cancel all arrangements.[285]

Mrs Elizabeth MacNamara, widow of Henry Vincent MacNamara of Ennistymon, was awarded a total of £7,750 by the Irish Grants Committee. Gore Hickman submitted a claim for compensation to the Irish courts in 1924, and the documents signed by Simon McInerney and Frank Barrett were produced in court at Ennis as evidence. Gore Hickman originally put in a claim for the destruction of Kilmore House, the furniture and other properties on the demesne of 500 acres for a sum of £50,000, but he subsequently reduced this claim to £39,647. Gore Hickman claimed that there were twenty-eight apartments in the mansion, that his wife and daughter were threatened and had to go to London, and that walls were knocked down, cattle were driven and 1,900 trees were destroyed. Gore Hickman was awarded £17,777 for damage done to the house, furniture, out-offices, trees and fisheries, and for rentals lost and cattle sold illegally.[286]

On 22 June 1921, towards the end of the War of Independence – just nineteen days before the truce – the IRA GHQ issued the following order, authorising reprisals against active enemies of Ireland:

Republican Army Orders, 1921

On every occasion in which the enemy destroys house property or contents, the following counter-reprisals may be taken:

a   A similar number of houses belonging to the most active enemies of Ireland may be destroyed in the Battalion area;

b   They should have their lands confiscated;

c   They should be ordered out of the country.

No person shall be regarded as enemies of Ireland, whether they be described locally as unionist, Orangemen, etc., unless they are actively anti-Irish in their actions.[287]

The Army Executive used this order to justify their attacks on several property owners in Clare in letters signed by their officers there, Commandant Simon McInerny and General Frank Barrett.

Shortly after the Treaty was ratified in the Dáil, a meeting of Clare unionists was held at Harmony Row Schoolhouse on Tuesday, 17 January 1922. The following resolution was proposed by R.J. Stacpoole, DL, seconded by William J. McNamara, a barrister, and passed unanimously:

That we the unionists of County Clare assembled at Ennis this 17 January 1922, recognise that a new form of government, accepted by a majority of the Irish people has now been legally established, and we, therefore deem it to be both the duty and the interest of all loyal subjects and good citizens, as it will be our own most sincere wish, to do everything possible to strengthen the hands of the new administration and to assist them in the discharge of the arduous duties which they have undertaken.

We are gratified by the assurances given that their administration will be impartial, and we believe that this policy steadfastly adhered to, will prove to be the best means calculated to produce general peace and contentment and ultimately to bring the whole of Ireland under one form of government again, as we feel that the best interests of the whole country must suffer so long as its people remain divided, and therefore in many respects, disunited.[288]

Despite this statement, many Protestant mansions were also burnt during the civil war. The Protestant mansions and other properties burnt around this time included: Roslevan House, Barefield; Kilmore House, Knock; Glenwood, Sixmilebridge; Ballinahinch House, Scariff; and a lodge at Paradise House, Ballynacally. It must be remembered that these and other properties may have been destroyed by land agitators who hoped to drive out landlords and break up Protestant estates. Besides the burnt properties, Mount Callan House was ransacked and Eden Vale House was commandeered by republicans for about three weeks in 1922. Many Protestants lived in fear that their properties would be burnt, and some of them, such as the Keanes of Beech Park, the MacDonnells of Newhall and the Stacpooles of Eden Vale, sold their estates and left the country.[289]

Lord and Lady Inchiquin of Dromoland Castle, who were among the leading unionists and Protestants in the county, also experienced this fear. Some of their private letters reflect the psychological stress of this 'reign of terror' on their lives. The government forces offered them some protection in June 1922; writing to her son Donough, Lady Inchiquin stated:

> We have four men from the Free State army and they stay at Carr's house and remain here all night but return to the barracks in the village [Clarecastle] during the day. We give them breakfast and supper. They are very young men but seem quite nice, they have got rifles and revolvers. Two nights ago, at around 2 am I heard a shot, a man on a cart passed through during the night and the man had failed to answer their challenge until a shot was fired over their heads [...] I told you that Everett saw De Valera driving around in our De Dion. As soon as he got out at the barracks Everett asked the chauffer who owned the car? The man turned on him rudely and said: 'mind your own business!' I hear that the Stackpooles [Eden Vale] have gone to Wales, we, and the Ballyalla O'Briens and the Keanes [Beech Park] are about the only people now left.[290]

Her fears intensified around the end of July, during the civil war, when she wrote:

One might as well be in east Africa – we are really going through the most extraordinary times, one can hardly believe that the people are a civilised people or a Christian people, they behave more like savages than anything else they can be compared to [...] This last week has been a horrid week as we heard that this place was going to be burned down. Personally, I have become more nervous during the last week than I have been for all the time since the rebellion in 1916. Cullinan, the yard man with 7 others of our workmen have volunteered to watch the place from twelve to six for a few nights [...] some are on the roof, some hidden in bushes, and all are armed, so that on the approach of a body of men they can fire on them and give the alarm so that the big bell can be rung and the Free State army warned at once to come from the village. It is horrid waking up in the night fearing one may hear the shots. The fire hoses are all in order. Lord Dunally's house has been burnt down and we hear rumours that Adare, Lord Dunraven's house has been burnt. Surely this cannot last much longer, it is incredible that it has gone on for so long. The people are worse than the savages in Africa. Well, the only thing to do is to stay here quietly until peace is established, or until we are driven out.[291]

The records of the Irish Distress Committee and the Irish Grants Committee indicate that many people in Clare suffered physically, psychologically and financially during the War of Independence, the truce and the civil war due to the actions of republicans and others. These records, along with other contemporary accounts, also show that many Protestants suffered because of sectarian actions against them, their properties and their churches during these years. It is generally accepted, however, that the IRA leadership did not sanction such sectarian atrocities as the burning of churches in Clarecastle and O'Briensbridge during the War of Independence, and the burning of Miltown Malbay church during the civil war.

It is remarkable that the Army Executive of the anti-Treaty IRA, with an army order issued on 22 June 1921, authorised the confiscation of the properties of leading Protestants in Clare in the period between the acceptance of the Treaty and the civil war. In letters sent to Gore Hickman and Henry Vincent MacNamara, the local officers in Clare, Commandant Simon McInerney and General Frank Barrett, used the terms 'Orangemen', 'loyalists' and 'Freemasons' to justify their actions against several Protestant families in Clare – including the Gore Hickmans of Kilmore, the MacNamaras of Ennistymon and the Molonys of Kiltannon – as reprisals for sectarian outrages in Northern Ireland. In Clare, they cloaked their sectarian policies and deeds with a philanthropic policy of helping the homeless and starving in Northern Ireland who were suffering at the hands of Orangemen. With these policies and actions, they breached a core principle of Irish republicanism attested by everyone from Wolfe Tone to the signatories of the 1916 proclamation: to unite Protestant, Catholic and dissenter under the common name of Irishmen and to respect the religious freedom of all Irish people.

Despite their acceptance of the Treaty, the Protestant community were being targeted, officially and unofficially, by the republicans in Clare during the civil war. Between February and August 1922, they experienced a 'reign of terror'. Their churches and other religious properties were burnt or seriously vandalised in places such as New Quay, Miltown Malbay, Lahinch, Kildysart and Ennis; they were publicly warned to leave Kilrush within twenty-four hours; their businesses were boycotted and damaged; and some of their estates were threatened with confiscation and commandeered by republican forces. There were also threats to their homes, several of which were maliciously burnt, and they lived under constant fear of threats to their lives and properties.

The worst time for the Protestant community in Clare during the civil war was in the early months of that conflict, when republican forces were very active in the county and the government forces had not yet taken control. After several years of conflict, darker and perhaps latent sectarian forces were unleashed upon the minority Protestant community in the county. David Fitzpatrick's statement about Protestants in Clare during the War of Independence highlights their plight:

> from 1919 onwards, Protestants had good reason to complain that their properties and lives were no longer secure, though none was murdered in Clare. To many of them emigration seemed to be the only tolerable course [...] for those who remained the psychological pressure was terrible.[292]

On Sunday, 12 May 1923, in a powerful statement, Bishop Fogarty of Killaloe condemned the treatment of Protestants, 'Their Protestant fellow countrymen, I regret to have to say it, were persecuted and dealt with in a cruel and coarse manner.'[293]

There was some truth in what President Michael D. Higgins stated in August 2016:

> We must recognise the atrocities of the Civil War for what they were on both sides – cruel, vicious and at times infused by vengeance rather than by compassion. They reveal the jagged ends of land hunger, envy, and indeed it should be no longer denied, the opportunity was taken for a sectarian identification of targets.[294]

APPENDICES

Appendix I: Brigandine and armed robberies in Clare in 1922 and 1923

Despite the fact that the republicans had robbed the Bank of Ireland in Ennis of a sum of money amounting to over £18,000 in April 1922, they carried out many more armed robberies in the county during the civil war, as the following table of robberies reported in the local press indicates:

13 July 1922, armed raid for foodstuffs at Lahinch and Ennistymon.

4 November 1922, bank raid at Kilrush; on Tuesday morning, 10 a.m., three armed men disguised as women raided the National Bank and secured £1,606.

4 November 1922, armed raids on shops in Mullagh.

11 November 1922, armed robberies in Ennistymon and Quilty.

18 November 1922, armed raids in Tubber for whiskey, bacon and clothing.

25 November 1922, armed raid on Ballyvaughan post office, £100 taken. During this raid the postmistress, Ms Grant, collapsed and died.

30 December 1922, armed robberies on private houses in Clarecastle and Sixmilebridge.

5 January 1923, armed robbery of Clarecastle post office; the armed robbers stated that they were seeking 'funds for the cause'.

6 January 1923, armed robberies of houses in Mullagh and near Miltown Malbay.

20 January 1923, robbery of Colonel Tottenham's car at Mount Callan.

27 January 1923, armed robbery of mail train near Ennistymon.

5 February 1923, robbery of R.J. Stacpoole's car at Edenvale.

31 March 1923, robbery of post offices at Maurice's Mills and Inagh.

7 April 1923, armed robbery of J. Kett, rent collector at Kilkee.

Source: Based on contemporary reports in the local papers, the *Clare Champion* and the *Saturday Record*, between July 1922 and April 1923.

Appendix II: Calendar of ambushes during the civil war in Clare

5 July 1922, ambush at Drehidnagower, Ennis–Ennistymon road.

15 July 1922, engagement at Kilrush.

5 August 1922, attack at Meelick.

6 August 1922, attack on Clarecastle barracks.

12 August 1922, attack on Kildysart barracks.

19 August 1922, attack on Clarecastle barracks.

20 August 1922, attack at Kildysart.

22 August 1922, ambush at Moy; ambush at Effernan near Kildysart.

24 August 1922, ambush between Barefield and Crusheen.

26 August 1922, ambush at Kilrush.

17 September 1922, attack on Ennistymon workhouse; ambush at Lickeen, Ennistymon.

29 October 1922, attack at Ennis.

6 November 1922, ambush at Tullycrine.

18 November 1922, attack at Killaloe.

16 December 1922, attack at Clarecastle.

23 December 1922, attack at Miltown Malbay; attacks at Ennis.

16 January 1923, attack at Kilmihil.

27 January 1923, ambushes at Kilrush and Kilmihil.

27 January 1923, ambush at Miltown Malbay.

18 April 1923, ambush at Kildysart.

21 April 1923, attack at Ennis.

Source: Based on contemporary reports in the the *Clare Champion* and the *Saturday Record* between July 1922 and April 1923. Note also that some records of the 2nd Battalion Mid-Clare Brigade, compiled by Joe Barrett, were deposited in the Clare County Archives at Ennis. These records corroborate the ambushes in that battalion area.

Appendix III: Destruction of public buildings
Civic Guard stations:

Kilkee, 29 November 1922

O'Briensbridge, 27 December 1922

Coastguard stations:

Ballyvaughan, 5 July 1922

Quilty, 10 July 1922

Dough, 29 July 1922

Kilkee, 29 July 1922

Cappa (Kilrush), August 1922

Seafield, August 1922

Courthouses:

Mountshannon, September 1922

Broadford, 16 March 1923

RIC Barracks:

Tiermaclane, 13 April 1922

Clarecastle, 1 July 1922

Ennis, 1 July 1922

Lisdoonvarna, 1 July 1922

O'Briensbridge, 5 July 1922

Rockvale, 11 July 1922

Feakle, 19 July 1922

Kilkee, 29 July 1922

Kilrush, 29 July 1922

Mountshannon, November 1922

Workhouses:

Kildysart workhouse, 1 July 1922

Corofin workhouse, 25 July 1922

Scariff workhouse, July 1922

Ennistymon workhouse, August 1922

Source: Files for the Damage to Property (Compensation) Act, 1923, *passim.*

Appendix IV: Deaths during the civil war

Civilians	Ex-RIC	Government troops	Republicans	Total
3	1	22	13	39

Appendix V: IRA arms holdings in Clare on 1 October 1921
West Clare Brigade

Rifles:
Lee–Enfield (.303): 8 guns, 150 rounds
Howth Mauser (single shot, 9mm): 2 pistols, rounds unknown
Mauser (magazine, .776mm): 2 revolvers, rounds unknown
Miniature (.22): 2 guns, rounds unknown

Shotguns:
Double-barrelled shotgun: 24 guns, 200 rounds
Single-barrelled shotgun: 36 guns

Handguns:
Revolver (.45): 10 guns, 15 rounds
Automatic (colt, .38): 5 guns, 12 rounds
Parabellum (short): 2 guns, 11 rounds

Mid-Clare Brigade

Rifles:
Lee–Enfield (.303): 48 guns, 2,000 rounds
Martini (.303): 20 guns
Miniature (.22): 3 guns, 300 rounds

Shotguns:
Double-barrelled shotgun: 80 guns, 100 rounds
Single-barrelled shotgun: 100 guns

Handguns:
Revolver (.45): 50 guns, 200 rounds

Grenades:
Grenades: 43

East Clare Brigade

Rifles:
Lee–Enfield (.303): 38 guns, 1,500 rounds
Martini (.303): 20 guns
Mauser: 8 guns, rounds unknown
Miniature: 7 guns, rounds unknown

Shotguns:
Double-barrelled shotgun: 60 guns, 1,000 rounds
Single-barrelled shotgun: 80 guns

Handguns:
Parabellum: 6 guns, 100 rounds
'Peter the Painters': 4 guns, no rounds
Colt (.45): 4 guns, 70 rounds
Colt (.32): 3 guns, 7 rounds

[Note: The Howth Mausers were retrieved from the Howth gun-running on 26 July 1914, when the Irish Volunteers secured a delivery of about 1,500 Mauser rifles, which were brought from Germany in Erskine Childers's yacht. 'Peter the Painter' was a popular name for a Mauser C96, also imported at Howth.]

Source: Reports from GHQ, Inspecting officers to Chief of Staff, 1 October 1921, Mulcahy Papers, UCD, Archives Collections, P7/A/11, P7/A/25 and P7/A/26.

Appendix VI: List of arms in the 1st Western Division
Weapons:
Rifles: 156.
Revolvers: 178.
Automatics: 37.
Bulldogs: 104.
Total: 475

Ammunition:
.303 rounds: 4,156.
Revolver rounds: 2,573.
Automatic rounds: 734.
Total: 7,463
Grenades:
Grenades: 109

Source: Joe Barrett Papers, 'Officers Training Camp Tubber,' dated 6/9/1921, courtesy of Dr Paul O'Brien, Mary Immaculate College, Limerick.

Appendix VII: Officers of the 1st Western Division from 11 November 1921

Commanding officer: Commandant-General Michael Brennan
Vice-commanding officer: Commandant Frank Barrett
Adjutant: Joe Barrett
Information Officer: James Hogan

Brigade officers

Position	East Clare Brigade	Mid-Clare Brigade	West Clare Brigade	South-east Galway Brigade	South-west Galway Brigade
Brigadier	A. Brennan	F. Barrett	J.J. Liddy	L. Kelly	D. Reynolds
Vice-brigadier	T. McGough	P. O'Loughlin	C. Whelan	unknown	unknown
Adjutant	H. O'Mara	J. Clohessy	W. Haugh	N. Pullen	unknown
Quarter-master	J. Hannon	S. O'Keefe	T. Marrinan	unknown	unknown

Source: Based on Joe Barrett's Operations Book, courtesy of Dr Paul O'Brien, Mary Immaculate College, Limerick.

BIBLIOGRAPHY

Books

Abbott, R., *Police Casualties in Ireland, 1919–1922* (Cork: Mercier Press, 2000).

Andrews, C.S., *Dublin Made Me* (Cork: Mercier Press, 1979).

Augusteign, J., *From Public Defiance to Guerrilla Warfare: The Experience of Ordinary Volunteers in the Irish War of Independence, 1916–1921* (Dublin: Irish Academic Press, 1996).

Barry, T., *Guerrilla Days in Ireland* (Cork: Mercier Press, 1955).

Béaslaí, P., *Michael Collins and the Making of a New Ireland* (London: The Phoenix Publishing Co., 1926).

Breen, D., *My Fight for Irish Freedom* (Tralee: Anvil Books, 1989).

Brennan, M., *The War in Clare 1911–1921* (Dublin: Four Courts Press, 1980).

Browne, K.J., *Eamon de Valera and the Banner County* (Clare: Glendale, 1982).

Buckland, P., *Irish Unionism 11: Ulster Unionism and the Origins of Northern Ireland, 1886–1922* (Dublin: Gill and Macmillan, 1973).

Bury, R., *Buried Lives: The Protestants of Southern Ireland* (Dublin: The History Press Ireland, 2017).

Byrnes, O., *Around the Square: The Story of Ennis Hurling* (Clare: published by the author, 2003).

Carroll, A., *Sean Moylan: Rebel Leader* (Cork: Mercier Press, 2010).

Coogan, T.P. and G. Morrison, *The Irish Civil War* (London: Weidenfeld and Nicholson, 1998).

Crowley, J., D. O'Droisceoil and M. Murphy (eds), *Atlas of the Irish Revolution* (Cork: Cork University Press, 2017).

Deasy, L., *Brother against Brother* (Cork: Mercier Press, 1998).

Deasy, L., *Towards Ireland Free* (Cork: Mercier Press, 1972).

Devas, N., *Two Flamboyant Fathers* (London: Collins, 1966).

Dooley, T., *The Irish Revolution, 1913–1923: Monaghan* (Dublin: Four Courts Press, 2017).

Dorney, J., *The Civil War in Dublin: The Fight for the Irish Capital, 1922–1924* (Dublin: Merrion Press, 2017).

Dwyer, T.R., *Tans, Terror and Troubles: Kerry's Real Fighting Story, 1913–23* (Cork: Mercier Press, 2001).

Durney, J., *The War of Independence in Kildare* (Cork: Mercier Press, 2013).

Enright, S., *The Irish Civil War: Law, Execution and Atrocity* (Dublin: Merrion Press, 2019).

Ferriter, D., *A Nation and Not a Rabble: The Irish Revolution, 1913–1923* (New York: The Overlook Press, 2015).

Fitzpatrick, D., *Politics and Irish Life, 1913–1921* (Dublin: Gill and Macmillan, 1977).

Fitzpatrick, D., *The Two Irelands, 1912–1939* (Oxford: Oxford University Press, 1998).

Foster, R.F., *Modern Ireland, 1600–1972* (London: Penguin, 1988).

Foster, R.F. (ed.), *The Oxford History of Modern Ireland* (Oxford: Oxford University Press, 2001).

Garvin, T., *1922: The Birth of Irish Democracy* (Dublin: Gill and Macmillan, 1996).

Griffin, G., *The Collegians* (London: Atlantic Books, 2008).

Hart, P., *The IRA and Its Enemies: Violence and Community in Cork, 1916–1923* (Oxford: Clarendon Press, 1998).

Hayes, B., *The IRA: A Documentary History* (Dublin: Gill and Macmillan, 2010).

Heffernan, B., *Freedom and the Fifth Commandment* (Manchester: Manchester University Press, 2014).

Herlihy, J., *Royal Irish Constabulary Officers, 1816–1922* (Dublin: Four Courts Press, 2005).

Herlihy, J., *The Royal Irish Constabulary* (Dublin: Four Courts Press, 2016).

Hopkinson, M., *Green against Green: The Irish Civil War* (Dublin: Gill and Macmillan, 1988).

Hopkinson, M., *The Irish War of Independence* (Dublin: Gill and Macmillan, 2002).

Jackson, A. (ed.), *The Oxford History of Modern Ireland* (Oxford: Oxford University Press, 2014).

Keane, F., *Wounds: A Memoir of War and Love* (London: William Collins, 2017).

Keane, H., *Memories of My Childhood in Co. Clare* (printed for private circulation, 1990).

Kee, R., *Ireland: A History* (London: Abacus, 2000).

Kee, R., *The Green Flag* (Penguin: London, 1989).

Kennedy, G., *The Crusheen Volunteers and Their Role During 1916* (published by the author, in Crusheen, 2013).

Kissane, B., *The Politics of the Irish Civil War* (Oxford: Oxford University Press, 2005).

Laffan, M., *The Resurrection of Ireland: The Sinn Féin Party, 1916–1923* (Cambridge: Cambridge University Press, 1999).

Lyons, F.S.L., *Ireland Since the Famine* (Glasgow: Fontana, 1971).

MacLysaght, E., *Changing Times: Ireland since 1898* (Buckinghamshire: Colin Smythe, 1978).

McArdle, D., *The Irish Republic* (London: Victor Gollanz, 1937).

McCarthy, C., *Cumann na mBan and the Irish Revolution* (Cork: The Collins Press, 2007).

McCarthy, D., *Ireland's Banner County: Clare from the Fall of Parnell to the Great War, 1890–1918* (Clare: Saipan Press, 2002).

Mac Conmara, T., *Days of Hunger: The Clare Volunteers and the Mountjoy Hunger-strike of 1917* (Clare: Dallan Publishing, 2017).

Mac Conmara, T., *The Time of the Tans: An Oral History of the War of Independence in County Clare* (Cork: Mercier Press, 2019).

Matthews, A., *Dissidents: Irish Republican Women, 1923–46* (Cork: Mercier Press, 2012).

Morrison, G., *The Irish Civil War: An Illustrated History* (Dublin: Gill and Macmillan, 1981).

Mulcahy, R., *My Father, the General: Richard Mulcahy and the Military History of the Revolution* (Dublin: Liberties Press, 2014).

Murphy, J.A., *Ireland in the 20th century* (Dublin: Gill and MacMillan, 1975).

Murray, P., *Oracles of God: The Roman Catholic Church and Irish Politics, 1922–37* (Dublin: UCD Press, 2000).

Neeson, E., *The Civil War in Ireland* (Cork: Mercier Press, 1966).

O'Brien, G.R., *These My Friends and Forebears: The O'Briens of Dromoland* (Clare: Ballinakella Press, 1991).

O'Brien, P., *The Glynns of Kilrush County Clare, 1811–1940: Family, Business and Politics* (Dublin: Open Air, 2019).

O'Brien, P., *Havoc: The Auxiliaries in Ireland's War of Independence* (Cork: The Collins Press, 2017).

O'Callaghan, J., *The Irish Revolution, 1913–23: Limerick* (Dublin: Four Courts Press, 2018).

O'Callaghan, S., *The Informer* (London: Transworld Publishers, Ltd., 1998).

O'Conchubhair, B., *Limerick's Fighting Story, 1916–21: Told by the Men Who Made It* (Cork: Mercier Press, 2000).

O'Corrai, C., and S. O'Corrai, *Peadar Clancy: Easter Rising Hero, Bloody Sunday Martyr* (Galway: Cranny Publications, 2016).

O'Doherty, G. (ed.), *With the IRA in the Fight for Freedom: The Red Path of Glory* (Cork: Mercier Press, 2010).

O'Donoghue, F., *No Other Law: The Story of Liam Lynch and the Irish Republican Army, 1916–1923* (Dublin: Irish Press Ltd., 1954).

O'Flaherty, L., *The Informer* (Dublin: Wolfhound Press, 2006).

O'Gadhra, N., *Civil War in Connaught, 1921–23* (Cork: Mercier Press, 1999).

O'Leary, C. and P. Maume, *Controversial Issues in Anglo-Irish Relations 1910–1921* (Dublin: Four Courts Press, 2004).

O'Malley, E., *On Another Man's Wound*, (Tralee: Anvil Books, 1990).

O'Malley, E., *The Singing Flame* (Dublin: Anvil Books, 1978).

O'Malley, K.H. and A. Dolan (eds), *No Surrender Here: The Civil War Papers of Ernie O'Malley, 1922–24* (Dublin: Lilliput Press, 2007).

O'Reilly, S., *Clare GAA: The Club Scene, 1887–2010* (Clare: published by the author, 2010).

O'Reilly, T. (ed.), *Our Struggle for Independence: Eyewitness Accounts from the Pages of An Cosantoir* (Cork: Mercier Press,

2009).

Ó Ruairc, P.Ó., *Blood on the Banner: The Republican Struggle in Clare* (Cork: Mercier Press, 2009).

Ó Ruairc, P.Ó., *Revolution: A Photographic History of the Revolutionary Ireland, 1913–1923* (Cork: Mercier Press, 2011).

Ó Ruairc, P.Ó., *Truce: Murder, Myth and the Last Days of the Irish War of Independence* (Cork: Mercier Press, 2016).

Ó Ruairc, P.Ó. (ed.), *The Men Will Talk to Me: Clare Interviews by Ernie O'Malley* (Cork: Mercier Press, 2016).

O'Sullivan, D.J., *The Irish Constabularies, 1822–1922* (Kerry: Brandon Books, 2000).

Pakenham, F., *Peace by Ordeal* (London: Weidenfeld and Nicholson, 1935).

Power, J., *A History of Clare Castle and Its Environs* (Clare: published by the author, 2004).

Power, J., *The GAA in Clare Castle, 1887–1987* (Clare: GAA, 1987).

Power, J., *Clare and the Great War* (Dublin: The History Press, 2015).

Price, D., *The Flame and the Candle: War in Mayo, 1919–1924* (Cork: The Collins Press, 2012).

Ryan, M., *Tom Barry: IRA Freedom Fighter* (Cork: Mercier Press, 2003).

Ryan, M., *Liam Lynch: The Real Chief* (Cork: Mercier Press, 2005).

Shanahan, E., *The Hand that Held the Gun: Untold Stories of the War of Independence in West Clare* (Clare: Clare Books, 2019).

Share, B., *In a Time of Civil War: The Conflict on the Irish Railway* (Cork: The Collins Press, 2006).

Sheedy, K., *The Clare Elections* (Dublin: Bauroe Press, 1993).

Spellissy, S., *The Ennis Compendium: From Royal Dun to Information Age Town* (Clare: The Book Gallery, no date).

Smith Walsh, E., *Kilkenny in Time of Revolution, 1900–1923* (Dublin: Merrion Press, 2019).

Stacpoole, J., *Stacpoole: The Owners of a Name* (Auckland: published for private circulation, 1991).

Stewart, A.T.Q., *The Shape of Irish History* (Belfast: The Blackstaff Press, 2001).

Townshend, C., *The Republic: The Fight for Irish Independence, 1918–1923* (London: Allen Lane, 2013).

Valiulis, M.G., *Portrait of a Revolutionary: General Richard Mulcahy and the Founding of the Irish Free State* (Kentucky: University of Kentucky Press, 1992).

Walsh, M., *Bitter Freedom: Ireland in a Revolutionary World, 1918–1923* (London: Faber and Faber, 2015).

Williams, T.D., *The Irish Struggle, 1916–1926* (London: Routledge & K. Paul, 1966).

Weeks, L. and M. O'Fhartaigh (eds), *The Treaty: Debating and Establishing the Irish State* (Dublin: Irish Academic Press, 2018).

Younger, C., *Ireland's Civil War* (London: Fontana/Collins edition, 1970).

Articles cited in journals

Cahill, S., 'The life and death of Thomas Shannon', *The Other Clare*, 41 (2017), pp. 26–9.

Clancy, C., 'The experiences of a Sinn Féin priest: Fr Pat Gaynor and self-government in Clare 1919–1921', *The Other Clare*, 31 (2007), pp. 51–8.

Fitzpatrick, D., 'Protestant depopulation and the Irish Revolution', *Irish Historical Studies*, 38, 152 (2013), pp. 643–70.

Hart, P., 'The Geography of Revolution in Ireland 1917–1923', *Past and Present*, 155 (May 1997), pp. 142–55.

Hayes, M., 'Dail Eireann and the Irish Civil War', *Studies* (Spring 1969).

Hopkinson, M., 'The Irish Civil War, 1922–23 from a pro-Treaty Perspective', *The Irish Sword, Journal of the Military Society of Ireland*, 20, 82 (Winter 1997), pp. 287–92.

Murphy, E.D., 'The Patrick Hennessy Letters', *The Other Clare*, 30 (2006), pp. 13–15.

Murphy, B.P. 'The Irish Civil War 1922–23, An anti-Treaty Perspective', *The Irish Sword, Journal of the Military Society of Ireland*, 20, 82 (Winter 1997), pp. 293–307.

O'Dea, S., 'Clare in 1920', *The Capuchin Annual*, 14 (1970), pp. 276–86.

Mac Conmara, T., 'These four Claremen have taken on the British

Empire, the Clare Volunteers and the transformation of Ireland in 1917', *The Other Clare*, 36 (2012), pp. 27–32.

O'Murcadha, C., 'Dr Donough MacNamara's memoir of the War of Independence', *The Other Clare*, 40 (2016), pp. 16–26.

O'Murcadha, C., 'Prison letters of Canon O'Kennedy', *The Other Clare*, 37 (2013), pp. 21–5.

Ó Ruairc, P., 'The distinction is a fine one, but a real one: Sectarianism in County Clare during the War of Independence', *The Other Clare*, 34 (2010), pp. 35–42.

Ó Ruairc, P., 'Missing in action-British servicemen secretly buried in Clare during the War of independence', *The Other Clare*, 36 (2012), pp. 77–80.

Newspapers
Clare Champion
Saturday Record
Cork Examiner
Freeman's Journal
Galway Advertiser
Irish Independent
Irish Times
Limerick Leader

Magazines
Capuchin Annual
History Ireland
The Irish Sword
The Other Clare

Clare County Archives
Clare County Council Minute Books CC/12/6, Minutes from 6 November 1920–September 1923.

Clare County Council Finance Committee Minute Books, CC/GMIN/7, 10 December 1917–1 November 1920.

Clare County Council Finance Committee Minute Books, CC/GMIN/8, 14 December 1920–29 September 1923.

ENDNOTES

1 J. Power, *The GAA in Clare Castle 1887–1987* (Clare: Clarecastle GAA, 1987), pp. 95–6.
2 E. Smith Walsh, *Kilkenny in Time of Revolution, 1910–1923* (Dublin: Merrion Press, 2019), pp. 97–100.
3 Police reports for County Clare, October–December 1917, National Archives of Ireland (NAI), MFA/54/62.
4 *Saturday Record* (*SR*), editorial, 10 December 1921; *Clare Champion* (*CC*), editorials, 10, 24 December 1921.
5 *SR*, 31 December 1921. Those for the motion included: Thomas Hogan, J.J. Scanlan, P. O'Loughlin (Liscannor), Thomas McGrath (O'Callaghan's Mills), H. O'Mara, B. Crowley, Thomas McGrath (Farrihy), Michael McMahon, J. O'Connor, M. Casey, P. Kelly, M. Quin, H.J. Hunt, Sean O'Keefe, A. Brennan, J.D. Moony and the chairman Michael Brennan. Those against: M. Murray, P. O'Loughlin (Kilfenora), J.D. Kenny, P. Devitt (Ennistymon) and S. Madigan.
6 *SR*, 31 December 1921.
7 *Irish Independent*, 28 December 1921; *SR*, 31 December 1921; *Freeman's Journal*, 9 December 1921; *Irish Independent*, 9 December 1921; Bishop Fogarty's letter to Childers is cited in P. Murray, *Oracles of God: The Roman Catholic Church and Irish Politics, 1922–37* (Dublin: UCD Press, 2000), p. 44, originally found in the Childers Papers, Trinity College Dublin, Fogarty to Childers, 8/12/21; Edward MacLysaght's letter to Bishop Fogarty, Killaloe Diocesan Archives (KDA), box 15. The letter is undated, but must have been written on or about 10 December 1921. P. Murray, *Oracles of God*, pp. 238–99.
8 *SR*, 31 December 1921.
9 Clare County Council Minute Book from 1 November 1920 to 29 September 1923, Clare County Archives, CC/Min/12/9; Sean O'Keefe to Éamon de Valera, 22 December 1922, Richard Mulcahy Papers, UCD Archives Collections, PT/A/32; Report by Michael Brennan to the chief of staff, dated 6 February 1922, Richard Mulcahy Papers, P7/A/33; *SR*, 7 January 1922. On the second occasion, those voting for the Treaty included: T. Hogan, John J. Scanlan; P. O'Loughlin (Liscannor), T. McGrath (O'Callaghan's Mills), H. O'Mara, T. Wall, B. Crowley, T. McGrath (Farrihy), M. McMahon, J. O'Connor, M. Casey, P. Kelly, M. Quinn, P. Kearse, P. Clancy, J.D. Moloney, A. Brennan and the chairman Michael Brennan. The councillors who voted against the Treaty were: M. Murray, P. O'Loughlin (Kilfenora), J. O'Dwyer, J.D. Kenny, Sean McNamara, Sean O'Keefe, P. Devitt, S. Madigan and M. Molony. The IRB, led by Michael Collins, the president of that revolutionary body, did issue a directive on 12 December to all members to support the Treaty, but elected representatives were given freedom of action to accept or reject the Treaty, see C. Younger, *Ireland's Civil War* (London: Fontana/Collins edition, 1970), p. 216.
10 *CC*, 7 January 1922; *SR*, 7 January 1922. For the motion: M. Brady (chairman), John Doyle, M. Gleeson, P. Hill, D. McNamara, J. Noonan, M.T. Moloney, M. Corbett, J. O'Halloran, T. Wall (county councillor), J. Reddan, S.A. Minogue, M.

McMahon, M. Cleary, P. McMahon, J. Dinan, T. Hayes, J.D. Moloney (county councillor), C.J. Clancy, T. Hogan, P. McCarthy and M. Finagan. Against: T. Kelly (county councillor).

11 *SR*, 7 January 1922; *CC*, 7 January 1922. For the motion: B. Mescall (Clarecastle), John Hehir (Kilmaley), John Malone (Kilmaley), M. Keane (Ennis), P.J. McNamara (Ennis), M. O'Grady (Ballynacally), Denis O'Loughlin (Corofin), James Lalor (Doora), James Clohessy (Ennis), Denis Keogh (Newmarket-on-Fergus), M. Brennan (Tradaree), H.J. Hunt (Corofin), T.V. Honan (Ennis), Rev. Fr Crowe (Barefield), Rev. Fr Breen (Ruan), Rev. Fr Hamilton (Ennis) and M. Donnellan (O'Callaghans Mills). The following members did not vote or else abstained on the motion: J. Keating (Kilnamona), M. Hegarty (Kilnamona), M. Hogan (Inch), Frank Cullinan (Inch), D.H. McParland (Ennis), James Kierse (Corofin), Michael Casey (Ruan), R.T. Molony (Newmarket-on-Fergus) and Rev. Fr D Flynn (Lissycasey).

12 *SR*, 7 January 1922; *CC*, 7 January 1922.

13 *SR*, 7 January 1922; *CC*, 7 January 1922.

14 *Irish Independent*, 7 January 1922; *CC*, 7 January 1922.

15 Intelligence summary, secret report, 20 August 1921, Mulcahy Papers, UCD Archives Collection, P7/ A/23; Intelligence Officer to Director of Intelligence, 16 September 1921, Military Archives, Michael Collins Papers, IE/MA/CP/5/2/21 {xxv}; County Inspector's report, NAI MFA/54/72, 30 October 1921.

16 In November 1921, the Minister for Defence, Cathal Brugha, issued a special memorandum regarding the collection of levies, effectively banning all forced collections (Papers of the East Limerick Brigade, University of Limerick, Special Collections, P46/7, dated 25/11/1921); Chief of staff to OC Mid-Clare Brigade, Richard Mulcahy Papers, UCD Archives Collection, P7/A/26: 'Frank Barrett has authority to raise a levy for the support and administration of the Volunteers'; County inspector's reports for July–September 1921, NAI, MFA/54/72-4; instructions for fund-raising issued by O/C, HQ, 1st Western Division, ref no 2, 2-11-1921, a copy of this instruction is in the Local Studies Centre, Ennis.

17 'Operations of the First Western Division,' Joe Barrett Papers, Mary Immaculate College, Limerick, courtesy of Dr Paul O'Brien; Police reports, November 1921, NAI, MFA 54/72; Michael Ryan to Director of Intelligence, 8 August 1921, Military Archives, Michael Collins Papers, IE/MA/CP/3/40(iii).

18 *CC*, 7 January 1922; *SR*, 7 January 1922; *Irish Independent*, 8 January 1922; L. Weeks and M. O'Fathartaigh (eds), *The Treaty: Debating and Establishing the Irish State* (Dublin: Irish Academic Press, 2018), p. 187. Note: on 8 December 1938, seven surviving members of the Second Dáil calling themselves the executive council of Dáil Éireann, who had not accepted the Treaty and who had not joined Fianna Fáil after 1926, presumptuously delegated the 'authority' of the declaration of the Irish Republic, which they asserted 'reposed in the second Dáil', to the army council of the IRA. They stated that they were the custodians of the republic declared by the Second Dáil. This transfer of authority of the 'Republican trust' to the army council of the IRA was announced in *Saoirse Éireann, The Wolfe Tone Weekly*, 2, 18 (December 1938). The lead headline of that edition, under the masthead, was, 'IRA take over the Government of the Republic'. The seven signatories, who claimed to be custodians of this 'Republican Trust', were: John Kelly, George Noble (Count Plunkett), Brian O'Higgins, Charles Murphy, Thomas McGuire and Maire MacSweeney. Brian O'Higgins had been Sinn Féin TD for west Clare between 1918 and 1924. He was the editor of *Saoirse Éireann* in 1938. B. Hayes, *The IRA: A Documentary History* (Dublin: Gill and Macmillan, 2010), p. 100, shows a copy of *Saoirse Éireann,* dated 17 December 1938, courtesy of the National Library of Ireland.

19 *SR*, 14 January 1922.
20 *CC*, 14, 21 January 1922.
21 *SR*, 21 January 1922; *CC*, 21 January 1922.
22 *CC*, 28 January 1922.
23 *CC*, 11 February 1922.
24 *CC*, 21 January 1922; *CC* 3 December 1921.
25 *CC*, 4 February 1922.
26 *CC* 4, 11 and 25 February 1922; *SR*, 4, 11 and 25 February 1922.
27 *CC*, 29 April, 10 June 1922; K.J. Browne, *Éamon de Valera and the Banner County* (Clare: Glendale, 1982), p. 162; P.Ó. Ó Ruairc (ed.), *The Men Will Talk to Me: Clare Interviews by Ernie O'Malley* (Cork: Mercier Press, 2016), p. 105; É. Gaynor, *Memoirs of a Tipperary Family: The Gaynors of Tyone, 1887–2000* (Dublin: Geography Publications, 2008), p. 203; telephone conversations with Sean Spellissy, 19–20 August 2020, who told me that Jimmy Mahony, an old IRA man from Ennis, told him this story in 1988.
28 K.H. O'Malley and A. Dolan (eds), *No Surrender Here: The Civil War Papers of Ernie O'Malley, 1922–24* (Dublin: Lilliput Press, 2007), p. 337. For a comprehensive account of political developments in Ireland, see C. Townshend, *The Republic: The Fight for Irish Independence, 1918–1923* (London: Allen Lane, 2013), pp. 347–447, passim.
29 *CC*, 29 April 1922; *SR,* 29 April 1922.
30 *CC*, 4 February 1922.
31 *SR*, 24 June 1922; *CC*, 24 June 1922; B. O'Cathaoir, 'Another Clare: Ranchers and Moonlighters, 1700–1945' in M. Lynch, W. Nolan and P. Nugent (eds), *Clare History and Society* (Dublin: Geography Publications, 2008), pp. 359–425.
32 *CC*, 29 April 1922.
33 *CC*, 4 March 1922; Witness Statement, Captain Michael Fogarty of Crusheen, later O/C of North Galway Brigade, 1920–1921, WS 673; F.S.L. Lyons, *Ireland Since the Famine* (Glasgow: Fontana, 1971), p. 454; also, *Irish Independent* 17, 18 and 20 March 1922, for de Valera's militant speeches at Dungarvan, Carrick on Suir, Thurles and Killarney; David McCullough, *De Valera, vol. 1, Rise, 1882–1933* (Dublin: Gill and MacMillan, 2017), pp. 232–3; Ronan Fanning, *Eamon de Valera: A Will to Power* (London: Faber and Faber, 2015), pp. 133–4.
34 *SR*, 3 December 1921; *CC*, 4 March 1922; Michael Collins' letter to Bishop Fogarty, KDA, box 15, dated 13 January 1921.
35 *CC*, 6 May 1922.
36 *CC*, 6 May 1922.
37 In their Lenten pastorals, the Catholic bishops of Galway and Limerick also appealed for peace in Ireland. *CC*, 4 March 1922; Dr Berry's statement is quoted in *CC*, 13 April 1921; *SR*, 13 April 1921.
38 *CC*, 22, 29 April 1922.
39 *SR*, 8 April 1922; D. McArdle, *The Irish Republic* (London: Victor Gollanz, 1937), p. 696.
40 *CC*, 6 May 1922.
41 *CC*, 22 November 1924; *SR*, 22 November 1924.
42 É. Gaynor, *Memoirs of a Tipperary* Family, pp. 203, 205. Tom Garvin cites a Garda report found in the Desmond Fitzgerald Papers, UCD (p. 850–1), from County Clare in 1929, referring to former IRA men who had set themselves up on the proceeds of bank raids, T. Garvin, *1922: The Birth of Irish Democracy* (Dublin: Gill and Macmillan, 1996), p. 102.
43 *CC*, 13 May 1922; *SR*, 15, 22 April 1922.
44 C. Townshend, *The Republic*, pp. 394–6; M. Coleman, *The Irish Revolution, 1916–*

1923 (London: Routledge, 2014), p. 107; John O'Callaghan, *Limerick, The Irish Revolution, 1912–23* (Dublin: Four Courts Press, 2018), pp. 103–5.
[45] *SR*, 17 June 1922; *CC*, 17 June 1922.
[46] *CC*, 15, 22 April, 10 June; C. Townshend, *The Republic*, p. 403.
[47] C. Townshend, *The Republic*, p. 397; T. Garvin, *The Birth of Irish Democracy*, p. 18.
[48] *CC*, 29 April, 6 May 1922.
[49] *CC*, 15, 22, 29 April, 13 May 1922. Ó Ruairc states that the barracks at Broadford was taken over by government troops in February 1922. He also states that the barracks was captured by local IRA Volunteers on Friday 21 April but was recaptured by government troops on the following Sunday, and that William O'Brien was shot dead on Sunday, 23 April during an attempt to disarm him, P.Ó. Ó Ruairc, *Blood on the Banner: The Republican Struggle in Clare* (Cork: Mercier Press, 2009), pp. 294–5.
[50] *CC*, 6 May, 22, 3 June 1922.
[51] *CC*, 3 June 1922; *SR*, 3 June 1922; Police reports for September/October 1921, dated 3 November 1921, NAI/MFA/54/72.
[52] Damage to Property (Compensation) Act, 1923, the National Archives of Ireland, copy in Local Studies Centre, Ennis.
[53] P. Murray, *Oracles of God*, pp. 57, 61, 152; *CC*, 30 April 1922; *Irish Independent*, 11 April 1922; Also, K. Sheedy, *The Clare Elections* (Dublin: Bauroe Press, 1993), p. 345.
[54] P. Murray, *Oracles of God*, pp. 53, 446, 450.
[55] É. Gaynor, *Memoirs of a Tipperary Family*, p. 268.
[56] Records of the Irish Distress and Irish Grants Committee, British National Archives, Kew, London, file ref. no. CO 762, copy in Local Studies Centre, Ennis, ref. 118/19, pp. 2048–9.
[57] Irish Distress and Irish Grants Committee, ref. 93/20 and 93/21, pp. 1555 and 1556.
[58] Irish Distress and Irish Grants Committee, ref. 44/7, p. 679.
[59] Irish Distress and Irish Grants Committee, ref. 118/20, p. 2050; 120/11, p. 2078.
[60] Irish Distress and Irish Grants Committee, ref. 138/5, p. 2328.
[61] Irish Distress and Irish Grants Committee, ref. 128/6, p. 2194.
[62] Irish Distress and Irish Grants Committee, ref. 18/12, p. 225.
[63] Irish Distress and Irish Grants Committee, ref. 187/7, p. 3291.
[64] Irish Distress and Irish Grants Committee, ref. 158/1, p. 2670.
[65] Irish Distress and Irish Grants Committee, ref. 68/20, p. 1112.
[66] Irish Distress and Irish Grants Committee, ref. 94/21, p. 1581.
[67] Irish Distress and Irish Grants Committee, ref. 94/21, p. 1581.
[68] Irish Distress and Irish Grants Committee, ref. 109/5, p. 1875.
[69] Irish Distress and Irish Grants Committee, ref. 122/4, p. 2098.
[70] Irish Distress and Irish Grants Committee, ref. 172/1, p. 2958.
[71] Irish Distress and Irish Grants Committee, ref. 157/20, p. 2668.
[72] Irish Distress and Irish Grants Committee, ref. 95/1, p. 1584.
[73] Irish Distress and Irish Grants Committee, ref. 171/17, p. 2948.
[74] Irish Distress and Irish Grants Committee, ref. 55/10, p. 840.
[75] Irish Distress and Irish Grants Committee, ref. 80/2, p. 1305.
[76] Irish Distress and Irish Grants Committee, ref. 42/18, p. 653.
[77] Irish Distress and Irish Grants Committee, ref. 96/3, p. 1609.
[78] Irish Distress and Irish Grants Committee, ref. 68/1, p. 1093.
[79] Irish Distress and Irish Grants Committee, ref. 172/1, p. 2958.
[80] Irish Distress and Irish Grants Committee, ref. 43/9, p. 663.
[81] Irish Distress and Irish Grants Committee, ref. 64/15, p. 1018.

82 Irish Distress and Irish Grants Committee, ref. 72/4, p. 1173.
83 Irish Distress and Irish Grants Committee, ref. 158/1, p. 2670.
84 Irish Distress and Irish Grants Committee, ref. 158/2, p. 2671.
85 Irish Distress and Irish Grants Committee, ref. 162/16, p. 2756.
86 Irish Distress and Irish Grants Committee, ref. 164/6, p. 2783.
87 Irish Distress and Irish Grants Committee, ref. 126/15, p. 2175.
88 Irish Distress and Irish Grants Committee, ref. 200/7, p. 3622.
89 Irish Distress and Irish Grants Committee, ref. 47/1, p. 719.
90 Irish Distress and Irish Grants Committee, ref. 86/2, p. 1401.
91 Irish Distress and Irish Grants Committee, ref. 128/11, p. 2199; also, *SR*, 31 January, 7, 14 February 1914.
92 Irish Distress and Irish Grants Committee, ref. 160/11, p. 2717; 157/3, p. 2651.
93 Irish Distress and Irish Grants Committee, ref. 117/5, p. 2008.
94 Irish Distress and Irish Grants Committee, ref. 104/12, p. 1782.
95 Irish Distress and Irish Grants Committee, ref. 138/6, p. 2329; 199/19, p. 3612.
96 Irish Distress and Irish Grants Committee, ref. 116/3, p. 1991.
97 Irish Distress and Irish Grants Committee, ref. 92/20, p. 1533.
98 Irish Distress and Irish Grants Committee, ref. 167/8, p. 2846.
99 Irish Distress and Irish Grants Committee, ref. 193/22, p. 3443.
100 Irish Distress and Irish Grants Committee, ref. 4/9, p. 20.
101 Irish Distress and Irish Grants Committee, ref. 72/3, p. 1172.
102 See files under the relevant names.
103 A. Bielenberg, 'Southern Irish Protestant experiences of the Irish Revolution' in J. Crowley, D. O'Droisceoil and M. Murphy (eds), *Atlas of the Irish Revolution* (Cork: Cork University Press, 2017), pp. 770–80.
104 T. Garvin, *1922*, p. 164.
105 F. O'Donoghue, *No Other Law: The Story of Liam Lynch and the Irish Republican Army, 1916–1923* (Dublin: Irish Press Ltd., 1954), appendices 9 and 10. The proclamation was signed by Liam Lynch, Liam Deasy, Ernie O'Malley, Con Moloney, Tom Derrig, Sean Lehane, Frank Aiken, Frank Barrett, Seamus Robinson, Tom Barry, Sean Moylan, P. Whelan and Joe O'Connor. See also, E. Neeson, *The Civil War in Ireland* (Cork: Mercier Press, 1966), pp. 327–8.
106 L. Deasy, *Brother against Brother* (Cork: Mercier Press, 1998), pp. 45, 48; C. Younger, *Ireland's Civil War* (London: Fontana/Collins edition, 1970), p. 326.
107 C. Townshend, *The Republic*, p. 450; A. Dolan, *Commemorating the Irish Civil War: History and Memory, 1923–2000* (Cambridge: Cambridge University Press, 2003), p. 200.
108 F.S.L. Lyons, *Ireland Since the Famine*, p. 460.
109 D. Ferriter, 'After commemoration comes the hard part', *Irish Times*, 2 April 2016.
110 C.S. Andrews, *Dublin Made Me* (Cork: Mercier Press, 1979), p. 306.
111 Captured Military Documents, Lot 232/1, no date, Military Archives, Cathal Brugha Barracks.
112 *CC*, editorial, 8 July 1922.
113 T. Garvin, *1922*, pp. 25, 39–43, 63, 70, 104.
114 C. Townshend, *The Republic*, pp. 359, 361.
115 R. McGreevy, 'Fianna Fáil's emergence', *Irish Times*, 2 June 2018; *CC*, 19 August 1922.
116 *SR*, 27 January 1923.
117 É. Gaynor, *Memoirs of a Tipperary Family*, pp. 178–80, 213, 217.
118 M. Hopkinson, *Green against Green: The Irish Civil War* (Dublin: Gill and Macmillan, 1988), p. 155.
119 B. Kissane, *The Politics of the Irish Civil War* (Oxford: Oxford University Press,

2005), p. 4.

[120] P.Ó. Ó Ruairc (ed.), *The Men Will Talk to Me*, pp. 46–7, 69–70, 153.

[121] E. MacLysaght, *Changing Times: Ireland since 1898* (Buckinghamshire: Colin Smythe, 1978), p. 134.

[122] Statement of Patrick Keane, Kilnamona, copy in Local Studies Centre, Clare County Library, Ennis.

[123] *CC*, 28 January 1922.

[124] Cited in N. O'Gadhra, *The Civil War in Connaught, 1922–1923* (Cork: Mercier Press, 1999), p. 51.

[125] Captured Documents, Military Archives, Cathal Brugha Barracks, Lot 232/1, no date.

[126] Files for the Damage to Property (Compensation) Act, 1923, the National Archives of Ireland, copy in Local Studies Centre, Ennis, FIN/COMP/2/3/65.

[127] Reports from Clare to IRA Chief of Staff, dated 12 July 1922, Maurice 'Moss' Twomey Papers, Archive Collections, UCD, P 69/28 (155), P 69/28 (129).

[128] M. Hopkinson, *Green against Green*, pp. 146–50; P.Ó. Ó Ruairc, *The Battle for Limerick City* (Cork: Mercier Press, 2010), pp. 80–2. See also C. Younger, *Ireland's Civil War*, pp. 370–5; M. Ryan, *Liam Lynch: The Real Chief* (Cork: Mercier Press, 2005), p. 179. John O'Callaghan, in *Limerick: The Irish Revolution, 1912–1923* (Dublin: Four Courts Press, 2018), p. 108, states that General Liam Lynch 'dawdled [...] and made a major tactical miscalculation' in his military dealings at Limerick, which allowed a 'distinct advantage to the pro-Treaty forces'; telephone conversation with Des Long, Limerick, on 20 August 2020.

[129] *CC*, 29 July 1922.

[130] *SR*, 29 July 1922.

[131] *CC*, 5 August 1922.

[132] Report from Clare, Maurice Twomey Papers, Archive Collections, UCD, P 69/28 (137), dated 13 July 1922; Report from Clare, P 69/28 (152), dated 11 July 1922. See Captured Documents, Military Archives, Cathal Brugha Barracks for various dates, from 15 July to 28 July, Lots 24/5; 24/6; Lot 24/11; 27 July 1922; 24/7; 24/8; 24/9; 24/11; 24/12; 24/15 and 24/16. For references to the theft of cars and motorcycles, see Files for the Damage to Property (Compensation) Act, 1923, passim.

[133] Letter from Seamus Hennessy, Commandant 4th Batt, 4th Brigade to Commandant General Frank Barrett, OC 4th Brigade, late July 1922, Captured Documents, Military archives, Dept of Defence, Cathal Brugha Barracks, Lot 24 /1.

[134] Commandant Hennessy to O/C, 18 July 1922, Captured Documents, Military Archives, Cathal Brugha Barracks, Lot 24/1; 24/2; 24/3; Lot 24/12.

[135] P.Ó. Ó Ruairc (ed.), *The Men Will Talk to Me*, pp 69–70.

[136] *SR*, 14 April 1923.

[137] *SR*, 29 July 1922.

[138] Maurice Twomey Papers, Archive Collections, UCD, P69/28 (38), dated 8 p.m. 24 July to 3 p.m. 25 July 1922.

[139] *SR*, 5 July 1922.

[140] *CC*; *SR*, 8 July 1922.

[141] Report from Clare to IRA GHQ, Clonmel, 13 July 1922, Maurice Twomey Papers, Archive Collections, UCD, P69/28 (102).

[142] *CC*, 15 July 1923; Maurice Twomey Papers, Archive Collections, UCD, P 69/28 (102), dated 13 July 1922.

[143] *CC*, 15 July 1923.

[144] Maurice Twomey Papers, Archive Collections, UCD, P 69/28 (103), dated 13 July 1922.

[145] Reports from Clare, dated 24–25 July, Maurice Twomey Papers, Archive Collections, UCD, P69/28 (63), P69/28 (38); Reports from Clare, dated 27–29 July 1922, Maurice

Twomey Papers, Archive Collections, UCD, P69/28(3–4); Humphrey Murphy to HQ, ref. no A/8, to O.C., 8th Battalion (North Kerry), Captured Documents, Military Archives, Cathal Brugha Barracks; see also E. Neeson, *The Civil War*, pp. 258–9; P. O'Brien, *The Glynns of Kilrush County Clare, 1811–1940: Family, Business and Politics* (Dublin: Open Air, 2019), pp. 137–9.

[146] James Adam & Son, Auctioneers, 26 St. Stephen's Green, Dublin 2, Auction Catalogue description, Lot 561, auction date 20 April 2010, First Western Division; Report from Clare, dated 13 July 1922, Maurice Twomey Papers, Archive Collections, UCD, P69/28 (102); Con Moloney, adjutant to assistant chief of staff, Ernie O'Malley, 29 July 1922, Maurice Twomey Papers, UCD Archives, P69/39.

[147] *Irish Times*, 3 August 1922; CC, 12 August 1922.

[148] CC, 23 July, 5 August 1922.

[149] CC, 19 August 1922.

[150] Meda Ryan, *The Day Michael Collins Was Shot* (Dublin: Poolbeg Press, 1989), pp. 122–3; SR, 26 August 1922; CC, 2 September 1922.

[151] SR, 9 September 1922.

[152] See reports in the *Clare Champion* and *Saturday Record* on 15 July, 12 August, 9, 23 September, 7 October, 2, 9, 17 December 1922, 20 January, 3, 14 February, and 14 April 1923; B. Share, *In a Time of Civil War: The Conflict on the Irish Railway* (Cork: The Collins Press, 2006), p. 99; Summary of official reports received on 13/14 January 1923, Military Archives, Cathal Brugha Barracks, Lot 28, Box 6-9.

[153] Reports in *Saturday Record* and *Clare Champion*, 22, 29 July, 5, 12, 26 August, 9 September, 7, 21, 28 October, 11, 18 November, 23 December 1922, 16 January, 17 February, 31 March, 14 April 1923; *The Motor*, 12 September 1922, p. 275; 'Civil War Papers', dated 1 February 1923, Joe Barrett Papers, Mary Immaculate College, Limerick (MIC), courtesy of Dr Paul O'Brien.

[154] CC, 22 July 1922.

[155] O'Brien family papers, letter courtesy of Grania Weir, née O'Brien, Whitegate.

[156] CC, 9 September 1922; SR, 9 September 1922.

[157] Files for the Damage to Property (Compensation) Act, 1923, FIN/COMP/2/3/307.

[158] From Patrick Keane's Military Service Record Pension Application, copy in Local Studies Centre, Ennis.

[159] CC, 5 August 1922; SR, 5 August 1922; *Irish Times*, 3 August 1922; CC, 12 August 1922; J. Power, *The GAA in Clare Castle 1887–1987*, p. 94.

[160] CC, 12 August; SR, 12 August 1922.

[161] CC, 26 August 1922. Note: William Blake, an elderly resident of Clarehill, Clare-castle, told me *c*.1974 that the attackers fired from the village side of the bridge, from behind Sheedy's garden wall and the embankment in Devine's field. He said that the fusillade continued up Main Street and the Pound (Patrick Street) as the attackers retreated by the Kildysart Road. There was little sleep for the people of Clarecastle during these attacks.

[162] CC, 18 November 1922; SR, 16 December 1922.

[163] From the *Freeman's Journal*, copied by CC, 5 August 1922.

[164] CC, 5 August 1922.

[165] CC, 9 September 1922. See the local papers, the *Clare Champion* and the *Saturday Record*, for the dates between August 1922 and April 1923 for reports of sweeps in the county.

[166] T. Garvin, *1922*, p. 164.

[167] SR, 29 July; CC, 29 July 1922.

[168] O'Brien family papers, letters courtesy of Grania Weir, née O'Brien, Whitegate; also, G.R. O'Brien, *These My Friends and Forebears: The O'Briens of Dromoland* (Clare: Ballinakella Press, 1991), pp. 209–18

169 *CC*, 5, 19, 26 August 1922; Operations File, Military Archives, Cathal Brugha Barracks, CW/OPS/9/07, Box 25, dated 19 May 1923.

170 Capt M. Moloney OC Inagh Coy 4th Batt to F. Barrett, 21 July 1922, Captured Documents, Military Archives, Cathal Brugha Barracks, Lot 24/10.

171 Files for the Damage to Property (Compensation) Act, 1923, see claims under the following names: Henry Bindon Alton (agent for McAdams), William Hawkins Ball, Annie Gore, John Hastings, Helen Henn, F.W.G. Hickman, Anastasia Joyce, Marcus Keane, E.S. O'Brien, Robert J. Parker, Robert Thompson, Edith Vereker, Gilbert Willis (agent for Lord Leconfield), Edith Stacpoole and G.W. Stacpoole; J. Stacpoole, *Stacpoole: The Owners of a Name* (Auckland: published for private circulation, 1991), pp. 158–61.

172 *SR*, 29 July 1922; Letter from Anthony Malone, Miltown Malbay to HQ 4th Batt, dated 15 July 1922, Captured Documents, Military Archives, Cathal Brugha Barracks, Lot 24/4; also, *CC*, 12, 19 August 1922.

173 T. Garvin, *1922*, p. 114.

174 *CC*, 30 September 1922; *SR*, 21, 28 October, 4 November 1922, 12 May, 7 October 1923.

175 *CC*, 23 February 1923; *SR*, 31 March 1923; *SR*, 14 April 1923; *SR*, 2 June 1923; *SR*, 12 July 1924. Files for the Damage to Property (Compensation) Act, 1923, see under William Charles Doherty, and Ellie O'Callaghan.

176 *CC*, 26 August 1922; *SR*, 7 October 1922, 2 February 1923; anecdote told to me by his son, Dermot Gleeson of Carnelly. Justice D.F. Gleeson, MRIA, was a distinguished historian and wrote a history of the Diocese of Killaloe among other works. Files for the Damage to Property (Compensation) Act, 1923, see under Susan McDonnell.

177 *CC*, 29 July 1922; *SR*, 29 July 1922.

178 *SR*, 6 January 1923; *CC*, 2, 16 September 1922; *SR*, 2, 16 September 1922; Gemma Clark, 'Violence against women in the Irish Civil War, 1922–3: gender-based harm in global perspective', *Irish Historical Studies*, XLIV, 165 (May 2020), pp. 75–90; Joe Barrett Papers, Mary Immaculate College, Limerick, Civil War Papers, dated 14 February 1923, courtesy of Dr Paul O'Brien.

179 Files for the Damage to Property (Compensation) Act, 1923, FIN/COMP/2/3/403; FIN/COMP/2/3/280; FIN/COMP/2/3/398; FIN/COMP/2/3/133; FIN/COMP/2/3/374; FIN/COMP/2/3/396; and FIN/COMP/2/3/319.

180 Files for the Damage to Property (Compensation) Act, 1923, FIN/COMP/2/3/178; FIN/COMP/2/3/374.

181 Files for the Damage to Property (Compensation) Act, 1923, FIN/COMP/2/3/41; FIN/COMP/2/3/180; FIN/COMP/2/3/311; FIN/COMP/2/3/99; FIN/COMP/2/3/373; and FIN/COMP/2/3/379.

182 Files for the Damage to Property (Compensation) Act, 1923, FIN/COMP/2/3/226; FIN/COMP/2/3/227; FIN/COMP/2/3/336; FIN/COMP/2/3/231; FIN/COMP/2/3/317; and FIN/COMP/2/3/135.

183 *CC*, 3 February 1923.

184 *CC*, 19 March, 7 April 1923; Military Archives, Cathal Brugha Barracks, CW/OPS/9/07, Box 25.

189 *SR*, 14 March 1922; 27 January, 22 September 1923

185 P. Murray, *Oracles of God*, pp. 407–8.

186 *CC*, 5 August; *SR*, 12 August 1922.

187 See the full text of the pastoral in R. Aldous and N. Puirséil, *We Declare: Landmark Documents in Ireland's History* (London: Quercus Books, 2008), pp. 140–5; *CC*, 14, 28 October; *SR*, 14, 28 October; *The Freeman's Journal*, 11 October 1922; *Irish Independent*, 11 October 1922; *Irish Times*, 11 October 1922.

188 C.S. Andrews, *Dublin Made Me*, pp. 250, 253. M. Ryan records that the threat of

excommunication caused much suffering among the republicans, but 'in spite of the men's strong religious feelings they were prepared to continue the struggle even under the threat of excommunication' (M. Ryan, *Liam Lynch*, p. 48).

189 P. Murray, *Oracles of God*, p. 240.

190 P.Ó. Ó Ruairc, *Blood on the Banner*, pp. 311–12, 314.

191 *CC*, 23 December 1922.

192 *CC*, 17 February 1923; *SR*, 17 February 1923; *Irish Independent*, 18 August 1923; *Sinn Fein*, 21 August 1923; https://theirishrevolution.wordpress.com/.

193 *CC*, 8 July, 5 August 1922; P.Ó. Ó Ruairc, *Blood on the Banner*, p. 299.

194 *CC*, 12 August 1922; P.Ó. Ó Ruairc, *Blood on the Banner*, pp. 309, 310, 325, 329; Notes compiled by Maurice 'Moss' Twomey *c*.1930, University of Limerick, Glucksman Library, Special Collections, West Clare Brigade papers, P 45/18(2); P 45/16(2).

195 *CC*, 30 September 1922; P.Ó. Ó Ruairc, *Blood on the Banner*, pp. 316–17, 325–7; *SR*, 22, 29 July; *CC*, 12 August 1922; *SR*, 14 April; *CC*, 21 April 1923; *Irish Times*, 26 September 1922; J. Dorney, *The Civil War in Dublin: The Fight for the Irish Capital, 1922–1924* (Dublin: Merrion Press, 2017), pp. 181–2; Mulcahy Papers, Archive Collections, UCD, P7/B/60; S. Enright, *The Irish Civil War: Law, Execution and Atrocity* (Dublin: Merrion Press, 2019), p. 104, n. 19 p. 167.

196 *CC*, 26 August 1922; *SR*, 26 August 1922.

197 *SR*, 30 September 22; *CC*, 30 September 1922; S. Enright, *The Irish Civil War*, p. 17. Enright does not cite a source for this information.

198 *CC*, 8, 15, 29 July 1922; *SR*, 29 July, 9 September, 7, 29 October 1922, 20 January 1923.

199 *CC*, 2 September; *SR*, 2 September, 7 October 1922; *Cork Examiner*, 1 January 1923; T. Doyle, *The Summer Campaign in Kerry* (Cork: Mercier Press, 2010), pp. 45, 142–4; Townshend, *The Republic*, p. 443; J. Dorney, *The Civil War in Dublin*, pp 245–6; T. Doyle, *The Civil War in Kerry* (Cork: Mercier Press, 2008), see several references to the massacres in Kerry; J. Dorney, *The Civil War in Dublin*, pp. 245–6.

200 *CC*, 11, 18 November 1922; *SR*, 11, 18 November 1922; *SR*, 2 December 1922; *SR*, 20, 27 January 1923; *CC*, 5 May 1923; *SR*, 5 May 1923.

201 *SR*, 21 October 1922; *SR*, 22 September 1922; *CC*, 22, 29 September 1923; *SR*, 8 December 1923.

202 B.T. Murphy, 'The Government's Executions Policy during the Civil War 1922–1923', PhD thesis, NUI Maynooth, October 2010, pp. 3–4, 183, 241, 288.

203 *CC*, 12 August 1922; *SR*, 12 August 1922; *Irish Times*, 10 August 1922.

204 C.S. Andrews, *Dublin Made Me*, p. 247; See also M. Ryan (in *Liam Lynch*, pp. 191–2) cites Lynch in a letter to Liam Deasy, 'Dev's mission was to try and bring the war to an end. Give him no encouragement.'; Mulcahy Papers, UCD, Archive Collection, P7/8/2.A; *CC*, 9, 23 September 1922; *SR*, 30 September 1922.

205 *CC*, 21 October 1922.

206 *CC*, 14 October, 9 December 1922; *SR* 14 October, 9 December 1922; *Irish Times*, 12 October, 7 December 1922.

207 Mulcahy Papers, UCD, Archive Collection, P7/A/83, 30 November 1922; See instructions issued to all commands, divisions and independent brigades regarding executions, from the adjutant general of the republican forces on 3 March 1923, 'It is essential that each brigade Commandant in Divisional areas has already prepared a list of residences and personnel against whom action will without delay be taken should any Volunteers captured in their area be executed. Reprisals will be more effective if carried out on the same day as the executions.' (copy found among Joe Barrett Papers, MIC, Limerick); Clare County Council Minute Book, from 1 November 1920 to 29 September 1923, CC/Min/12/9, in Clare Local Archives.

[208] *SR*, 16, 22 December 1922, 6 January 1923; Instructions from GHQ to destroy houses and kill named Senators in reprisal for execution of republican Volunteers, dated 26 January 1923, see Civil War Papers among the Joe Barrett Papers, MIC, Limerick.

[209] Summary of Official Reports received on 15 January 1923, Military Archives, Cathal Brugha Barracks, Lot 28, Box 6–9; *CC*, 20 January 1923; *SR*, 20 January 1923.

[210] Summary of official reports, 20 January 1923, Military Archives, Cathal Brugha Barracks, Lot 28, Box 6–11.

[211] *CC*, 27 January 1923; *SR*, 27 January 1923. S. Enright, *The Irish Civil War*, pp. 72, 73 and 103. Enright does not give his sources for the information about Seán Darcy. Enright also mentions two other Clare men who were arrested for allegedly carrying arms. He states that Mike Hassett, from Clarecastle, was convicted of the possession of a revolver, but that he seems to have been released in error. Thomas Murphy, from Clarecastle, was charged with, but acquitted of, being in possession of a shotgun. Enright does not give the dates or sources for the trials of these two men (pp. 102, 171).

[212] E.D. Murphy, 'The Patrick Hennessy letters', *The Other Clare*, 30 (2006), pp. 13–14; also, *SR*, 24 February 1923.

[213] C. Younger, *Ireland's Civil War*, pp. 497–8; M. Ryan, *Liam Lynch*, pp. 207–8; *CC*, 17 February 1922; *Cork Examiner*, 13 February 1923; *Irish Times*, 13 February 1923; *Irish Independent*, 13 February 1923.

[214] Letter from Frank Barrett O/C 1st Western Division to Major General Deasy, dated 5 February 1923, Ernie O'Malley Papers, National Library of Ireland, Mss No., 10,973/16/3; C. Younger, *Ireland's Civil War*, pp. 488–9.

[215] Frank Barrett to Liam Lynch, dated 11 February 1923, UCD Archives, Maurice Twomey Papers, P69/39/18.

[216] Letters from General Frank Barrett O/C 1st Western Division to the Chief of Staff, General Liam Lynch, 2 February, 19 February, 1 March 1923, catalogue of documents from 1st Western Division for sale, James Adam, Auctioneers, Lot 561, auction date, 20 April 2010. This historic collection was not sold on that date; also, Mulcahy Papers, UCD Archive Collection, P 69/8/(118-119); P69/39/(119–121); 124 125-127), dated 11 February 1923; P69/44. Incidentally, General Liam Lynch was also upset by de Valera's Document No 2. When he saw it, he replied to de Valera, 'Your publicity as to sponsoring Document No. 2 has had a very bad effect on the army and should have been avoided. Generally, they do not understand such documents. We can arrange a peace without referring to past documents', cited in Earl of Longford and T.P. O'Neill, *Eamon de Valera* (Dublin: Gill and Macmillan, 1970), pp. 215–16.

[217] Fogarty to Hagan, 10 January 1923, cited in P. Murray, *Oracles of God*, p. 91.

[218] *Irish Independent*, 9 February 1923; *Irish Times*, 9 February 1923; *CC*, 17 February 1923; *SR*, 17 February 1923; Copy of Republican Executive's response to Liam Deasy's appeal, issued 12 February 1923, Joe Barrett Papers, MIC, Limerick, courtesy of Dr Paul O'Brien; Copy of Order No 17, dated 8 March 1923, Joe Barrett Papers, MIC, Limerick, courtesy of Dr Paul O'Brien.

[219] *SR*, 17 February 1923.

[220] *SR*, 3 March 1923.

[221] *CC*, 17 February 1923; P.Ó. Ó Ruairc, *Blood on the Banner*, pp. 315, 329.

[222] *CC*, 28 April 1923.

[223] *CC*, 5 May 1923.

[224] *CC*, 28 April 1923; *SR*, 28 April 1923; P.Ó. Ó Ruairc, *Blood on the Banner*, p. 318; S. Spellissy, *The Ennis Compendium: From Royal Dun to Information Age Town* (Clare: The Book Gallery, no date), p. 51. Spellissy told me that Jimmy Mahony was

the source of that information regarding Miko Casey. Mahony also told Spellissy that Miko Casey went to America shortly afterwards and joined the fire department in Chicago

[225] *CC*, 5 May 1923.

[226] Military Archives, Cathal Brugha Barracks, CW/OPS/9/07, Box 25.

[227] *CC*, 28 April, 15 May 1923; *SR*, 28 April, 15 May 1923.

[228] *SR*, 28 April; *CC*, 5 May 1923, 1, 8 November 1924; Joe O'Muirceartaigh in *Clare People*, 30 April 2013, pp. 48–49. E. Neeson (in *The Civil War*, p. 258) states that the documents relating to the trials of the 'seventy-seven' were burnt by the outgoing administration in the Phoenix Park, Dublin in 1932.

[229] *CC*, 1 November 1924; *SR*, 1 November 1924.

[230] *CC*, 20 May 1933. For a contemporary insight into commemoration of the War of Independence and civil war, see B.M. French, *Narratives of Conflict, Belonging, and the State: Discourse and Social Life in Post-war Ireland* (New York: Routledge, 2018), Chapter Five, 'War Commemorations, the IRA and Uncertain Futures'.

[231] E. O'Malley, *The Singing Flame* (Dublin: Anvil Books, 1978), p. 168.

[232] C.S. Andrews, *Dublin Made Me*, pp. 269, 285–93.

[233] É. Gaynor, *Memoirs of a Tipperary Family*, p. 278.

[234] D. Breen, *My Fight for Irish Freedom* (Tralee: Anvil Books, 1989), p. 186.

[235] *CC*, 21 April 1923; *SR*, 21 April 1923.

[236] *Irish Independent*, 28 April 1923; *Irish Times*, 28 April 1923; *CC*, 5 May 1923; *SR*, 5 May 1923.

[237] C. Younger, *Ireland's Civil War*, p. 509.

[238] Catalogue of documents relating to the 1st Western Division, letter from Sean Casey to the Chief of Staff Frank Aiken, 29 June 1923, James Adams Auctioneers, Lot 561, auction date 20 April 2010.

[239] *CC*, 26 May 1923.

[240] *SR*, 25 August 1923.

[241] *CC*, 8 July, 4 August 1923.

[242] *SR*, 25 August 1923.

[243] P. Murray, *Oracles of God*, p. 240; K. Sheedy, *The Clare Elections* (Dublin: Bauroe Press, 1993), pp. 345, 351.

[244] *CC*, 18 August 1923; *SR*, 18 August 1923; K.J. Browne, *Éamon de Valera and the Banner County* (Clare: Glendale, 1982), pp. 187–98.

[245] Captured Documents, Military Archives, Cathal Brugha Barracks, Lot 145, Nos 13, 15 and 16, dated 12, 22 and 24 August 1923.

[246] *CC*, 31 August 1923. The *Clare Champion* of 6 September 1923 has a table showing transfer of preferences.

[247] *CC*, 25 August, 1, 8 September 1923; *SR*, 25 August, 1, 8 September 1923; K. Sheedy, *The Clare Elections*, pp. 351–6; K.J. Browne, *Eamon de Valera and the Banner County*, pp. 194–5; C. Younger, *Ireland's Civil War*, pp. 510–11; N. O'Gadhra, *The Civil War in Connaught*, p. 105.

[248] Barron family papers, courtesy of Declan Barron, Newpark House, Ennis, November 2018. Incidentally, Declan Barron informed me in a telephone conversation on 17 August 2020 that his grandfather, Aimee Barron, told him that he had killed Constable Lougheed in self-defence during the arms raid on Ruan Barracks by the Mid-Clare Brigade in October 1920. Sean Spellissy corroborated this story.

[249] M. Hopkinson, *Green against Green*, pp. 268–9.

[250] *SR*, 20 October 1923; *CC*, 27 October, 5, 12, 24 November 1923.

[251] S. Gaynor, *Memoirs of a Tipperary Family*, pp. 282–4; C. Younger, *Ireland's Civil War*, p. 511; Frank Barrett was released in November 1923 (according to obituary in *CC* and *SR*, 18 April 1931); See also, Peadar O'Donnell, *The Gates Flew Open*:

An Irish Civil War Prison Diary (Cork: Mercier Press, 2013), pp. 152–81; For another insight into conditions endured by internees, see J. Durney, 'The Curragh internees 1921–24: from defiance to defeat' in *Journal of the County Kildare Archaeological Society 2010–2011*, 20 (2), pp. 6–24.

252 See 'Courtmartial of Frank Barrett', Mulcahy Papers, UCD Archive Collection, P69/103(1-24); See also, Catalogue of First Western Division Documents 1922–1923, for sale, James Adams Auctioneers, Dublin, Lot 561, auction date 20 April 2010.

253 A. Mathews, *Dissidents: Irish Republican Women, 1923–46* (Cork: Mercier Press, 2012), pp. 269, 275.

254 Lieut. General L. Hogan, 'Civil strife and the hunger-striker from Cratloe,' in *Clare Champion*, 11 May 2001; S. McCoole, *No Ordinary Women: Irish Female Activists in the Revolutionary Years, 1900–1923* (Dublin: O'Brien Press, 2016), p. 121; *Clare People*, 25 May 2010; T. Mac Namara, *Days of Hunger: The Clare Volunteers and the Mountjoy Hunger-strike of 1917* (Clare: Dallan Publishing, 2017), p. 182n; Maurice Twomey, West Clare Brigade Papers, Glucksman Library, University of Limerick, P45/6(2).

255 Frank Barry, 'Death on the small bridge, the shooting dead of Michael Hartnett at Kerin's Cross, Clarecastle on 15 August 1924' in *Land and People* (Clare: Clarecastle & Ballyea Heritage and Wildlife Group, 2014), pp. 157–9; *CC*, 23, 30 August 1924; *SR*, 23, 30 August 1924.

256 M. Cronin, 'The GAA in a time of Guerrilla War and Revolution in Ireland 1913–1923' in G. Ó Tuathaigh (ed.), *The GAA and Revolution in Ireland 1913–1923* (Cork: The Collins Press, 2015), p. 168. Note: Cronin does not give any source for this information. S. O'Reilly, *Clare GAA the Club Scene 1887–2010* (Clare: published privately, 2010); J. Power, *The GAA in Clare Castle 1887–1987*, p. 54; *CC*, 1 March 1924; See also *CC* editions of June–July 1924.

257 M.G. Valiulis, '"The man they could not forgive," the view of the opposition: Eamon de Valera and the Civil War' in J.P. O'Carroll and J.A. Murphy (eds.), *De Valera and His Times* (Cork: Cork University Press, 1983), pp. 92–100; Earl of Longford and T.P. O'Neill, *Eamon de Valera*, pp. 253–4.

258 F.S.L. Lyons, *Ireland Since the Famine*, pp. 496–9. Lyons referred to de Valera as 'the constitutional Houdini of his generation'. D. McCullagh, *De Valera: Rise, 1882–1932* (Dublin: Gill, 2017), p. 357.

259 K. Sheedy, *The Clare Elections*, pp. 361–6; A. White, *Irish Parliamentarians: Deputies and Senators, 1918–2018* (Dublin: Institute of Public Administration, 2018); P. Maume, 'Keeper of the Flame: Brian O'Higgins and the Wolfe Tone Annual 1932–1962' in *History Ireland*, January/February 2019.

260 Correspondence letter from Frank Barrett to T.M., 7 June 1926, Archives of the Fianna Fáil Party, UCD Archives Collection, P176/23(19).

261 K. Sheedy, *The Clare Elections*, pp. 334, 339; Joe O Muircearthaigh, *Chronicle of Clare, 1900–2000* (Clare: Fag and Bealach, 2000), pp. 69, 73–4; *CC*, 28 April 1931. One of Frank Barrett's sons, Sylvester Barrett, was elected as a Fianna Fáil TD for Clare in 1968. He remained as a TD for Clare until 1984. He served as Minister for the Environment (1977–80) and as Minister for Defence (1980–2). He was elected as an MEP for the Munster constituency from 1984 until 1989, after which he retired from politics.

262 *CC*, 4 April 1965; Wikipedia references to Patrick Brennan and Sean Liddy; Colonel T. Hobson, *The Portrait Collection of the Irish Defence Forces* (Dublin: The History Press, 2011), pp. 86–7.

263 *Molua* (Clare: Diocese of Killaloe, 1954), pp. 15–29, photo pp. 32–34, courtesy of the Irish Press.

264 O. Byrnes, *Around the Square: The Story of Ennis Hurling* (Clare: published by the

author, 2003), pp. 37–40.

265 President Michael D. Higgins, speech at Michael Collins's memorial event at Béal na mBláth, 21 August 1916, *Irish Times*, 23 August 2016. John Higgins, from Ballycar, Newmarket on Fergus, father of President Michael D. Higgins, was a lieutenant in the IRA during the War of Independence, serving mainly in the Cork region. After the war was over, he joined the anti-Treaty forces, was arrested in January 1923, and was interned until November 1923. His brother Michael from Ballycar supported the Treaty and joined the National Army. Both men were awarded military service pensions. Their sister, Kitty, was a member of Cumann na mBan and also received a military service pension, though she stayed neutral in the civil war. President Michael D. Higgins was reared with his uncle and aunt at Ballycar from the age of 5 years and was educated at Ballycar National School and at St Flannan's College, Ennis. See the Military Service Pension Applications for these members of the Higgins family from Ballycar. Also, *Irish Times*, 11 December 2011.

266 *SR*, 24 April, 1 May, 19 June 1920; *CC*, 24 April, 10 June 1920; *Irish Times*, 20 April 1920; Police reports for County Clare, June 1920.

267 A. Bielenberg, 'Southern Irish Protestant experiences of the Irish Revolution', pp. 770–80.

268 Irish Distress and Irish Grants Committee, ref. 138/6, p. 2329; 199/19, p. 3612.

269 Irish Distress and Irish Grants Committee, ref. 184/7, p. 3221.

270 Irish Distress and Irish Grants Committee, ref. 66/18, p. 1061.

271 Irish Distress and Irish Grants Committee, ref. 80/8, p. 1311.

272 Irish Distress and Irish Grants Committee, ref. 185/7, p. 3253.

273 *SR*, 29 July 1922; *CC*, 19 August 1922; Anthony Malone to Frank Barrett, Captured Documents, Military Archives, Lot 24/4.

274 Files for the Damage to Property (Compensation) Act, 1923, FIN/COMP/2/3/36; *SR*, 16 February 1924.

275 Files for the Damage to Property (Compensation) Act, 1923, FIN/COMP/2/3/285; *SR*, 16 February, 10 May 1924.

276 Files for the Damage to Property (Compensation) Act, 1923, FIN/COMP/2/3/352.

277 Files for the Damage to Property (Compensation) Act, 1923, FIN/COMP/2/3/364.

278 Files for the Damage to Property (Compensation) Act, 1923, FIN/COMP/2/3/359.

279 *CC*, 5 June 1922; *SR*, 5 June 1922.

280 D. Fitzpatrick, *Politics and Irish Life, 1913–1921*, pp. 77–9. Also see P.Ó. Ó Ruairc, 'The distinction is a fine one, but a real one: Sectarianism in County Clare during the War of Independence', in *The Other Clare*, 34 (2010), pp. 35–41.

281 A.T.Q. Stewart, *The Shape of Irish History* (Belfast: Blackstaff History, 2001), pp. 181–2.

282 *SR*, 10 June 1920.

283 *Irish Times*, 21 September 1920; *SR*, 25 September 1920; *Irish Times*, 23 September 1920; *SR*, 25 September 1920.

284 *CC*, 17 June 1922.

285 See letter from H.V. MacNamara in the *Morning Post* of 14 July 1923; also, *SR*, 1 September 1923. A copy of the threatening letter to H.V. MacNamara, signed by Frank Barrett on behalf of the executive council of the IRA, and the letter from Gore Hickman to H.V. MacNamara are published courtesy of the Local Studies Centre, Clare County Library, Ennis. The letter was given to the county librarian, Noel Crowley by James B. MacClancy of Kerin, Hickman and O'Donnell, Solicitors, Ennis on 6 November 1987.

286 *SR*, 1 March 1924.

287 N. O'Gadhra, *Civil War in Connaught*, pp. 169–70.

288 *SR*, 21 January 1922; *CC*, 21 January 1922.

[289] *SR*, 22 July, 5, 23 August 1922, 24 September, 12 November 1923, 16, 24 February, 10 May 1924.

[290] Lady Inchiquin to her son Donough, 10 June 1922, courtesy of Grania Weir, née O'Brien, Whitegate.

[291] Lady Inchiquin to her son Donough, 23 July–5 August 1922, courtesy of Grania Weir, née O'Brien, Whitegate.

[292] D. Fitzpatrick, *Politics and Irish Life*, pp. 77–9.

[293] *CC*, 18 May 1923.

[294] President Michael D. Higgins, speech at Michael Collins's memorial event at Béal na mBláth, 21 August 1916, *Irish Times*, 23 August 2016.

INDEX OF NAMES

INDEX

Culligan, Bart, 44, 46
Culligan, Fr Charles, 31, 133, 159
Cullinan, F.F., 74
Dalton, Emmet, 52
Daly, Michael, 79
Daly, Rev. Henry S., 157
Darcy, John, 81, 116, 192 (n211)
de Valera, Éamon, x, 1–6, 8, 14–16, 18,
    21–3, 25, 27–9, 33–4, 51–6, 104–5,
    110, 113, 118, 124, 128, 130–6,
    144, 146–50, 152, 166
Deasy, Liam, 19, 51, 118–20, 122
Devitt, Martin, 23
Doherty, William Charles, 45–6
Dolan, Anne, 52
Donnellan, Guard, 95
Doyle, Thomas, 156
Duggan, Stephen, 99
Duggan's Hotel, Scariff, 12
Egan, Joseph, 115
Elliott, Rev. David, 157
Ellis, E.A.G., 86
Ellis, Robert Goold, 49
Enright, Seán, 108, 112, 116
Falshee, M., 142
Findlay, David, 19
Fitzgerald, Patrick, 45
Fitzpatrick, David, 159, 168
Fogarty, Bishop Michael, 4, 5, 17, 22–
    5, 32–3, 38, 53, 56, 75, 103–4,
    121–2, 133, 149–50, 152, 168
Frawley, Martin, 63, 87
Frawley, Tom, 81
Gallagher, S., 63, 87
Gallery, Christy, 86
Galvin, Fr M.J., 33
Gardiner, T., 17
Garrihy, Michael, 42
Garvin, Tom, 49, 54, 88, 94
Gaynor, Fr Patrick, 19, 26, 33, 55, 94
Gaynor, Michael, 45
Gaynor, Sean, 130–1, 140
Gelston, Mr, xi, 154
Gleeson, Dermot, 96
Glynn Fr J., 133
Glynn, M. & Co, 15, 71
Going, James D., 49
Goodwin, Mary, 99
Gore Hickman, F.W., 48–9, 158, 161–
    2, 164, 167–8
Gore, Annie J., 89
Gore, Reginald, 49

Griffin, J., 81
Griffin, Rev. J., 157
Griffith, Arthur, 1, 14, 23, 24, 27, 75
Hagan, Monsignor, 33, 121
Hales, Seán, 112
Hales, Tom, 20
Hamilton, Fr Michael, 7, 17, 145, 185
    (n11)
Hanley, Maura, x
Hanrahan, Lt, 89
Hartigan, Thomas, 109
Hartnett, Michael, 144, 195
Haugh, Bill, 21, 57, 69, 176
Hayes, Fr, 78
Hehir, Joseph, 97
Hehir, Michael, 6, 17, 20, 132, 136
Hehir, Pat, 86
Henn, Helen, 91, 191
Hennessy, Michael, 111
Hennessy, Patrick, 115–18, 122, 128,
    145
Hennessy, Seamus, 62, 63
Hibbert, Mrs, 90
Higgins, Anne, 196 (n265)
Higgins, John, 196 (n265)
Higgins, Michael D., 153, 169, 196
    (n265)
Higgins, Michael, 196 (n265)
Hillery, Dr, 63
Hogan, Annie, 61, 143–4
Hogan, Conor, 28, 97, 136, 138
Hogan, John, 100
Hogan, Patrick, 136
Hogan, W., 45–6
Honan, Stephen, 98
Honan, T.V., 5, 7, 21, 134, 136, 149,
    185
Hopkinson, Michael, 56, 106, 137, 139
Hourihan, Michael, 39
Hunt, Henry J., 183 (n5)
Hunt, John, 123–4
Hunt, T.J., 65, 67
Hynes, Frank, 21
Hynes, George, 45
Inchiquin, Lord, 31, 48, 80, 88, 166
Joyce family, 91
Keane, Marcus, 47–8, 166
Keane, Michael, 110
Keane, Patrick, 8, 57
Keane, Thomas, 90
Kearns, Patrick, 82
Kelly, Patrick, 107, 135

INDEX

INDEX OF PLACES

INDEX